CONTENTS

HOW THE DESTINATION CONTENT WORKS

Each destination includes a short introduction, an A–Z of practical information and recommended points of interest, split into 4 different categories:

- Highlights
- Accommodation
- Eating out
- What to do

You can view the location of every point of interest and save it by adding it to your Favourites. In the 'Around Me' section you can view all the points of interest within 5km.

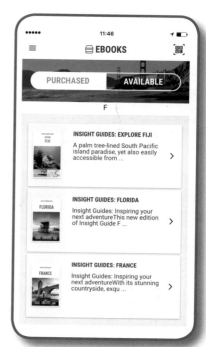

HOW THE EBOOKS WORK

The eBooks are provided in EPUB file format. Please note that you will need an eBook reader installed on your device to open the file. Many devices come with this as standard, but you may still need to install one manually from Google Play.

The eBook content is identical to the content in the printed guide.

HOW TO DOWNLOAD THE WALKING EYE APP

1. Download the Walking Eye App from the App Store or Google Play.
2. Open the app and select the scanning function from the main menu.
3. Scan the QR code on this page – you will then be asked a security question to verify ownership of the book.
4. Once this has been verified, you will see your eBook and destination content in the purchased ebook and destination sections, where you will be able to download them.

Other destination apps and eBooks are available for purchase separately or are free with the purchase of the Insight Guide book.

INSIGHT ● GUIDES

CROATIA

Walking Eye App

YOUR FREE DESTINATION CONTENT AND EBOOK AVAILABLE THROUGH THE WALKING EYE APP

Your guide now includes a free eBook and destination content for your chosen destination, all for the same great price as before. Simply download the Walking Eye App from the App Store or Google Play to access your free eBook and destination content.

HOW THE WALKING EYE APP WORKS

Through the Walking Eye App, you can purchase a range of eBooks and destination content. However, when you buy this book, you can download the corresponding eBook and destination content for free. Just see below in the grey panels where to find your free content and then scan the QR code at the bottom of this page.

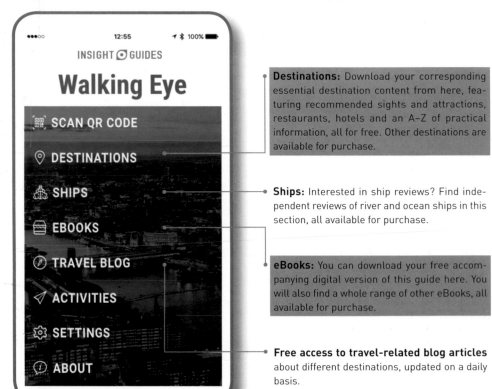

Destinations: Download your corresponding essential destination content from here, featuring recommended sights and attractions, restaurants, hotels and an A–Z of practical information, all for free. Other destinations are available for purchase.

Ships: Interested in ship reviews? Find independent reviews of river and ocean ships in this section, all available for purchase.

eBooks: You can download your free accompanying digital version of this guide here. You will also find a whole range of other eBooks, all available for purchase.

Free access to travel-related blog articles about different destinations, updated on a daily basis.

LEGEND
🔍 Insight on
📷 Photo Story

THE BEST OF CROATIA: TOP ATTRACTIONS

△ **St Donat**. Dating from the 9th century, Zadar's magnificent, round pre-Romanesque church has exceptional acoustics that are exploited on summer musical evenings. Roman stones were used in its construction. See page 157.

▽ **Golden Horn beach (Zlatni rat)**. This beautiful shore, near Bol on Brač island, is the most famous in Croatia. Nearly 600 metres/yds long, it is constantly shifting with the wind and tide. See page 184.

△ **Rovinj**. The star of Istria is a fishing port with Venetian-inspired architecture. The highlight of a visit is simply exploring the old town and wandering around its narrow lanes, visiting its galleries and cafés. See page 106.

▷ **Stari Grad plain**. The agrarian society that toils here on the beautiful, lavender-growing island of Hvar has not changed since the Greeks arrived in the 4th century BC. This 'cultural landscape' has made it a Unesco World Heritage Site. See page 188.

△ **Diocletian's Palace**. Eat, sleep and drink in the footsteps of a Roman emperor in Split. Between AD 295 and 305 Diocletian built his waterfront retirement home here on a grand scale. See page 176.

△ **Dubrovnik**. The Pearl of the Adriatic doesn't disappoint. You've seen it in pictures – now go and walk the walls, and find out all about this fabled maritime republic. See page 198.

◁ **Naïve Art**. The first museum in the world dedicated to it opened in Zagreb in 1952, and is still attracting attention today. Check out, too, the gallery in Hlebine, where many of the painters came from. See pages 226 and 258.

△ **Plitvice Lakes National Park**. An 8km (5-mile) stretch of dams, caves, waterfalls, of 16 lakes and countless streams and brooks, are at the heart of this water wonderland full of wildlife, including wolves and 126 bird species. See pages 239 and 243.

▽ **Zadar's public art installations**. Side by side on the edge of the peninsula are the flashing *Greeting to the Sun* and the haunting sound of the Sea Organ. See page 153.

△ **Varaždin**. A musical town with wonderful Baroque flourishes – both in its architecture and its concert performances. A town guard and uniformed burghers love to show their Habsburg heritage. See page 230.

THE BEST OF CROATIA: EDITOR'S CHOICE

Meštrović Gallery, Split.

MARKETS

Bjelovar. Bjelovar's daily farmers' market brims with produce and game, and hosts big food fairs. See page 256.

Dubrovnik. The morning market in Gundulić Square has everything fresh from the field and orchard. See page 203.

Rijeka. The Art Nouveau city market is a great place to see the Adriatic's bounteous seafood. See page 139.

Split. The market in Split is one of the biggest and liveliest in Dalmatia. See page 177.

Zagreb. Dolac is one of the finest markets. Its stalls of produce, plants and textiles are set up from 5am. See page 222.

Stall holder at Dolac market, Zagreb.

ISLANDS

Cres. The long, thin island in the Kvarner Gulf is where rare griffon vultures breed. See page 148.

Korčula. Korčula town is a mini Dubrovnik, with the added ghost of Marco Polo. There are good beaches on the island, too. See page 210.

Kornat. Kornat, a centre for agritourism, is the largest uninhabited island in Croatia. See page 163.

Pag. This barren, treeless island is worth visiting as the source of famous cheese and lace. See page 148.

Rab. Pine forests, sandy coves and lagoons make this a fabulous island, and it's hard not to fall in love with Rab town, one of the most beautiful in Croatia. See page 145.

Vis. This wonderfully rugged mountainous island is a favourite with divers, who have the Blue Grotto and other caves to explore. See page 190.

Korčula town.

MUSEUMS AND GALLERIES

Mimara Museum, Zagreb. Exhibits include a fine art collection, the world's longest Etruscan inscription and the Vučedol Dove, a potent national emblem. See page 223.

Museum of Croatian Tourism, Opatija. The story of the country's hospitality industry is told in permanent exhibitions at the Villa Angiolina and Juraj Šporer Arts Pavilion in Opatija. See page 133.

Meštrović Gallery, Split. The gallery of Croatia's greatest 20th-century artist, Ivan Meštrović, is in the house to which he intended to retire, before deciding to emigrate to the US. See page 180.

Place of Memory, Hospital Museum, Vukovar. Chilling reminders of what happened here in 1991, when Vukovar became the first European city to be entirely destroyed since World War II. See page 255.

Rector's Palace, Dubrovnik. This lovely Renaissance building gives an idea of daily life in the heyday of the Ragusan republic. See page 201.

Staro Selo Ethnographic Museum, Kumrovec. An open-air museum forming part of the village of Tito's birth. See page 236.

Museum of Broken Relationships, Zagreb. Offers poignant glimpses into dozens of heartbreaks. See page 227.

Veliki Tabor castle.

CASTLES

Kamerlengo Fortress, Trogir. Bristling with castellated walls and towers, the castle is a major feature in this lovely medieval city. Dating from the 15th century, it was once the Venetian governor's palace. See page 172.

Nehaj Fortress, Senj. This was the stronghold of the Uskoks, the pirates of Senj, who fought valiantly for life and liberty against both Turks and Venetians. See page 139.

Spanish Fortress, Hvar. There are brilliant views over Hvar from the top of this imposing fortress. See page 187.

Trakošćan. A wonderful fairy-tale castle created from the 16th to the early 20th centuries, when it was in the hands of the Drašković dynasty. See page 233.

Veliki Kaštio, Ston. The great fortress that links the Mali Ston and Ston across the Pelješac isthmus, built as a defensive wall by Ragusa. See page 209.

Veliki Tabor, near Krapina. This picturesque castle, one of the best preserved Renaissance forts in Croatia, has been turned into a museum and is also the setting for an international festival of short films every June. See page 235.

A Meštrović exhibit.

Lower Falls, Plitvice National Park.

Sunset at the 'Greeting to the Sun' installation, Zadar.

Trogir's waterfront.

A DIVERSE NATION

Croatians are fiercely proud of their country, though geography and history have made it a land of several parts, each with its own specificity.

However much emphasis Croatians put on a single identity, the country's odd shape has created a nation of several distinct flavours. One part of the country stretches inland across Continental Croatia to the capital, Zagreb, and here the cultural legacy of the Habsburgs is evident. Another large strip, lapped by the blue Adriatic from Istria down through hundreds of islands and the Dalmatian coast, reveals the stamp of the Venetians and – more recently – the Italians. Then there's the rugged interior, with dramatic limestone mountain ranges towering over canyons, gorges, waterfalls and rivers.

Resident in the Zagorje region.

This incredible diversity offers a dizzying choice to today's holidaymaker, and Croatia's entry to the European Union in 2013 has made the country even easier to visit. The difficult part is deciding on which region to explore. Even the idea of a simple beach holiday becomes pleasantly complicated when choosing between Istria's Italianate resorts, the elegant Opatija Riviera, the islands that dot the coast from Kvarner southwards, sophisticated Hvar and Dubrovnik with its jewel-like islands.

Active types can hike and climb in some of Europe's most scenic national parks – from the karst peaks of Velebit to the rushing waters of Krka. Cycle paths and walking trails wind through Istria's tranquil landscapes of vineyards, olive groves and orchards. The 16 lakes and countless

Worker in a vineyard, Vukovar.

waterfalls of Plitvice are an extraordinary sight and one of the many reasons to veer away from the sea and head inland. The Adriatic coast is a dream for sailors, where the multitude of islands forms an enchanting backdrop. Zagreb, the European Union's newest capital, teems with a lively café culture spread around its historic old town. Follow the path of the Romans in the wonderfully preserved amphitheatre in Pula and among the bars colonising Diocletian's Palace in Split.

Although scars remain of the 1991–5 Homeland War that ripped the former Yugoslavia apart, Croatia has spent the intervening years quietly turning itself into one of the most sought-after destinations in Europe.

Vineyard in inland Istria, near Beram.

LAND AND PEOPLE

Three vast empires – Austro-Hungarian, Venetian and Ottoman – have mingled to create a varied country that is full of character, where the population is as diverse as the landscapes it inhabits.

Croatia amounts to around 146,000 sq km (56,500 sq miles), about the size of England and Wales, or the US state of Iowa. Though it's not large, it often seems less like a single country than a league of nations and small city-states. This partly reflects its odd boomerang shape: one arm flung eastwards along the verdant Pannonian plain, cupping the soft underbelly of Hungary, the other stretching south over the dry mountains that run like a spinal cord along the Adriatic Sea. Then there are the scores of islands that are strung out along the length of the Adriatic coast.

Croatia's borders today lie along five countries, clockwise from the north: Slovenia (455km/285 miles), Hungary (329km/204 miles), Serbia (241km/150 miles), Bosnia Herzegovina (932km/580 miles) and Montenegro (25km/16 miles).

One part was ruled for centuries by the Habsburg Austro-Hungarians and another was governed for a similar length of time by Venice. No wonder that the 4.2 million population scattered around continental and maritime Croatia has evolved into such different societies – one more reserved, another more Mediterranean.

ITALIANATE ISTRIA

Istria, the tear-shaped peninsula, is yet another country. Geographically it spreads over its Croatian border to Slovenia. It also touches Italy just below Trieste, making this

At the market in Split.

the land entry point to the country for Italians. Ceded to Italy after World War I and returned to Yugoslavia after World War II, Istria had first an influx, then an exodus of Italians. A number still remain, and Grožnjan is the only town in the country where non-Croatians (Italians, representing 51 percent of the population) outnumber Croatians.

Istria's undulating landscape, vineyards, the hilltop towns and the soaring campaniles on the village churches evoke frequent and understandable comparisons with Tuscany. Istrians, however, consider themselves first and foremost Istrian. Street signs written in Italian in the main town of Pula reflect their relaxed patriotism and easy-going relationship with their neighbour – a sentiment that worries and angers more orthodox Croat nationalists living further east. Strong pro-autonomy movements, the Istrian Democratic Party and the Istrian Social Democratic Forum, reflect most people's determination not to be pushed around by Zagreb.

KVARNER

Istria's immediate neighbour provides the link between the peninsula and the beginning of the Dalmatian coast to the south. The major sea-

Farmer in the Zagorje region.

port of Rijeka sits at the head of the Kvarner Gulf, its history as an Austro-Hungarian and then Italian outpost evident in its architecture and atmosphere. The resorts of the Opatija Riviera have been drawing tourists since Habsburg days, its visitors basking in the unique microclimate. Several of Croatia's greenest islands are dotted in the gulf, notably Krk and Cres (which share the title of Croatia's biggest islands), as well as exquisite Rab, Lošinj and Pag. Kvarner is also the starting point for Croatia's largest mountain range, Velebit, which begins near the port of Senj and towers over the Adriatic coast for 145km (90 miles) to northwest of the fortress town of Knin in inland northern Dalmatia.

DALMATIA AND ITS HINTERLAND

Carry along the coast road in Dalmatia and you will have crossed the Dinaric Alps, which run for 645km (400 miles) along the Adriatic coast, sheltering it from cold easterly winds and hemming much of it tightly against the sea. Corroded by water, these rocks are Swiss cheeses of caves, canyons and grottoes. They produce the dramatic gorges of rivers such as the Cetina, while other rivers spring up from their depths, fully formed, their sediment-free waters sparklingly clear.

> *At 1,392 metres (4,570ft) deep, Lukina jama in the northern Velebit massif is the deepest cave in Croatia. Discovered in 1992, it was named after Ozren Lukic, a keen caver and volunteer who had been shot by a sniper the previous year.*

The limestone crags of Velebit tumble deeply into the sea, only to emerge again shortly afterwards in a series of islands that make this coast so appealing. Here the contrast between the old world and the new are nowhere more striking than on the island of Hvar, where the main town attracts the mega-yacht brigade and Hollywood stars, while the island's Stari Grad Plain has a cultural landscape so little changed since the times of the ancient Greeks that it has become a Unesco World Heritage Site.

The Adriatic, a spur of the Mediterranean, is an omnipresent influence on life in Dalmatia. It has shaped the inhabitants' dreams and poems, inspired their art and architecture and informs their religion. It shapes the music of this maritime nation, most notably in the klapa a cappella songs.

It has also fed them. Seafood is an important part of Dalmatian life. Forget *schnitzels* and the other Austrian winter-warmers that are so beloved further north. This is the land of fish, sold fresh from the quaysides at the crack of dawn every morning. Visitors may opt for tourist menus offering pork chops and pizza; the locals will be eating their favourite dish of squid risotto, washed down with some of the Mediterranean's most delicious – though least known – wines, the best of which are produced on the islands and on the Pelješac peninsula.

Here the dark hair and eyes of the local people reveal centuries of intermingling with Italians and, before them, Greeks. This is a no-holds-barred Mediterranean society that has little time for what the Dalmatians see as Zagreb's stiffness and 'hauteur'. Dalmatians take their manners and their fashion sense

Croat refugees from Bosnia were encouraged to resettle the town, and today they make up most of the population.

CONTINENTAL CROATIA

Central Europe's great Pannonian plain, once a sea, comes down from Hungary into central and eastern Croatia, and into Serbia. Taking its name from the Roman province of Pannonia, the Croatian part of this plain largely accords with the ancient region of Slavonia (not to be confused with Slovenia, the country to the

Zagreb residents in traditional clothing.

from neighbouring Italy. Immaculately pressed white shirts and dark glasses are de rigueur for the suave, not to say arrogant, young men swaggering through the narrow streets of Split on the evening korzo, or revving up their motorbikes on the seafront.

Though the Homeland War happened a generation ago, there are still a few unhealed scars left on the coast. Serbs formed more than three-quarters of the population of Knin, a former Croatian capital, and a main transport hub between Zagreb and the coast. In 1991 they seized control of the city, declaring the region the Republic of Serbian Krajina. Croatia's Operation Storm drove them out, and leaders on both sides were charged with war crimes.

⊙ PALAGRUŽA ISLAND

If you head due south from the Dalmatian coast towards Italy, the most southerly part of Croatia is Palagruža, an island 1.4km (1 mile) long and 300 metres/yds wide with a subtropical climate. At its 90-metre (295ft) summit is a lighthouse, which offers accommodation in one of the most remote spots in Europe. Palagruža is a nature reserve, with two beaches. The island and its islets lie between Italy's Gargano peninsula and Lastovo, the island to the south of Korčula, from where boats bring visitors on a 2.5-hour journey. It was an important stop in Mesolithic times; an archaeological dig is tracing the island's past.

north, though both roughly mean a region settled by Slavs). This is mostly flat land of forests and farms, and their bounty can be seen in the big markets at Bjelovar, as well as in the daily Dolac market in Zagreb. The islands in this ancient sea are now hills, such as those in Papuk Nature Park where the volcanic pillars of Rupnica became the first geological monument in the country to have a protected status. Other former islands are Psunj, Slavonia's highest peak at 986 metres (3,235ft), and the 152-metre (500ft) hill at Požega, which provided

300km (190 miles) north of Croatia, occupied much of Slavonia for around 150 years. As they retreated, the Hungarians carved out this military border to shield their empire from Turkish invasions, populating the region known as Lika with conscript volunteers. Heavily settled over several centuries by Orthodox Serbs, the character of Lika changed drastically in 1991 when Serb separatists drove out all the local Croats. It changed drastically again in July 1995, when the Croatian army drove out most of the Serbs. Almost overnight, a Serb population of 150,000 or so fled to Bosnia or

Captain of one of the many boats that ply the waters between Hvar town and the Pakleni islands.

the fortress on the River Sava between Vukovar and Zagreb.

The Sava is Slavonia's drain in the south, the Drava in the north, both running east to reach the Danube at, respectively, Vukovar and Serbia's capital Belgrade. The Danube, Europe's great water highway, forms Croatia's eastern border, creating a flood plain by its confluence with the Drava that is described as 'Europe's last remaining wetlands'. The Danube delta is designated a Wetland of International Importance.

The southern part of Slavonia is part of the Vojna Krajina, a military buffer zone that stretched from the Adriatic all along the border and into modern Bosnia Herzegovina, and east into Serbia. The Ottomans, who had reached the gates of Vienna

⊘ THERMAL SPAS

In the wooded interior of Croatia, water bubbles up from underground at high temperatures in spa centres that have been enjoyed since Roman times. In the north there are traces of a Roman settlement by the baths at Varaždinske Toplice in the woods above Varaždin, where sulphurous waters come out of the ground at 37°C (98.6°F). There are a number of spa retreats between here and Zagreb, in the Zagorje. In the countryside north of Istria, Istarske Toplice has large indoor and outdoor pools. Many of the modern spas date from the late 19th century, when railways and better roads brought rich Viennese in search of cures.

Serbia, leaving many towns and villages empty. The Serb population overall in Croatia is down now from around 12 percent before the war to around 4 percent of the total.

The greatest problem facing Lika is its poor economy. Its major tourist draw is the popular Plitvice Lakes National Park (a Unesco World Heritage Site), but there are few job prospects. The global recession has not helped. With a small, elderly population, it is difficult to see this ruggedly beautiful region ever realising its massive tourist potential.

reflect centuries of intermarriage between Croats, Germans, Hungarians and a dozen other nationalities settled in the region by the Empress Maria Theresa in the 18th century, including Czechs, Slovaks, Ruthenes and Ukrainians. Many of these settler communities maintain a distinct identity, which distinguishes the places where they have settled: the Czechs around Daruvar and Pakrac in western Slavonia; the Hungarians in the Baranja region, north of Osijek; and the Slovaks in Ilok, on the border with Serbia.

Raising a glass of Dalmatian wine on the island of Vis.

WESTERN CROATIA

By contrast, the Zagorje in western central Croatia has a healthy economy that comes from a rolling landscape of green hills, elegant castles and popular spas, which bring weekenders from Zagreb. Stretching north of the capital to the most northerly city, Varaždin, this is a favourite place of escape, not much explored by foreign visitors. Further stretches of quiet countryside lie west of Zagreb in the sparsely populated Žumberak mountain range, where conditions are ideal for growing vines, especially around the Samobor hills.

Almost 90 percent of Zagreb's 1.1 million inhabitants are identified as Croats. But the fair complexions of so many Slavonians

The stamp of Habsburg rule and the cultural influence of Vienna hang heavily over this part of the world in the monumental neoclassical architecture of Zagreb's National Theatre and the other grand civic buildings of the capital as well as in nearby cities such as Osijek and Baroque Varaždin. But it is not just the buildings. Much of Zagreb looks and feels like a slice of Old Vienna that has been airlifted south, from the *schnitzels* and *strudels* served in the restaurants to the formidable old ladies dressed in porkpie hats walking tiny fluffy dogs through the parks in the morning. That other pillar of Viennese life – coffee and cream cake consumed over the daily newspaper in cafés – remains sacrosanct to many Zagrebians.

DECISIVE DATES

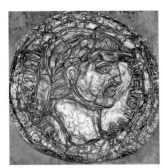

Gold medallion showing the Roman Emperor Diocletian.

EARLIEST TIMES

2500 BC
The statue of the Vučedol dove confirms Neolithic settlements in the region.

4th century BC
Greeks established on the coast, living side by side with native Illyrians.

1st century BC
Roman colony of Illiricum established, divided into Dalmatia (southern) and Pannonia (northern) provinces.

AD 300
Roman Emperor Diocletian builds palace at Spalatum (Split).

365
Collapse of Roman Empire. Eastern (Orthodox) church established in Constantinople (Byzantium).

7th century
Slav invasions. Croats settle in Dalmatia and Pannonia.

852
First use of the name Croatia. Around the same time, Greek brothers Cyril and Methodius were converting Slavs to Christianity.

c.910
Tomislav crowned king of Croatia.

FOREIGN RULE

1089
Invasion by Hungary.

1094
Bishopric of Zagreb founded.

1102
Croatian autonomy under Hungary with its own *ban* (governor, or viceroy) and *sabor* (parliament).

1126
The destruction of Biograd by Venice.

1202
The sack of Zadar by Fourth Crusaders.

1238
Mongol invasion destroys Zagreb cathedral.

Saints Cyril and Methodius holding the Cyrillic alphabet.

The Battle of Kosovo.

1320–30
Seizure of Split, Trogir and Pula by Venice.

1389
Serbs defeated by Ottoman Turks at battle of Kosovo.

1493
Croat nobles slaughtered by Ottomans at the Battle of Krbava Fields.

1526
Most of Croatia falls to the Ottoman Turks.

HABSBURG EMPIRE

1527
Croatian crown goes to Habsburg Archduke Ferdinand of Austria.

1593
Ottomans repulsed at Battle of Šišak, south of Zagreb, and the tide turns.

1630
Serb Orthodox settlers in Krajina offered freedoms in exchange for a life of military service.

1671
Execution of heads of Zrinski and Frankopan families for

conspiring against the Habsburg crown.

1699
Croatia mostly liberated from Ottoman rule.

1797
Dalmatia comes under French rule as the Illyrian Provinces.

1815
The Congress of Vienna: Dalmatia incorporated into Austrian Empire following the defeat of Napoleon.

NATIONAL REVIVAL
1847
Croatian becomes official language.

1848
Josip Jelačić made *ban* of Croatia and leads Croats against Hungarians.

1861
Party of Rights founded by Ante Starčević who opposes the idea of South Slav, or 'Jugoslav', union proposed by his rival, Bishop Strossmayer.

1867
Austrian Empire divided into Austria-Hungary. Inland Croatia becomes part of Hungary. Dalmatia remains under Austria.

1883–1903
Rule of Charles Khuen-Hedervary as *ban* of Croatia, who advances Hungary's interests.

20TH CENTURY
1905–6
Croatian-Serbian coalition wins elections in Dalmatia and Croatia.

1914
Assassination of Archduke Ferdinand in Sarajevo (Bosnia

Ferdinand I was Holy Roman Emperor from 1558 until his death in 1564.

Herzegovina) brings Croats into World War I on the side of Austria-Hungary.

1918
The kingdom of Serbs, Croats and Slovenes proclaimed in Belgrade by Serbian Prince Aleksandar.

1934
Assassination of King Aleksandar.

1939
Croatian autonomy within Yugoslavia.

1941–5
World War II: German invasion. Ustaše proclaim Independent State of Croatia, Nezavisna Država Hrvatska (NDH).

1945
Partisans enter Zagreb. The Nezavisna Država Hrvatska army massacred. Croatia becomes a federal republic of Yugoslavia under the Partisan leader Tito.

1990
Multi-party elections in Croatia and Slovenia end Communist rule. Franjo Tuđman and his Croatian Democratic Union (HDZ) win power. Serb revolt in Knin, northern Dalmatia, backed by Slobodan Milošević and Yugoslav Army.

1991–5
Homeland War: Croatia proclaims its independence. Dubrovnik shelled. Vukovar destroyed. The conflict ends with Operation Storm (known in Croatian as Oluja) in the summer of 1995.

1944 propaganda poster for the Partisans: 'Everybody fight for the freedom of Croatia'.

21ST CENTURY
2003
New parliamentary elections held and reformed HDZ party wins under leadership of Ivo Sanader, who becomes prime minister.

2008
Croatia joins Nato.

2009
Jadranka Kosor becomes first woman prime minister.

2013
Croatia joins the European Union on 1 July.

2015
Kolinda Grabar-Kitarović becomes the first female Croatian president.

2016
The centre-right coalition government, headed by Andrej Plenković, is formed.

2017
A new airport terminal opens in Croatia's capital, Zagreb.

GOLDEN GATE.

INTERIOR COURT.

EARLY DAYS

The Slavic Hrvati, one of the tribes that arrived in the Balkans from far Eastern Europe after the Roman Empire fell, formed the first Croatian state.

Visitors to Croatia may notice posters and pictures of a squat stone bird and wonder what it is. This ancient drinking vessel is the Vučedol Golubica, the Vučedol dove. It was discovered in 1938, and its role as a symbol of the nation was given added poignancy during the siege of Vukovar (see page 257) in 1991–2. Dating from at least 2,500 BC, it came to represent a nation's ancient heritage under threat.

The dove is one of many finds to suggest that a rich Neolithic culture flourished in what is now the Eastern Slavonia region of Croatia. Other artwork from the same period has been found on the coast of Dalmatia (*Dalmacija* in Croatian), where Neolithic settlers gave way first to Phoenicians and, by the 4th century BC, to Greeks. The Greeks left many traces of their presence on the coast. Their settlements can be plotted in place names that come from Greek words, such as the island of Hvar, from *pharos*, meaning lighthouse, while vineyards on the nearby island of Korčula dating from classical times produce famous wines called Grk, which simply means 'Greek'. In 2012, archaeologists found what they believe is the world's oldest astrologer's board, which had been shut away in a cave near Nakovana on the Adriatic coast for more than 2,000 years. It just shows how much more there is to discover.

ROMAN DALMATIA AND PANNONIA

By the 3rd century BC, Greek cultural and economic dominance over the Adriatic was giving way to the superior force of Rome. Expanding steadily into what they called Illyricum, Roman armies gradually subdued the Illyrians of the interior, incorporating the region into the empire by around 59 BC. Illyrians not absorbed into

Ceramic Vučedol dove, Zagreb's Archaeological Museum.

Roman society pushed deep into the mountains, and the inhabitants of modern Albania may well be their descendants.

Most of modern Croatia and Bosnia became part of the Roman province of Dalmatia, while the north became part of the province of Pannonia. Greek settlements on the islands of Hvar and Korčula evolved into Latin towns and the Romans developed new cities on the mainland. Many Croatian coastal towns date their continual settlement from the Roman era, including Zadar (*Jader* in Latin), Trogir (*Tragurium*) and Dubrovnik (near *Epidaurum*, modern Cavtat).

Roman Dalmatia's most famous son was the Emperor Diocletian, who retired to his home town of Salona (now Solin, a suburb of Split)

around AD 300 and built a vast home for himself a few miles away at Spalatum, overlooking the harbour. Ironically, the octagonal mausoleum of this dedicated persecutor of Christians eventually became Split's cathedral. The thick walls, soaring arches and massive supporting columns of the immense compound where Diocletian spent his retirement survive to this day, framing Split's old city like an exoskeleton.

The old city of Split is, perhaps, Rome's most impressive legacy in Croatia. But it has a great rival in the north, in the forum at Pula, in Istria.

Around 3,000 Christians are thought to have died under Diocletian's purges. The last pagan Roman Emperor, Diocletian was succeeded by Constantine, who converted to Christianity and founded Constantinople.

Istria of the general distress he had witnessed in this time of trouble. 'Bishops have been captured, priests killed, horses tied to Christ's

Roman amphitheatre, Pula.

Constructed from about 20 BC to AD 70, Pula's amphitheatre – three tiers high with 72 arches – is considered second only to the Colosseum in Rome in terms of size and preservation. It is still used today as a theatre and film venue.

After the division of the Roman Empire in AD 395 into an eastern half governed from Constantinople (Byzantium) and a western half ruled from Rome, Dalmatia was awarded to the west. But as Rome buckled under the weight of successive invasions, security in Dalmatia collapsed. Christian Visigoths, Germanic Vandals, Central Asian Avars and other tribes raced through, looting and sacking the wealthy towns en route.

In 396, St Jerome, the great biblical scholar who was born in Strido, wrote movingly from

altars and martyrs' relics cast around,' he declared. 'Everywhere there is sorrow, horror and the image of death.'

The fact that by the 5th century Pula's magnificent arena was functioning as a menial cattle market shows how far the region's economy and culture had declined. Some of the more exposed Roman settlements in Dalmatia shrank into insignificance.

Others, like Salona, disappeared altogether and people were forced to move elsewhere. In the early 7th century, in search of security, refugees from ravaged Salona began pouring into the ruins of the walled palace at Spalatum, transforming Diocletian's palace into a town. Further south, the inhabitants of Epidaurum fled their old home to build a new city a few miles away in a marshier, less accessible position. In so doing they laid the foundations of what would later become the great merchant city of Ragusa, or Dubrovnik.

SLAVIC HRVATI (CROATS) ARRIVE

While the Latin, or Latinised, inhabitants of the Dalmatian coast struggled to adapt to their deteriorating circumstances, momentous demographic changes were taking place in the interior. Emigrating from their homeland in modern Ukraine and Belarus, Slavs had begun to surge between the surviving Latins on the coast and the Croats in the neighbouring interior. In fact, the Croats seemed to have assimilated easily, rapidly taking on board the Christian faith of their Latin neighbours – though their mass evangelisation may have owed more to the Frankish army of Charlemagne, which conquered the area in the 9th century. The earliest surviving examples of *starohrvatski* (Old Croatian) architecture, such as the 9th-century Holy Cross Cathedral in Nin, suggest that the Croats were much more interested in imitating Latin civilisation than attacking it.

Church of the Holy Cross, Nin.

into the Balkan peninsula. These migrants may have come, at least initially, at the invitation of the Byzantine emperors, who saw the Slavs as a potential bulwark on the empire's depopulated frontier against invading barbarians.

Regardless of whether this was fact or legend, from the 7th century onwards the shattered Latin settlements of the Dalmatian coast found themselves living in proximity to the Slavic Croats. Their name, Hrvati, may point to distant Iranian antecedents, for Greek writers of around 200 BC described the Horvatos as an Iranian tribe. But they were undoubtedly a Slavic society by the time they settled Dalmatia and Pannonia.

The immigrants seem to have acted as a stabilising force, as there is no record of armed conflict

⊘ ISLAND ESCAPES

The islands around the Adriatic provided protection for the Latinised communities when the Slavic invasions began. In Italy, they formed the first settlements on Venice's lagoons. Dubrovnik, an island at the time, was founded as a retreat, with the Slavs settling on the coast nearby. Nin, one of Croatia's major early centres, occupied an island that covered just half a square kilometre. But some islands had long been occupied: seafaring Liberians had a stronghold on three rocky outcrops that became Zadar. Illyrian Rovinj, also an island settlement, was unconnected to the mainland until 1763.

From a mass of small principalities, a single Croatian polity began to merge in the 8th and 9th centuries. By the 820s, a ruler called Vladislav was styling himself Duke of the Croatians and Dalmatians. Thirty years later, a successor, Trpimir, invited the Benedictine order to Croatian lands, a significant step in strengthening ties between the Croats and western Christendom.

THE FIRST KING OF CROATIA

The early Croatian state reached its apogee under Tomislav, who, according to legend, was

The Glagolitic alphabet commemorated in the village of Hum in central Istria.

crowned first King of Croatia in 910. The legend may be apocryphal, as there is no contemporary surviving evidence that this ceremony ever took place. What is certain is that Croatia's rise to power had attracted international attention. In his contemporary handbook, Porphyrogenitus describes Croatia as a substantial power. The early Croatian state did not maintain its independence, however. The more advanced states of Hungary to the north and Venice to the west both cast acquisitive glances over the strategically important Dalmatian coastline. Of the two, Venice was the more dangerous, and by the beginning of the 11th century the doges ominously had assumed the title of dukes of Dalmatia.

GREGORY OF NIN

A significant weakness of the infant Croatian state had been its failure to promote an autonomous church, which could act as a pillar of the state. Gregory (Grgur) of Nin, a Slav bishop, had championed the use of an indigenous Croatian alphabet, known as Glagolitic (see page 143), as well as the performance of Mass in the vernacular. As a result there was an attempt to make Nin, just north of Zadar, the ecclesiastical centre of the kingdom. But the Latin clergy in other coastal towns in Dalmatia fiercely resisted the idea. After appeals to Rome, the papacy sided with the established Latins against the Croat newcomers, elevating Split, instead of Nin, to the rank of archbishopric in 925. In spite of this setback, the Croat kingdom enjoyed an Indian summer from 1058 to 1074 under Kresimir IV, who moved the capital from Knin, in the Dalmatian interior, to Biograd na Moru on the coast. He also founded a new Slav city on the coast south of Biograd to rival the older Latin foundations. This was Šibenik. Kresimir's death without an heir left the kingdom rudderless and divided. Power fell into the hands of Zvonimir, the *ban* (governor) of the northern Pannonian region.

THE HUNGARIANS MOVE IN

On Zvonimir's death in 1089, Croatia's northern neighbour seized the opportunity to invade. Claiming the crown as the brother of Zvonimir's surviving queen, Jelena, King László of Hungary moved an army south, seizing much of Croatia's northern plains and founding a bishopric in 1094 at Zagreb, which was then an insignificant settlement. His brother, Koloman (in Hungarian Kálmán, King of Croatia 1095–1116), continued the campaign to subdue the Croats but decided to buy off the resistance of the Croat nobles rather than wage a protracted war of conquest.

The fruit of Koloman's deliberations was the *Pacta Conventa* of 1102, under which Hungary pledged to respect the ancient rights of the Croatian kingdom. Koloman's coronation in Biograd was a victory of sorts for the Croat noble class. The ceremony confirmed that the Croat kingdom would retain a separate identity under the Hungarian crown. The Croats would have their own *ban* to govern them in the king's name and would keep their own *sabor* (parliament). Nevertheless, the Croats were no longer masters of their own destiny. They would not rule themselves again for another eight centuries.

'The Capture of Cattaro' (modern-day Kotor in Dalmatia) by the Venetians under Vittorio Pisani in 1378, from a painting by Andrea Micheli (1539–1614).

THE MIDDLE AGES

The Croatian crown passed from the Hungarians to the Habsburgs, but the biggest upset was the Ottomans, enemies of Venice and the Pope.

The union of the Croatian and Hungarian crowns under Koloman did not bring the Croats security against Venice, or any other invaders. After Koloman's death in 1116, Venice attacked Šibenik, Zadar and Biograd na Moru, practically demolishing the old coronation town in 1126. The most infamous assault occurred in 1202, when thousands of soldiers who had arrived in Venice for the Fourth Crusade were given supplies in return for the prize of Zadar. The city surrendered after a punishing bombardment. Ignoring the crosses hanging from its walls as a sign of submission, the crusaders simply massacred many of the city's inhabitants. The slaughter and looting of churches so outraged Pope Innocent III that he excommunicated the Venetians for their infamy.

The sack of Zadar was only the beginning of Venetian expansion in the Adriatic. In the 1320s and 1330s, the Italian city-state took control of Split, Trogir, Šibenik and Pula. In 1409, King Ladislas of Naples, claimant to the Hungarian crown, sold his rights over Zadar and the rest of Dalmatia to Venice for 100,000 ducats. In little more than 10 years, Venice had obtained control of most of Dalmatia, which it retained until the French revolutionary army terminated Venice's own independence in 1797.

THE MONGOL INVASION

The Hungarian crown had been equally ineffective in resisting an invasion of Mongols from the east, who tore through Hungary and Croatia in 1238 with devastating effect, demolishing Zagreb cathedral, which had been completed just 21 years earlier. King Bela IV of Hungary-Croatia was chased as far down as the Dalmatian city of Trogir, which risked sharing Zagreb's

Mongolian warriors in a Persian miniature.

fate when it refused to hand him over. Mysteriously, however, the Mongol army abruptly retreated east and Trogir was spared.

One consequence of these debilitating invasions was a decline in royal power and the growth of semi-independent feudal lordships. Two families that would long exercise quasi-royal authority over much of Croatia were the Frankopans and the Šubićs, later known as the Zrinskis. The base of the former was the island of Krk, while the Šubić fastness was located at Bribir, near Knin. The other consequence of colonisation was that Croatia's axis shifted north from Dalmatia to the plains of Pannonia, now known as Slavonia (Slavonija in Croatian). As Dalmatia declined under Venetian rule and its cities lost their lustre,

Zagreb began its slow rise to pre-eminence. In spite of the severity of the Mongol assault, the cathedral was rapidly rebuilt in the new Gothic style and in 1242 Zagreb was awarded the status of a royal free city by King Bela IV.

Medieval Zagreb was soon large and prosperous enough to afford the luxury of vigorous territorial battles, pitting the clerical lords of the Kaptol area, surrounding the cathedral, against the lay masters of the town, known as Gradec. The bone of contention usually concerned control over the mills in the stream dividing the two areas. The

was only slowed, not reversed. At a decisive battle at the Krbava Fields in the Lika region of western Croatia in 1493 the Turks routed a Croatian force and cut down the flower of its nobility.

At the turn of the 16th century, armies of Ottoman Turks had penetrated the Dalmatian coast and were rapidly overrunning everything in their path, except for those coastal cities held by Venice and the prosperous city-state of Dubrovnik, which offered the Ottoman Sultan nominal allegiance in 1526 in exchange for retaining effective independence.

Turkish forces under the command of Suleiman the Magnificent.

street that bears the name Krvavi Most, or Bloody Bridge, recalls the spot where one of these furious encounters took place in 1295.

THE MUSLIM OTTOMANS

In the 14th century, a new threat from the east appeared in the shape of the Ottoman Turks. This danger was to prove far more durable than that posed by the Mongol hordes. The Battle of Kosovo in 1389, though an indecisive military encounter, marked the beginning of the end of neighbouring Serbia as an independent state. By temporarily reoccupying much of Bosnia, which had collapsed by 1463, King Matthias Corvinus (1458–90) of Hungary-Croatia energetically repelled the Ottoman advance, but the process of Muslim conquest

By then the Turkish advance was only a few kilometres south of Zagreb. The ecclesiastical authorities had already frantically supervised the erection of defensive towers and high city walls in expectation of a siege, completing them by 1520. This gave the cathedral the appearance of a fortress, which it retained until the walls were finally torn down in the 19th century.

Suleiman, victor at Mohács, was the Ottomans' greatest ruler, who doubled the size of the empire during his reign (1520–66). Dubbed 'The Magnificent', he preferred the title of 'Lawgiver'.

The piecemeal occupation of Croatia by the Ottomans was relentless but it encountered fierce resistance. From Rome, an anxious papal court watched the country's steady collapse with a mixture of alarm for the security of Italy and admiration for the Croats' valour in defence of their land. When the military genius Suleiman the Magnificent became Sultan in 1520, Hungary-Croatia suffered a further series of defeats and more land was overrun by the Turkish invaders.

Croatian nobles desperately canvassed outside powers for support. Bishop Šimun Kožičić

Mohács in southern Hungary, the Ottomans annihilated a joint Hungarian-Croat army, killing King Ludovik II and opening the way to the Hungarian capital of Buda. Most of Hungary fell quickly to the Ottomans. In December, a remaining portion in the northwest of the country accepted the Habsburg claim to the Hungarian crown. Croatia promptly followed suit. On New Year's Day 1527, the Diet of Cetin offered the Habsburg Archduke Ferdinand of Austria the Croatian crown.

The long era of Hungarian domination was thus over and the baton was passed to the Aus-

Turkish forces in battle.

of Modrus went to Rome to plead Croatia's cause before the Catholic bishops, who were attending the Fifth Lateran Council in 1513. Nobles such as the 82-year-old Bernardin Frankopan attended the Diet of Nuremberg, summoned by the Habsburg Holy Roman Emperor Charles V, in 1522. But the timing of their appeals was unfortunate. The papacy and the Holy Roman Empire were both weakened and distracted by the Lutheran revolt against the Church, which threatened to plunge the whole of Europe into civil war. Preoccupied with the religious chasm that was opening up within his own domains, Charles V left the Croats to their own fate.

Hungary-Croatia's end came five years after the fall of Belgrade. In August 1526 at the Battle of

trians. Few might have predicted that they would keep hold of it for almost 400 years.

OTTOMAN RULE

The Ottoman conquest had vast, overwhelmingly negative consequences for the Croats. Serbs, Greeks, Bosnians and Albanians all resented subjugation to a Muslim emperor but, deep inside the Ottoman domains, they were able to reap some material benefits from the imposition of a stable government. The Ottomans built roads and bridges through their lands and erected fine administrative local capitals. In addition, the Orthodox Christian Serb and Greek churches revived to a degree, taking advantage of the Ottoman Empire's tolerance of the

Orthodox faith. Many Albanians and Bosnians, meanwhile, converted to Islam, uniting their fates with that of the Ottoman Empire.

The Croats, on the other hand, were condemned to endure all the disadvantages of life on a shifting and unstable frontier. Their Roman Catholic religion was anathema to the Turks, who viewed the pope as one of their most dangerous political foes. The result was the virtual depopulation of many areas of Croatia and radical ethnic and religious changes in others. In the half-empty lands of Slavonia, new com-

Bosnia and Croatia to the city-state of Dubrovnik (then known as Ragusa) and to the Venetian-ruled towns in Dalmatia. Many were highly educated professionals and they quickened the pace of intellectual life, stimulating a new interest in the place that Croats held in the wider family of Slav nations.

The late 15th and early 16th centuries also saw the publication of numerous books in the Glagolitic script that Grgur of Nin had championed many centuries earlier. But the decision of poets such as Marko Marulić to use Latin

Ragusa, the name given to the independent republic of Dubrovnik, thrived as a trading hub between the 15th and 18th centuries, even rivalling Venice.

munities of Muslim Turks and Slav converts settled the deserted towns of Osijek and Ilok. Bihać, in western Bosnia, also underwent a complete change after the Ottomans captured and sacked the city in 1592, and repopulated it almost entirely with Muslims. While towns were restocked with Muslim settlers, the empty countryside was repopulated with migrating herdsmen and shepherds. Most were ethnic Vlachs who belonged to the Serbian Orthodox Church.

INTELLECTUAL FLOWERING

The Turkish occupation did have a few positive side effects for the Croats, however. There was an influx of thousands of Catholic refugees from

instead of Cyrillic letters (still used today in Serbia) was prescient. The dice were loaded against a permanent revival of Glagolitic. The Renaissance anchored Croatian culture more firmly than ever within a Western European orbit, where the use of the Latin alphabet was universal. Glagolitic would survive but it became increasingly marginalised, finally fading from the picture in the 19th century.

SUBORDINATE TO VENICE

While Croatian culture flourished in 16th-century Venetian Dalmatia – and benefited from Venice's role as a European centre for the book trade – the Croats were always conscious of their subordinate place in the hierarchy of the Italian city-state. Moreover, colonial rule brought few economic benefits to the Adriatic towns and cities, which were exploited as staging posts and military garrisons. Venice imported raw materials from Dalmatia – mainly wine, cheese, salt and animal skins – but strongly discouraged manufacturing. Under this unfavourable economic regime, many Adriatic cities took on an increasingly petrified appearance. In Trogir, new building work virtually ceased after Venice took over in the 15th

The word 'argosy' to describe a fleet of mercantile ships is derived from the word Ragusa, the old name for the seafaring city of Dubrovnik.

century. The great age of the Adriatic cities appeared to be over.

THE REPUBLIC OF DUBROVNIK

The shining exception to this overall picture of economic decline in the Adriatic was the Republic of Dubrovnik (Ragusa). Never a particularly large city, with a population of only a few thousand, it had retained its liberty, pride and wealth through its merchant fleet, which plied the shipping lanes from the Levant in the east to Flanders in the north. The city functioned as a great entrepôt for the Ottoman-ruled territories in the Balkans, where Dubrovnik's enterprising merchants established many commercial interests.

Though a republic, Dubrovnik was no democracy. As in Venice, power resided in the hands of a noble elite that controlled the Grand Council. But as a wealthy, beautiful, Slav and Catholic city, Dubrovnik provided a beacon for many Croatian writers and intellectuals at a time when all their other hopes appeared to be dashed.

Dubrovnik's golden age came to an abrupt end in 1667, when a massive earthquake levelled most of the city and killed half the population. Until then, the Croats serenaded the city as their 'Croatian Athens'.

Statue of poet Ivan Gundulić, Dubrovnik.

☉ THE CROATIAN RENAISSANCE

Many Renaissance writers and poets in Dubrovnik and Venetian Dalmatia explored ideas of racial solidarity among the Slavs, while others used the new medium of printing to write the first works in Croatian as opposed to Latin, marking the liberation of Croatian culture from purely religious themes. A landmark was the publication of *Judita* (Judith), the first epic poem in Croatian, by the Split poet Marko Marulić. It was written in 1501 and published in Venice in 1521. Marulić's poem enjoyed huge popularity. Its story of a widow struggling to retain her faith, dignity and independence in circumstances of extreme adversity was an obvious allegory of the plight of Croatia as a whole.

The Golden Age of Croatian literature was typified in the work of Ivan Gundulić (1589–1638), a poet from Dubrovnik, who celebrated the combined strengths of the Slavic nations in a famous epic, *Osman*. Another highly significant figure in this Croatian Renaissance period was the Benedictine abbot Mavro Orbini, from the island of Mljet. His book *Il Regno degli Slavi* (The Kingdom of the Slavs), published in Italy in 1601, provided the first comprehensive account of all the Slavic nations. This flowering of Slavic consciousness among the Croat intelligentsia, whose sons were often sent to be educated in Italian universities, stimulated the production of many books and plays.

THE HABSBURGS

Austrian measures to repel the Ottoman threat had important consequences for Croatia: it sowed the seeds for future conflict.

The first decades of Habsburg rule in Croatia began ominously. Further Turkish incursions led to the loss of more territory, so that by the end of the 16th century all that was left was a small patch of land surrounding Zagreb. This was the dismal inheritance that the Croatian Sabor mournfully referred to as the *Reliquiae Reliquiarum*, the 'Remains of the Remains' of the once great Kingdom of Croatia.

But in the second half of the century the tide began to turn. A seminal event was the Siege of Siget (Szigetvár in Hungarian) in southern Hungary in 1566, where for a month a Croat force under *the ban* Nikola Šubić-Zrinski held up a vastly superior army under Suleiman the Magnificent. Although the Ottomans eventually overwhelmed the town, the *ban's* exploits made him a hero among Croats and thrilled all Christian Europe, while the Ottomans' image of invincibility was dented by the death of the great Sultan himself at the siege. Then, in 1593, a powerful Turkish assault on the last Croatian stronghold south of Zagreb was repulsed in the landmark Battle of Šišak. Although the Turks would menace Croatia – and, indeed, Vienna – for another century, there was a sense that the Turkish Empire had reached a high-water mark.

THE VOJNA KRAJINA

The Austrians, meanwhile, strengthened their defences in Croatia. In a development of great significance for the nation's political future, they established a string of garrisons along the Croatian border with Ottoman territory, removing the surrounding area from the jurisdiction of the *sabor* (parliament) and placing it under the direct control of the Austrian military. The Vojna Krajina, or military border, was designed

Double-headed eagle (symbol of the Austro-Hungarian Empire) in Rijeka.

to act as a breakwater against further Ottoman incursions. Most importantly, the Austrians turned the entire population of the Krajina into a permanent standing army, obliged to spend their active lives in the emperor's direct service and beyond the jurisdiction of the *sabor*. Owing to the depopulation of the frontier zone, the Habsburgs also encouraged Orthodox Christian Vlachs and Serbs to migrate into Krajina, permanently altering Croatia's ethnic and religious composition.

The Croat nobles in the *sabor* resented their loss of control over such a large portion of Croatia's remaining territory and the immigration of so many non-Catholics. They also resented

The destruction of two of Croatia's leading families, Frankopans and Zrinskis, opened the way for a new German, or Germanised, aristocracy whose loyalties lay with the Habsburgs but who had none of their pretensions to national leadership.

the immigrants' status as free peasants exempt from feudal control. The *sabor* called for its own jurisdiction to be restored over the new inhabit-

two leading families, the Frankopans and Zrinskis, who hawked the Croatian crown around France and Poland. In desperation, they even offered it to the Sultan in exchange for the reconstitution of all or most of the old Croatian kingdom. Not surprisingly, there were no takers and when news of the plot was leaked, the heads of both families were arrested. On 30 April 1671, they were executed and their lands were broken up.

The longed-for end to Ottoman rule over Croatia followed remarkably soon, though it was the Turks, not the Austrians, who initiated the chain

The Battle of Vienna in September 1683 marked a turning point in the battle against the Turks.

ants of the Krajina who infinitely preferred their status as armed warriors serving the emperor to that of menial serfs serving the Croat nobility. Ignoring the demands of the *sabor*, Ferdinand II confirmed the incomers' civil and religious freedoms in the *Statuta Valachorum* (Statute of Vlachs) of 1630, and granted them the powers to elect their own judges and local chiefs.

Anger over the shape of the Vojna Krajina and a growing sense of disillusion over the Habsburgs' failure to roll back the tide of Ottoman conquest formed the background to a series of anti-Austrian plots by the Croatian nobles. Their frustration peaked when Austria defeated the Turks at Szeged in 1664, only to concede yet more territory. The conspiracy was headed by Croatia's

of events leading up to it. Their fatal tactical error was the siege of Vienna in 1683, which finally roused the Austrians to a decisive counterblow. After the siege was broken, Habsburg armies ploughed deep into the Balkans, reaching Kosovo in southern Serbia in 1689. Ten years later, the Peace of Srijemski Karlovci left Turkey with most of its Balkan empire intact but Hungary and Slavonia were reunited under the Habsburg sceptre.

To the annoyance of the *sabor*, most of liberated Slavonia was added to the Vojna Krajina, over which they had no control. However, thousands of Croats were able to settle the virgin lands, along with Orthodox Serbs, Germans, Hungarians and others, turning Slavonia into an ethnic mosaic.

PROSPEROUS PEACE

The century that followed proved to be a golden age for the new aristocracy and the middle classes. The towns of Croatia-Slavonia took on an appearance that many retain to this day, their skylines dominated by onion-domed Baroque churches and some impressive civic buildings. The Baroque chateaux that pepper the landscape, such as the massive and imposing Eltz castle in Vukovar, and the Odescalchi chateau in Ilok, show the prosperity of the new noble families who had been rewarded for their services to the dynasty with large estates.

Catholic convents and monasteries. They did not appreciate the new talk of being 'citizens' and they could not read the new progressive newspapers such as the *Kraljski Dalmatin* (The King's Dalmatian), which the French encouraged. They knew only that they were being heavily taxed.

The Illyrian experiment folded with the defeat of Napoleon and Dalmatia's incorporation into the Habsburg Empire in 1815. But there could be no outright return to the moribund political order that had prevailed before the 1790s. Though the Dalmatian peasants remained sceptical of

Napoleon and the French capture Venice in 1797 during his campaign to drive the Austrians out of northern Italy.

THE KINGDOM OF ILLYRIA

The years of peace and plenty – for the rich – came to an end after the French Revolution in 1789, though it was not so much the handful of Jacobins in Croatia who disturbed the old order as the French occupation of Venice in 1797. Overnight, the centuries-old Venetian Empire collapsed and Dalmatia was incorporated into a new Napoleonic creation, the Kingdom of Illyria, including Dubrovnik, which was overrun in 1806.

This French client state was not popular. Dalmatia's impoverished Catholic peasants believed in their priests, who told them that the French were atheistic devils come to rob them of their religion. They boycotted the schools and academies that the French set up in suppressed

French notions of progress, an urban minority had drunk deeply from the well of French thought and they became a restless element in the ultra-conservative Austria of Prince Metternich. Austria's failure to revive Dalmatia's economy and its firm refusal to allow Dalmatia's union inside the empire with Croatia-Slavonia fed a sense of national frustration. This was heightened as an increasingly assertive Hungary began to flex its muscles and promote its ancient claims to Croatia as part of the Hungarian crown.

NATIONAL REVIVAL

Hungarian pressure only stimulated a national revival among the Croats. The new national party in Croatia had its chance in 1848, the 'Year of

Revolutions', when bourgeois radicals toppled the French monarchy, drove the Pope from Rome and threw most of Europe's ruling houses on the defensive. In Hungary, a nationalist uprising under the radical parliamentarian Lajos Kossuth threatened the Habsburg Empire with destruction. It also gave the Croat reformers their opportunity. Pledging loyalty to the dynasty, Josip Jelačić, a popular army officer from the Vojna Krajina, was installed as *ban* of Croatia amid unprecedented popular rejoicing. A wave of changes followed, including the abolition of feudalism, the reform of

Karl Marx never forgave Jelačić for siding with Vienna against Hungary, scorning 'these dying nationalities…who had tried to profit from the confusion of 1848'. Jelačić's statue in Zagreb was removed in 1947, but restored in 1990.

the *sabor*, the unification of Croatia and Slavonia and the adoption of Croatian as the exclusive language of government and education.

Statue of Josip Jelačić, Zagreb.

⊘ THE LANGUAGE OF A NATION

Pressure from Hungary was one of the factors in Croatia's 19th-century national revival which centred on language. At this time a multitude of tongues was spoken throughout Croatia-Slavonia and Dalmatia. While the aristocracy and the urban elite spoke German or Hungarian in Croatia, their counterparts in Dalmatia used Italian. Several mutually incomprehensible Slav dialects were spoken among the peasants. In the 1920s and 1930s, a group of young intellectuals instigated the 'Illyrium Movement' with the aim of standardising the language.

Inspired by the example of neighbouring Serbia, where a talented lexicographer, Vuk Karadžić, reformed the Serbian language and alphabet with royal support,

Ljudevit Gaj attempted a similar reform in Croatia. Gaj himself spoke Kajkavian, the dialect of Zagreb, and though this had a strong literary tradition, he turned instead to the *stokavski* dialect of Dubrovnik, the national standard. It was also a language understood by Serbs, Bosnians and Montenegrins. The movement was popular and received the discreet support of the authorities in Vienna who were increasingly wary of Hungary's pretensions. As a result, Gaj's allies had no problems with the government when they published the first newspapers, *Novine Horvatske* (Croatian News) and a literary supplement, *Danica* (Morning Star) in their standardised Croatian.

But Croatia's moment of freedom did not outlive the crushing of the Hungarian uprising in 1849. Once Kossuth was safely defeated, with Russian aid, Vienna no longer felt it needed to indulge Jelačić and the Croats, and the Austrians had no intention of permitting Croatia and Dalmatia to unite into a powerful bloc. Most of the reforms in Croatia were undone and a new emphasis on Germanisation prevailed. In 1859, Jelačić died a broken man.

The ideas of the *narodnjaki*, or nationals, as the patriotic party was called, did not perish, even though their powerlessness encouraged constant

Strossmayer, proponent of pan-Slavism.

factional splits. In the last quarter of the 19th century, two broad strands developed in Croatian political thought. The Party of Rights under Ante Starčević (1823–96) rallied those who wanted Croatia to develop its national programme alone. Those hankering for a wider Slavic union embracing Croats, Serbs and others leaned to the National Party led by Josip Juraj Strossmayer (1815–1905), the Catholic Bishop of Đakovo. The difference between the two groups was exacerbated by intense personal rivalry between these two doughty old bachelors. Though their party ideologies were often blurred, they undoubtedly represented diverging answers to a perennial question: could a nation as small and weak as the Croats' survive as a self-contained entity, or did it need to subsume its identity into a larger Slavic association? The question would dog Croatia right up to independence in the 1990s.

> 'The Hungarians are a proud, egotistical and in the highest degree tyrannical race and my poor nation is persecuted, oppressed and ill-treated.' Strossmayer to William Gladstone

The empire's division into Austria-Hungary in 1867 increased popular pressure on all political factions in Croatia to form a common front. After a crushing military defeat at the hands of Prussia, Austria devised a 'dual monarchy', effectively splitting the empire between Vienna and Budapest. But Hungary gained its freedom from Vienna at the expense of the Croats, Serbs, Romanians and other nationalities, who found themselves under the thumb of a highly nationalistic government in Budapest. The Hungarians tried to head off Croatian unrest with a special agreement, the Nagodba. This granted Croatia a measure of self-government within an autonomous Hungary. In practice, the Nagodba was subverted because effective power resided not with the *sabor* but with the *ban* appointed by the Hungarian government.

The *ban* from 1883 to 1903, Charles Khuen-Hedervary, was a particularly devoted servant of Hungarian interests, manipulating the *sabor* and playing on the mistrust between the Catholic Croats and the large Serb Orthodox minority to divide and rule. Though outwardly successful in his aims, Khuen-Hedervary unintentionally closed the gap between the parties and nationalities in Croatia, who increasingly saw through his motives. The result was the formation of a historic coalition, uniting most Croat and ethnic Serb parties under a programme of national equality, and the union of Dalmatia and Croatia. In 1905–6, this Croatian-Serbian coalition swept the board in elections to both the Dalmatian and Croatian assemblies. These coalition victories alarmed the authorities in Vienna and Budapest. In Croatia-Slavonia, Hungary's puppet *bans* repeatedly dissolved the *sabor* and called for new elections in the hope of different results. In 1908, the authorities put 52 ethnic Serb politicians on trial for treason, sentencing 31 of them to jail.

EMIGRATION AND WORLD WAR I

Economic depression fuelled the sullen mood in Croatia and Dalmatia. While cities such as Zagreb expanded and were beautified in this period, modest industrialisation failed to absorb the landless poor who began emigrating to the New World. Between 1900 and 1913, about half a million Croats left for North America.

The outbreak of World War I in 1914, precipitated by the assassination at Sarajevo in Bosnia Herzegovina of the heir to the Austrian throne, the Archduke Ferdinand and his wife Sophie, by

London as a bribe for abandoning the Triple Alliance and entering the war on their side. Fear of Italian designs on the Adriatic was a powerful incentive for Croats to throw in their lot with neighbouring Serbia.

A YUGOSLAV STATE

At the Serbian headquarters in exile on Corfu in 1917, a Yugoslav Committee, comprising Croatian politicians, intellectuals and artists, set out to negotiate terms for a new south-Slav, or *jugoslav*, state with the Serbian prime minister,

Archduke Ferdinand before his assassination in Sarajevo, the event that triggered World War I.

Bosnian nationalists, was a dramatic distraction. Tens of thousands of Croats dutifully answered the call-up to the imperial army. Among them was a young Croat called Josip Broz, known later as 'Tito' when he became the Communist ruler of the new state of Yugoslavia. The empire was too weak to withstand a protracted war, however, and the death of the Emperor Franz Josef in 1916 effectively marked the end of the long Habsburg era. The new emperor, Charles, struggled on until Austria's defeat set the nationalities on paths to independence. The Croats' greatest worry was that the victorious Entente powers might bargain away their land. Britain and France had been ready to offer Istria and Dalmatia to Italy in the secret 1915 Pact of

Nikola Pašić. The Croats were encouraged by the entry of the United States into the war that year. President Woodrow Wilson stated his support for the principle of national self-determination.

In October 1918, the empire's southern front collapsed and Austria-Hungary sued for an armistice. The National Council of Croats, Serbs and Slovenes was set up in Zagreb as a provisional government for the empire's southern Slavs. The Croatian *sabor* declared independence and on 1 December a delegation in Belgrade presented the agreed terms for unification to Prince Aleksandar, the heir to the Serbian throne. Aleksandar I Karadordević then proclaimed the new state the Kingdom of Serbs, Croats and Slovenes.

THE MODERN AGE

After a turbulent and bloody road to independence, Croatia has quickly become one of Europe's most spectacular tourist destinations.

The Croats soon regretted the haste with which they had negotiated the terms of union with Serbia at the end of 1918 (see page 45). The Vidovdan (St Vitus Day) Constitution of June 1921 abolished Croatia as a separate entity and established a centralised state in Belgrade under Serbia's Karađorđević royal family. The Treaty of Rapallo with Italy the previous year was another disappointment, as it ceded Zadar, Istria and the islands of Lošinj, Cres and Lastovo to Italy. The city of Rijeka (Fiume in Italian) was made a League of Nations trusteeship but subsequently also fell into Italian hands.

Croatian resentment of the post-war political and territorial settlement was articulated through the Croatian Republican Peasant Party (HRSS) led by Stjepan Radić. The idol of the rural masses, Radić waged an unsuccessful, non-violent struggle for Croatian autonomy, his popularity increased by regular spells in jail. His assassination in 1928 in the Belgrade parliament by a Serbian nationalist deputy from Montenegro, Puniša Račić, threatened the country with civil war and gave King Aleksandar an opportunity to suspend parliamentary government and proclaim a royal dictatorship the following year.

Direct rule by the monarch failed to heal any of the bitter divisions, and the renaming of the Kingdom of Serbs, Croats and Slovenes as Yugoslavia was interpreted by the people merely as a cosmetic gesture.

THE FASCISTIC USTAŠE

Ethnic and political polarisation led to the creation of a right-wing authoritarian movement in Croatia modelled on Benito Mussolini's Fascists in Italy. The Ustaše (from *ustanak* meaning uprising), led by a lawyer, Ante Pavelić, rejected the

Aleksandar I, Prince of Serbia and King of Yugoslavia (1921–34).

Peasants Party's parliamentary politics, its programme of non-violent agitation and its willingness to accept autonomy rather than complete independence. Based mainly in Italy, the Ustaše were sponsored by Mussolini as a useful tool with which to destabilise his neighbour and keep the question of sovereignty over Dalmatia alive.

The assassination of King Aleksandar in Marseille in France in 1934, in which the Ustaše were implicated, opened the way for a new political settlement in Yugoslavia. The dead king's cousin, Prince Paul, became regent during the new King Peter's minority. With Hitler now in power in Berlin, and Mussolini in Rome, the regent resolved to prevent Europe's expansionist dictators from playing on Yugoslavia's divisions. For this, he engineered a historic compromise between the Serbs and Croats. The terms of the 1939 national *Sporazum*, or agreement, established a Croatian Banovina with considerable autonomy. The deal was a triumph for Vladko Maček, Radić's successor as head of the Peasant Party, but it did not have long to prove itself.

WORLD WAR II

The outbreak of World War II in September 1939 made it certain that Yugoslavia would

invasion in 1941 and hopes raised by the *Sporazum* were destroyed.

While the Germans occupied Serbia, setting up a puppet government under General Nedić, their Italian allies sponsored an Ustaše takeover of Croatia. The Independent State of Croatia, Nezavisna Država Hrvatska (NDH), was proclaimed in Zagreb on 10 April. The credibility of the new regime was boosted by a public blessing from Croatia's Catholic leader, the Archbishop of Zagreb, Alojzije Stepinac.

The popularity the new regime gained by proclaiming independence dwindled when

Ante Pavelić, leader of the Ustaše and later the NDH, in Zagreb in 1941.

be drawn into the conflagration, especially after Mussolini's abortive invasion of Greece in 1940. Succumbing to overwhelming German pressure, Yugoslavia signed the Tripartite Pact with Germany, Italy and Japan in the following March, triggering a British-inspired military coup in April. This led to a German

> Dalmatians became hostile to the new 'independent state of Croatia' when the regime was forced to hand over vast sections of the Dalmatian coast to Italy, including the area from Zadar to Split and the Kvarner islands.

the Ustaše's Italian patrons imposed a humiliating territorial settlement. In the Rome Agreement of 18 May 1941, Italy added the port of Susak, near Rijeka, the islands of Krk, Rab and Pag and the north Dalmatian coast from Zadar to Split to its Dalmatian domains. A much wider area was designated Italy's 'sphere of influence', in which the Italian military were paramount.

As compensation, the NDH was granted Bosnia Herzegovina, with a result that 2 million of the enlarged state's 6.3 million population were Orthodox Serbs. Serb hostility to the new order was guaranteed by Ustaše mass killings and deportations of Serbs and Jews and the establishment of concentration camps for the regime's political and racial enemies, most notoriously at Jasenovac, south of Zagreb.

By the summer of 1941, the NDH faced a full-scale revolt by Serb royalist 'Chetniks' under Draža Mihajlović. The NDH's problems were augmented after anti-Fascist Croats and Serbs rallied to a left-wing uprising proclaimed by the Yugoslav Communist Party leader, Josip Broz 'Tito', in June 1941. Tito's Partisans were initially a less important force than the Chetniks but in 1944, after a British secret agent, Fitzroy Maclean, parachuted into Yugoslavia and praised the Partisans' fighting

in Argentina in 1957. His army was less lucky. Fleeing to Austria to escape Partisan retribution, thousands of soldiers accompanied by their families were turned back at the border by British occupation forces. Partisans executed almost all of them at the village of Bleiburg.

TITO IN POWER

With the Partisans now in control of Yugoslavia, the pretence at a coalition government was abandoned and a strict Communist regime imposed. Non-Communists were rapidly eased out of the

A clandestine Partisan meeting, 1944.

abilities to the wartime leader Winston Churchill, the allies switched support from Mihajlović to Tito.

At a series of stage-managed conferences at Bihać in 1942 and at Jajce in 1943, the Anti-Fascist Council for the National Liberation of Yugoslavia (AVNOJ) presented its programme for a new settlement, based on Yugoslavia's division into six federal republics, Serbia, Croatia, Slovenia, Bosnia Herzegovina, Macedonia and Montenegro.

The Allied invasion of Normandy and Russia's advance westwards in 1944 heralded Germany's defeat and with it the fall of Pavelić's NDH and other satellite regimes. In November 1944, Tito entered Belgrade and on 8 May 1945, the day Germany surrendered, the Partisans entered Zagreb. Pavelić escaped and would die

government and their parties suppressed. A single-list 'election' in November 1945 gave Tito's Popular Front the predictable 95 percent of votes it sought. With the politicians jailed, silenced or exiled, the regime turned to the Catholic Church, arresting Archbishop Stepinac in 1946 for collaboration. Incriminated by his public support for the NDH in 1941, he was imprisoned, and then placed under house arrest, dying in 1960.

Purges were not restricted to non-Communists. In 1948 the former wartime leader of the Croatian Communists, Andrija Hebrang, was arrested and never seen again. The break with Stalin in 1948 and Yugoslavia's expulsion from the Cominform (Communist Information Bureau) brought no let-up in the repressive regime, or in the ubiquitous activities of the secret police, the OZNA, later known as the UDBA. However, the government's resistance to Soviet pressure was popular. In Croatia, the return of Italian-occupied Dalmatia, Istria and Rijeka also boosted the Communists' standing and gave them a more patriotic profile than Communists enjoyed elsewhere in Eastern Europe.

In the early 1960s, a political thaw set in. A vigorous debate on the virtues of economic decentralisation was permitted, and mass tourism was encouraged in Dalmatia, signalling a more general opening-up to the West. Within Croatia, the death of Archbishop Stepinac – and the impressive funeral the authorities permitted – eased the path towards a less fraught relationship between Church and State.

THE CROATIAN SPRING

At the same time, a new generation of Communist leaders emerged that was less timorous than its elders about pressing for greater autonomy and liberalisation. Led by Miko Tripalo and Savka Dabčević-Kučar, their movement would soon become known

Tito as a Partisan in 1942.

⊘ TITO

Born in 1892 in a small stone house in Kumrovec (see page 235) to a Croatian father and Slovenian mother, Josip Broz became a sergeant major in World War I. He was captured fighting the Russians and while in prison learned to speak their language. He met his wife, Pelagija Belousova, in Siberia and fought with the Red Guards in the Russian Civil War.

On his return, Broz became active in the Yugoslav Communist Party and was frequently imprisoned. Having to work clandestinely, he adopted the name Tito to conceal his identity. Tito is Croatian for Titus, but his wartime advocate Fitzroy Maclean maintains that he earned the name for ordering people about, pointing

first at them and then at what was to be done, saying: 'you' *(ti)* 'that' *(to)*.

As post-war leader of the country, he had an ability to hold the disparate elements of the Balkans together while refusing to ally the country with either the Soviet Union or the West. This made Tito one of the most remarkable figures in the history of the region. On his death in 1980, thousands of Croats lined the railway line to watch his famous Blue Train carry the presidential coffin back from the clinic in Ljubljana, where he had died, to Belgrade.

Even now Tito is remembered by many members of the older generation with affection.

as the Croatian Spring, or as the 'maspok', from *masovni pokret*, meaning mass movement.

At first Tito tolerated the reformists, especially when they offered him crucial backing against the Soviets during the invasion of Czechoslovakia in August 1968, which he condemned. In the same year, Savka Dabčević-Kučar became the head of the Croatian League of Communists and when, two years later, she fought off a challenge by party hardliners, she unleashed a wave of public rallies that made her a national heroine – a highly dangerous position in a Communist society.

The number of enemies of the Croatian Spring began multiplying to include many of Croatia's ethnic Serbs, who feared a revival of Croat nationalism, long-time Croatian Communist stalwarts, the Serb-dominated Yugoslav People's Army and the hardline leaders of neighbouring Bosnia Herzegovina. Abroad, the Soviet Union denounced events in Croatia and, on a visit to Yugoslavia in September 1971, Soviet leader Leonid Brezhnev virtually ordered Tito to remove anti-Communist elements.

The crunch came in November when radical students engulfed Croatian university campuses with strikes, enraging Tito who was then on a visit to the United States. On his return, he summoned the Croatian leadership to the old hunting lodge of the Serbian royal family at Karadordevo on 1 December and ordered them to resign. A widespread purge of the universities, newspapers, radio and television and the League of Communists followed. Thousands lost their jobs and hundreds served jail terms.

AFTER TITO

Tito's last decade was marked by ideological stagnation and a marked rise in living standards that took the edge off discontent. Most Yugoslavs turned away from politics towards the pursuit of the good life, their new prosperity underpinned by seemingly limitless Western credits. The ideological straitjacket was made more comfortable by greatly increased access to foreign holidays and consumer items that the inhabitants of other Communist countries could only dream about. But by the time of Tito's death in 1980, the artificial boom of the 1970s, purchased on the strength of foreign loans, had saddled the country with a US$20 billion debt.

Foreign media predictions that Yugoslavia would collapse without his guiding hand were at first

unfounded. The official slogan, *I Posle Tita – Tito!* (And after Tito there will be Tito), testified to the political elite's determination to maintain his legacy.

His final political settlement, the 1974 constitution, left the Yugoslav presidency to a rotating collective, representing all the republics. Within a few years, however, this inheritance began to unravel as a severe economic crisis hit home. As high inflation and wage cuts hit the workers and shortages of goods hit the shops, an acrimonious argument erupted between the republics on how to restore Yugoslavia's finances, pitting the four

Tito the statesman.

poorer republics against the two richest: Croatia and neighbouring Slovenia. These two demanded radical solutions, including greater autonomy for the republics, cuts in the massive army budget and an end to subsidies for failing enterprises.

In Slovenia, a new liberal Communist leadership under Milan Kučan took power in 1986 and began reaching out to non-Communists, ecological groups and other sympathetic parties, horrifying the guardians of Communist orthodoxy in Belgrade and the Yugoslav Army. They began to accuse the Slovene Communists of treason.

MILOŠEVIĆ'S BID FOR A GREATER SERBIA

In Serbia, affairs moved in a different direction. There, growing anger over the ethnic turmoil in the province of Kosovo propelled an authoritarian Communist, Slobodan Milošević, to assume the party leadership in 1986. The Kosovo crisis had been years in unfolding. It was poor, overcrowded and overwhelmingly Albanian, but the Serbs insisted that it was the medieval cradle of their state and had to remain inside Serbia. They bitterly resented the local Albanian-led government that had been given some autonomy under the 1974 constitution.

Serb frustration over their loss of control created a groundswell of opinion in favour of Milošević's 'big stick' tactics. The new Serbian

Tuđman posing with Croatian national basketball players during a triumphal visit to the liberated Serb capital, Knin, in August 2006.

leader encouraged massive tumultuous rallies throughout Serbia, where Kosovo's Albanian leaders and other 'enemies' of the Serbs were lambasted as traitors. With the support of the Yugoslav Army's mostly Serb leaders, Milošević scrapped Kosovo's autonomy in 1989 and crushed Albanian demonstrations. Celebrating his victory, he was the star of a rally in Kosovo of about a million of his supporters, held to mark the 600th anniversary of the Battle of Kosovo in June.

A growing fear outside Serbia that Milošević aimed at achieving a dictatorship over the whole of Yugoslavia on the back of Serbian populism propelled the Slovene Communists to

unveil their own trump card. In January 1990, they walked out of the last Yugoslav Communist summit, ditched their Communist labels, rebranded themselves as Social Democrats and announced that multiparty elections would be held in Slovenia in April. Croatia followed suit, announcing its own multiparty poll at the same time. Yugoslavia was set for a showdown.

A NEW CROATIAN PARTY

The Slovene and Croatian Communist leaders both planned to benefit at the polls from posing as champions of Western-style democracy against Serbian authoritarianism. But while Kučan coasted into office as Slovenia's first elected president, his Croatian counterpart, Ivica Račan, stumbled. The suppression of the Croatian Spring had left a legacy of bitterness in Croatia that Račan's winning manner could not overcome, and many Croats twinned Communist ascendancy, however it was reformed, with Serbian domination.

Victory swung instead to an elderly outsider, Franjo Tuđman, and his Croatian Democratic Union, Hrvatska Demokratska Zajednica (HDZ). Born in 1922 into a Peasant Party family, Tuđman had joined the Partisans in World War II, rising to the rank of general in 1961. In the Croatian Spring he was active within the Matica Hrvatska publishing house, receiving a two-year jail sentence for nationalism in 1972 (reduced to nine months) and another three-year term in 1981.

In spite of his Communist, Partisan background, Tuđman boldly reached out to the traditionally right-wing Croat diaspora in the US, Canada, Australia and Argentina for money, ensuring his campaign was well financed. Campaigning almost exclusively on a nationalist platform, the HDZ trounced the opposition.

THE HOMELAND WAR

Tuđman's triumph was short-lived. After using Serbian agitation to swallow up Kosovo, Milošević was working towards a Greater Serbia and set his sights on Croatia. Here, 600,000 ethnic Serbs, a majority in large parts of the old Vojna Krajina (the Austrian military frontier lands that were to be a buffer against the Ottomans), proved amenable to his rhetoric about the HDZ being the new Ustaše, bent on completing the genocide of 1941. The town of Knin in the Dalmatian interior became the centre of militant

Serb opposition to HDZ rule and the presence of a large Yugoslav Army base ensured the rebels could act with impunity.

By the summer of 1990, a full-scale Serb revolt had erupted in the Krajina, aided by supplies of weapons delivered by the army. With Serbian encouragement, the rebels, led by a former dentist, Milan Babić, and a former policeman, Milan Martić, proclaimed the Autonomous Province of Serbian Krajina in August, declaring independence from Croatia shortly after.

While Babić's men rolled unimpeded through the Krajina in 1990, Serb militants opened new fronts in the spring of 1991 in Eastern Slavonia, on the border with Serbia round Vukovar, and in Western Slavonia, round the town of Pakrac. Their advances almost cut Croatia into three segments and the government lost control of about 30 percent of its territory.

In spite of American and international opposition, Slovenia and Croatia decided further discussions with Milošević were useless and that it was time to go for independence. Both states proclaimed their sovereignty on 25 June 1991. The two new countries' circumstances could not have been more different. After a brief skirmish with the Slovenes, the Yugoslav Army evacuated Slovenia with hardly a murmur.

Croatia, on the other hand, found itself gearing up for a long hot summer of desperate fighting against a coalition of local Serbs, the Yugoslav Army and paramilitary formations from Serbia proper. While many towns suffered severe bombardment, the most savage fighting enveloped Vukovar, which for both sides became a symbol of victory (see page 257). By the time of the surrender of Vukovar on 17 November it had been reduced to rubble and thousands were dead. Its capture was followed by a brutal war crime – the massacre of almost 300 Croat patients in Vukovar hospital. Their bodies were buried in a mass grave on a nearby sheep farm.

However, from October 1991 international attention focused more on the Siege of Dubrovnik by the Yugoslav navy and Montenegrin troops, who trapped the 50,000 inhabitants behind the medieval city walls and shelled this priceless Unesco landmark.

That autumn, the Serbs' blatant aggression awoke sympathy in Germany and Austria, which had large Croat communities. Germany's Foreign Minister, Hans-Dietrich Genscher, emerged as a trenchant critic of the West's hands-off policy and of the arms embargo that hurt the lightly armed Croats much more than Serbia and the Yugoslav Army. Fearful of a split in EU ranks, both Britain and France dropped their opposition and agreed to Europe's joint recognition of Slovenia and Croatia in December 1991.

THE VANCE PLAN

Serbia's desire to wind down the war, partly to concentrate on Bosnia Herzegovina, which

Siege of Dubrovnik, 1991.

also now demanded independence, prompted Milošević to throw his weight behind a ceasefire signed on 3 January 1992 and a UN-brokered peace plan for Croatia. Drawn up by former US Secretary of State Cyrus Vance, the Vance Plan involved the withdrawal of the Yugoslav Army from Croatia and the deployment of UN peacekeepers in UN Protected Areas, known

The phrase 'ethnic cleansing', synonymous with the war in Yugoslavia, was first used by the Croatian Supreme Council in July 1991 to describe Serbian actions against Croatians.

as UNPAS. Controversially, in Croatia, the plan did not address the question of Krajina's sovereignty, or the return of refugees. Nor were the local Serbs disarmed. Dissatisfaction with a deal that left the Serbs in possession of their territorial gains destabilised the agreement, ensuring Croatia's first years of independence were dominated by demands for the recovery of the Krajina.

PACT WITH MILOŠEVIĆ

While public attention in Croatia focused on the Krajina, Tuđman pursued a disastrous

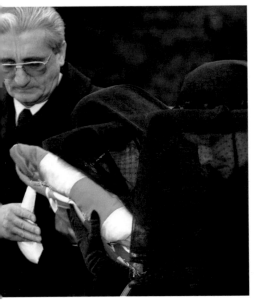

Tuđman's son, wife and daughter at his funeral in Mirogoj Cemetery, Zagreb, 1999.

adventure in Bosnia Herzegovina, effectively endorsing Milošević's partition policy on the understanding that Croatia would receive a chunk in the southwest, where many Bosnian Croats lived. Condemned in the West, Croatia's military intrigues in Bosnia lost it the sympathy it had briefly attracted over Vukovar and Dubrovnik. The policy was unpopular at home, too, where the idea of a tacit alliance with Milošević against the Bosnian Muslims revolted public opinion. Ordered by the US to disengage from a messy war in Bosnia in spring 1994, or face global sanctions, Tuđman watched his prestige hit an all-time low and the media clamoured for his removal.

The end of the Bosnian conflict, however, concentrated minds on the Krajina. By the spring of 1995, Tuđman's defence minister Gojko Šušak had transformed the ragged army of 1991 into a well-armed fighting force, which was confident it could take on the Krajina Serbs. In a test strike in April 1995, named Operation Flash (*Bljesak* in Croatian), the Croats overran the smallest UNPA, in western Slavonia, within hours. In retaliation, Krajina forces shelled Zagreb.

Milošević's impassive reaction to Operation Flash indicated a loss of interest in the Krajina. The *casus belli* for another strike came in July, when the Bosnian Serb army attacked and overran the UN-proclaimed 'safe areas' of Srebrenica and Zepa in eastern Bosnia, murdering some 7,000 Muslims. With US encouragement, Bosnia and Croatia signed a mutual defence pact in Split in July, and on 4 August Tuđman sent 200,000 soldiers into the Krajina on Operation Storm (*Oluja* in Croatian). The Croats routed the Serb forces within 24 hours, triggering an epic exodus of at least 150,000 Serbs, fleeing towards Serb-held Bosnia and Serbia. The recovery of the Krajina was severely marred by the killing of several hundred Serb civilians who had remained behind, many of them elderly, and resulted in several army officers being pursued for war crimes.

With the fall of the Krajina, the recovery of the rest of occupied territory was only a matter of time, and Milošević quickly backed a plan to return the last slice of Serb-held land around Vukovar to Croatia, in eastern Slavonia.

PEACE WITH SOME PROSPERITY

The war had savage economic consequences and, tired of nationalist slogans, people became restive about the rampant corruption that allowed a clique of HDZ officials to asset-strip state enterprises under the guise of privatisation. Although vast crowds attended Tuđman's funeral on 13 December 1999, the people wanted change. The subsequent elections restored the former League of Communists leader, Ivica Račan, to the helm as prime minister of a centre-left coalition. The vote for the presidency went to Stipe Mesić, a former Tuđman ally who had turned against him over his Bosnia policy.

The ruins of Vukovar and their surroundings were returned to Croatia in December 1995, within three years of the signing of the UN-mediated Basic Agreement at Erdut.

The new government showed its determination to improve Croatia's profile by pledging to cooperate fully with the International War Crimes Tribunal for former Yugoslavia, mend

years in prison. Unfortunately the general then fled the country.

The political fortunes of the HDZ waned as corruption was being exposed within the government – most notoriously with the 10-year jail sentence given to former prime minister Ivo Sanader in 2012. Discontent over the economy grew during the global downturn of 2008-9, which eventually led to the HDZ's defeat in 2011 when the centre-left coalition headed by new Prime Minister Zoran Milanović took over. The necessary austerity measures brought in by

Vukovar, scene of a horrific siege in 1991.

fences with Bosnia Herzegovina and facilitate the return of Serb refugees. The coalition was buffeted by large popular protests against the extradition of Croatian officers to face war crimes charges, and Croatia's application to join the EU in 2004 was held up until General Ante Gotovina was tracked down and indicted for crimes against humanity. Milošević was already on trial for genocide, but he died in 2006 amid the proceedings. But the authorities have also shown that they are capable of meting out justice at home: in May 2009 former General Branimir Glavaš became the first Croatian politician to stand trial for crimes against Serbs. A court in Zagreb found him guilty of torturing and murdering 12 Serbs in 1991 and sentenced him to 10

Milanović dampened national enthusiasm for membership of the European Union, but the country met all the conditions and was admitted to the EU on 1 July 2013. Following the 2015 parliamentary elections, Tihomir Orešković became Prime Minister, but his cabinet was plagued by grave conflicts and proved very short lived. In September 2016, new elections were held and Andrej Plenković, of the Croatian Democratic Union, formed the new centre-right coalition government. Unemployment rates are still high, but tourism continues to be a vital and growing part of the economy, bolstered by the opening of a new €300-million terminal at Zagreb's airport in 2017. Croatia remains one of Europe's most beautiful and alluring tourist destinations.

RELIGION AND SOCIETY

Even after decades of Communist atheism, Catholicism remains at the heart of Croatian identity, bolstered through folk traditions. But it doesn't mean everyone regularly goes to church.

According to Freud, the smaller the real difference between peoples, the larger it is bound to loom in their imaginations. This point is made by the writer/broadcaster Michael Ignatieff, son of a Canadian ambassador to Yugoslavia, in *Blood and Belonging*. The book describes his journeys to Croatia during the Homeland War, and to other world hotspots, to discover what binds nations and gives people their identity, and how they crave recognition of that identity.

When the social and political experiment that was Yugoslavia fell apart, its constituent populations sought to show their identities in large part through their faiths. For Croatians, to profess their Roman Catholicism was as much about telling the world that they looked to the West for their identity as it was to say that they turned their back on Eastern Orthodox Christianity – in other words, the Serbs, not to mention those who believed in Islam. This difference, to Croatians, is very important indeed.

Nun outside Zagreb's cathedral.

The Orthodox rite involves complex iconography, and the Icon Museum next to the Serbian Orthodox Church in Dubrovnik is a place to see it.

Statistically around 90 percent of the country is Roman Catholic, and statistically around 90 percent of the population is ethnic Croat. To many Croatians, it amounts to the same thing.

That does not mean most people go to church regularly, or that everyone likes the clergy. Church attendance in urban areas is low and Croatia has an old left-wing, anti-clerical tradition, which has no time for organised religion.

However, there is a strong Marian cult, and professions as well as towns and villages have patron saints. The popularity of annual pilgrimages and saints' festivals is a reminder of the powerful grip that the Roman Catholic Church still exercises over the Croat imagination, in spite of years of atheistic indoctrination under the Communists. Weddings in church have also become more common, though the union has first to be sanctioned by a civil ceremony.

There are eight active Benedictine convents for nuns in the country, mostly on the islands, and one monastery for monks on the island of Pašman near Šibenik. Nuns work in schools and hospitals and they are a common sight in the streets. Most people still grant the Church a leading position in society as the historic guardian of the nation's identity, a role cemented in the Communist era and increased to a still greater degree in the 1990s, when war with Serbia at times assumed the aspect of a religious as well as a national struggle.

The Church strongly supported the country's bid for independence and drummed up support for Croatia's diplomatic recognition in the Vatican. In return, the government of Franjo Tudman restored religious education in schools – though attendance is not compulsory – and returned much of the Church property that the Communists had seized since 1945. But in his effort to unite the nation, Tudman failed to condemn the wartime Fascist Ustaše – against whom he had fought.

The beatification in 1998 of Alojzije Stepinac, Croatia's wartime Archbishop of Zagreb, was a significant and controversial political event. Pope John Paul II's act delighted Catholics and nationalists as much as it angered the greatly diminished Serb and Jewish communities, many of whom have always seen Stepinac as an apologist for the wartime Fascist regime of Ante Pavelić.

RELIGIOUS DIFFERENCES

The Balkan peninsula has long been a great soup of peoples and faiths. Ottomans, who occupied much of it for more than 500 years, practised some religious tolerance, with the local governing councils (millets) being made up of leaders of each religious community. But until the 19th century, Catholicism would have no other god but its own, a god who responded only to a Latin liturgy. Diocletian, in his palace at Split, had been the last Roman Emperor to persecute Christians, which he did with a vengeance. His successor, Constantine, converted to Christianity and founded Constantinople and the Byzantine Empire where, at the fall of Rome, the Eastern Church grew under the Orthodox rite that was fundamentally Greek. In Croatia, Glagolitic rites were sanctioned by the pope, and the Latin, Western Church continued its missions from Aquileia down the Adriatic coast, where the outposts of Venice and Ragusa (Dubrovnik) kept the pope's torch burning.

The Cyrillic alphabet, invented in the 9th century by saints Cyril and Methodius to write down the speech of the Slavs, created a third language in the Christian church: Old Church Slavonic, which came to be used in the Serbian, Bulgarian and Russian Orthodox churches.

The Serbo-Croat language that evolved in the Balkans after the fall of the Ottomans became the official language of Yugoslavia, but in the break-up of the state, it was rejected by Croatia at the first opportunity. A written language with familiar Western Latin letters replaced the Cyrillic alphabet that was seen as an instrument of repression. And though today the language may sound pretty similar to Serbian – or to Russian or any other Slavic language – such a suggestion should never be made to a Croat.

During the Balkans conflict, ecclesiastical

Zagreb's Orthodox Cathedral.

buildings were seen as targets on all sides, especially when religious leaders gave support to the fighting forces. In Croatia during the Homeland War, dozens of Serbian Orthodox churches and some monasteries, along with their treasures and graveyards, and around 5,000 icons were destroyed, damaged or looted, and the *eparchies* (dioceses) of Karlovac, Slavonia and Dalmatia were abandoned. After 1995, priests and bishops returned and the buildings have been largely restored, but congregations are diminished.

Old Church Slavonic, with Cyrillic script, used in the Serbian Orthodox Church is also adopted in the Croatian Greek Catholic Church established in the Eparchy of Križevci in central Croatia, whose parish once extended through much of Yugoslavia. It still practises the Byzantine rite and has about 6,000 adherents.

Mosques in Ottoman-occupied Slavonia were all torn down by the Catholic Austrians at the start of the 20th century. Now there are around 63,000 Muslims in the country, 1.5 percent of the population, and they have three mosques and 15 *masjids* (small mosques). The first of the modern mosques was built in Zagreb at the end of the Communist era, in 1987. There are currently plans for several more in Osijek, Sisak and Karlovac.

The churches of Croatia to be seen today are

gender rights was never an issue under Communism, when women were used to salaried work and to taking high office in the League of Communists. Savka Dabčević-Kučar, a Dalmatian, famously led the ill-fated Croatian Spring reform movement in the late 1960s. Milka Planinc, a far less popular figure, was another Croatian woman in the driving seat as Yugoslav premier in the early 1980s. In July 2009, the Croatian Democrat Union (HDZ) leader Jadranka Kosor, a former journalist, became prime minister when Ivo Sanader stepped down. And in 2015, Kolinda Grabar-Kitarović

Imam leading afternoon prayers in Zagreb's mosque.

therefore almost exclusively Roman Catholic, and there are some very beautiful buildings among them – the Basilica of Euphrasius in Poreč and the Cathedral of St James in Šibenik are world-class treasures. Many have once again become places of prayer, but some remain museums or social spaces for concerts and other events. But any local church is appreciated by its congregation, especially during festivals, when it is obvious just how much they are a focus of daily life.

EQUALITY OF OPPORTUNITY

Religious tolerance and ethnic reconciliation have been among the demands for joining the European Union, though these may have been achieved to a greater or lesser extent anyway. Equality of

⊘ CUSTOMS AND MANNERS

On the whole, Croatians are formal, punctual, respectful and neatly dressed. They shake hands, speak their minds and put store by family and age. Except for close friends and family, they address each other formally, as Gospodin (Mr), Gospođa (Mrs) and Gospodice (Miss). Friends get an embrace or a kiss on each cheek. Invited to a house, guests will take flowers, but not chrysanthemums, and there should be an odd number of stems. Guests should eat with enthusiasm and try to agree to second helpings if pressed. All this is a generalisation, of course: the rules of a more reserved interior and a more Latin coast still apply.

became Croatia's first female (and youngest ever) president. Former Croatian ambassador to the United States, Grabar-Kitarović studied in the US and speaks fluent English.

Today, even in more conservative country districts, women are far from submissive. Indeed, many believe Croatia is really a matriarchy, a state of affairs summed up in the old Dalmatian proverb: *Žena drži tri kantuna kuće* – A woman holds three corners of the house. In 2005, the women of Ložišća on the island of Brač won all seven seats on the local council after proclaim-

depopulated if the trend is not reversed in the next quarter-century.

As in the rest of the West, women are also getting married later, and while many of the old religious taboos, such as no sex before marriage, seem to have crumbled away in urban areas, others remain pretty much in place. There is still pressure on women to get married and little respect for single women, childless women (unless they are nuns) or single mothers. Divorce is hardly unknown but it is not common.

Economic reality means that many people live at

Lighting candles in the cathedral, Zagreb.

ing they were sick of seeing the village men doing nothing for the community.

The Croats' selective approach to religion is also reflected in their attitude towards contraception. Long before the Communists began methodically to undermine religious teaching, the Catholic clergy was bemoaning the refusal of its flocks to take any notice of Rome's prohibition of birth control. The evidence for this was a rapid decline in the size of the average family from the early 20th century. It is a trend that continues to worry demographers, as constantly shrinking families fail to compensate for the death rate, resulting in an overall decline in population. There are predictions that many rural areas will continue to be

home until they are married, at which point sons are often given a house. In rural areas, where couples tend to marry at a younger age, traditional weddings can still last several days and visitors may well get caught up in them. The family remains the centre of everyday life, and relatives stay close, offering the first port of call for any help and support. Children are expected to look after their parents and the elderly are more likely to move in with their families rather than to be put in a home.

Same-sex relationships are recognised in law, and though homosexuality is still frowned upon by many, Pride is now a regular feature in Zagreb every June, with 10,000 participants in 2017. Each year more and more gay tourists, many of them Americans, are discovering the freedoms of the coast.

> *Croatian parents often go without to keep their children supplied with the latest prestige goods and clothes, and enough pocket money to show off in bars and clubs.*

FASHION FIENDS

While the demographers cite low wages and the small size of socially owned flats as some of the causes of the current baby shortage, aren't. The answer is that most Croats (and Serbs for that matter) would rather starve than wear last year's gear. And far more than in most Western countries, Croatian parents and grandparents unthinkingly sacrifice their own creature comforts for their children. There is another trick to the Croats' uncanny ability to go out a lot on next to nothing – much of the time all they need to do is walk up and down, and unlike in Britain or the US, where waiters usually drive out diners as soon as they have finished their meals, Croats cling undisturbed

Playing at a wedding in Samobor, central Croatia.

another factor is the national obsession with fashion. Croatians are fanatical followers of every latest trend, and there isn't much that the average female city dweller won't do to fill her wardrobe with designer-label clothes and spend as much time as possible in trendy bars and cafés. None of these activities is compatible with becoming the mother of a large brood, and even young mothers pushing prams can look as if they have just come off the catwalk. This obsession isn't limited to women; men are just as devoted to fashion.

Most foreign visitors wonder how the inhabitants of a country with such low average wages can afford to go out so often and dress up so glamorously. Are they secretly rich? No they to their seats in their favourite cafés for hours. If need be they will nurse a single coffee and ice cream all night to indulge the nation's favourite pastime – people-watching.

SPORT: THE OTHER RELIGION

Catholicism is not the Croats' only religion. The other is sport, and it's one that dovetails neatly with the national obsession with politics and regional pride. The only crowds large enough to rival political protest rallies and church pilgrimages are those watching Zagreb's Dinamo football team slug it out against Hajduk Split. In 2009, a group of 19 Benedictine nuns from a convent in Zadar bought around €3,600 worth of shares in Hajduk Split, making them one of the club's top 20 shareholders. Most nuns in the convent know little of football, but they promised to pray for their newly adopted team.

At a time when Croatia was isolated, and even reviled during the war in Bosnia, world-class footballers such as Davor Šuker and Zvonimir Boban – the two pillars of Croatia's World Cup bid in 1998 that took Croatia to the semi-finals – put the country on the world map in a positive way. Croatia marched all the way to third place in the World Cup that year, taking the scalps of Germany and Holland on the way and giving the hosts and eventual winners, France, a real run for their money in the semi-final. This was the 'Golden Generation' of Croatian football, but the team remains world class. It knocked England out of the 2008 World Cup qualifiers by beating them twice, making a hero out of Ivan Klasnić – though they suffered retribution when England removed them from the qualifiers for 2010.

Croats know that football supremos and tennis stars such as Goran Ivanišević have done far more for their country's image abroad than any number of diplomats, writers or singers. These days, Croatia's football stars such as Real Madrid midfielder Luka Modrić, FC Barcelona midfielder Ivan Rakitić and Juventus forward Mario Mandžukić tend to get poached by wealthy clubs outside the country, but they still wield a lot of political influence back home. When Šuker and Boban signed a protest letter in 2001 against the decision to surrender two war crimes suspects to the Hague tribunal, the government trembled.

PROFIT AND LOSS

The early days of cavalier capitalism are over, the warlords have returned to their restaurant businesses or their farms and the country has settled into capitalism's maw, with a strong role still from central government. Innovation and an ability to think for oneself outside safe bureaucracies and known rules from the past can take a generation to learn. But there is a new generation, one that knew neither Communism nor civil war. Young Croats are well educated – literacy is over 98 percent – and the majority of them speak English and

Choir boys outside the cathedral in Split.

⊘ FABRICS OF THE NATION

The wonderful traditional costumes of Croatia, in which women can wear up to three bodices and seven underskirts, are a chance to show off the skills of weavers, embroiderers, lacemakers, leatherworkers, silver- and goldsmiths, seamstresses and jewellers.

Silk has a long tradition in the country, which is why there are so many white mulberry trees, as the silk moth feeds on their leaves. Today the cravat or tie, Croatia's main fashion gift to the world, remains a good outlet for silk products. Dubrovnik's silver- and goldsmiths were once famous, and you can still find filigree buttons for sale there. But perhaps the most emblematic of the country's costume crafts are the wide-hatted

lacemakers in the town of Pag, on the island of the same name. You can see women at their doorsteps creating intricate patterns with their special needles.

Men aren't left out of the style stakes, as clients of Boris Burić will attest. The tailor's shop Gena in Trogir specialises in old-fashioned collarless suits, one of which was sent to Barack Obama. The embroiderer's art may seem arcane, but in Croatia it has been brought to new artistic heights by Ivan Rabuzin who designed the drop curtain for the Takarazuka Theatre in Tokyo. Measuring 1.4 by 24 metres (4ft 6in x 79ft), it depicts a naïve landscape of cherry trees, sunny hills and fluffy clouds. It took 24 weavers three months to make.

German. They tend to be optimistic and determined to succeed in a world that remains alien to many of their parents. They are computer-literate and technology-smart. Travelling overseas in search of money and experience is increasingly common, but so is coming back to set up small businesses in Croatia. They are not afraid of work, and may often have more than one job to try to make ends meet. They are also facing up to the reality that unemployment in Croatia is still very high. Germany and the US have the highest emigrant populations, with around half million in each.

In the aftermath of independence, some Croats worried that their distinctive traditions were crumbling under the impact of relentless exposure to Western mass media. Regional dialects, proverbs and traditional songs seemed to be fading and the country's wonderful regional costumes were sometimes put on only for the benefit of tourists or for 'Vinkovačke Jeseni' – the annual autumn folklore festival held in Vinkovci. But the reality of capitalism has set in, with the realisation that it is not a cure for all ills, that money does not turn up the moment that free markets

Football fans before Croatia's match against Ireland in UEFA Euro 2012.

⊘ SPORTING HEROES

Croatia's most famous sporting icon is the tennis player Goran Ivanišević, who surprised everyone in 2001 by becoming the first 'wild card' entry ever to win the Wimbledon men's singles championship. On his return to his native Split, more than 100,000 fans lined the waterfront and, in typically Goran style, he stripped off to his underwear to salute his slightly bemused followers. Following on Ivanišević's heels was Mario Ančić, who made his debut at Wimbledon on the centre court as a teenager, beating Switzerland's Roger Federer. He led the Croatian team that won the 2005 Davis Cup. And in 2014, Ivanišević-coached Marin Čilić won his first Gram Slam title, the US Open.

In Zagreb and northern Dalmatia, basketball competes with football for attention. Zadar and Šibenik both have excellent teams and have supplied players who have been successful in the National Basketball Association leagues in the United States. The Croatian Basketball Federation was founded in 1948.

Perhaps Croatia's most surprising sporting success of all time came in 2002 at the Salt Lake City Winter Olympics in America when Croatian skier Janica Kostelić not only won Croatia's first-ever Olympic medal, but also its second, third and fourth in a haul that included an impressive three golds. In swimming, Duje Draganja, an Olympic silver medallist, became the fastest man in the water in 2009 when he finished the 50-metre freestyle in just 20.81 seconds.

are introduced and five-star tourist hotels built. There were aspects of life under Tito's Communism that many still recall with nostalgia. Though towns remain by and large clean and orderly, much of the simple country life has gone.

As the quest for identity continues, traditions today are not just clung to, but are enriched. New festivals are introduced, old crafts resuscitated, and customs have re-emerged as popular as ever.

The pull of the West and the almost universal desire, especially prevalent among the young, to imitate everything American, from accents to

Organised crime, on the other hand, is a symptom of newly independent states. It began with the break-up of Yugoslavia when arms embargoes against the country led to criminal activity that would finance arms buying, and it continues through a murky underworld of drugs, prostitution, extortion and corruption.

According to journalist Goran Flauder, 'Where Italy is a state with a mafia, Croatia is a mafia with a state.' Flauder has suffered a number of physical attacks as a result of his investigative articles, including stories about the assassina-

People-watching whilst sunbathing in Brač.

dress sense, has created a more homogenised society. But swings in one direction are invariably followed by reactions in another. That is the one lesson in Croatian history. And as the country's favourite poet, Gustav Matos, once reassuringly put it: *Dok je srca bit če i Kroacije* – While people have hearts (or rather, courage) there will always be Croatia.

ORGANISED CRIME

Western ills as well as benefits have also infiltrated daily life. Violent crime – virtually unknown a generation ago – is creeping into cities. Even so, it remains comparatively low, and, beyond the usual safety precautions, visitors have little to concern themselves with.

tion by car bomb in Zagreb of Ivo Pukanić, editor of the *Nacional* newspaper, and its marketing chief Niko Franjić in 2008. Two weeks earlier, 26-year-old Ivana Hodak, the daughter of a prominent lawyer, was shot in the back of the head in Zagreb. These events led to the British Foreign Office issuing warnings to visitors about the threat from organised crime, and to the EU raising doubts about Croatia's fitness as a potential member. This is a threat the government must have viewed seriously. It took a while for Croatia to be recognised by the UN. Next to that, membership of the EU, acquired in 2013, was the highest accolade a fledgling European nation could aspire to and a big step towards confirming a national identity.

NAKED PASSIONS

Encouraged by the government and approved by romping royals from all over Europe, naturism on Croatia's thousands of bays and beaches has a long and healthy tradition.

Naturism and Croatia go back a long way, and the country could even claim to be the spiritual home of modern European naturism, with devotees flinging off their clothes on its Adriatic beaches as early as the start of the 20th century. But it was in 1936, when Edward VIII stripped down to his crown jewels on the Kvarner island of Rab that naturism really took off. The British monarch requested permission from the local authorities, which allowed him to bathe naked in Kandarola Bay (now dubbed 'English Beach'). It was not recorded whether Mrs Simpson chose to join him, but the musical *The Naked King* is based on Edward's notorious visit to Rab.

With the advent of mass tourism and jet airline travel in the 1960s, naturist resorts, beaches and camps sprang up all along the Croatian coastline as more than 100,000 naturists flocked to the coast every summer. Today, encouraged by government and the tourism boards, the numbers are probably not far short of this. But it's hard to draw a line between dedicated, paid-up naturists, and holiday-makers who briefly slip away from the textile world.

Croatians, however, are thought to make up only about 5 percent of naturists on the country's beaches. Some put this down to the effects of the Catholic Church, which preaches a more private attitude to their bodies. That said, compared with other Catholic countries, Croatia is fairly liberal when it comes to nudity. Even outside naturist areas it is common for local women to go topless.

OFFICIAL NATURIST CENTRES

More than 20 official naturist centres take various forms, and can be beaches, campsites, apartments, bungalows and hotels with plenty of sporting facilities and places to eat and drink. Istria has a string of naturist resorts around Umag, Poreč, Vrsar and Rovinj. The Alpe-Adria Encounter is a well-established sports gathering of national naturist associations with a standard diet of sporting contests, dinners and dances.

Casanova is said to have swum naked on both his visits to the islet Koversada, a fact that encouraged it to hold the 1972 World Naturist Congress. Vrsar, on the shore opposite, now has an annual Casanova festival of erotica.

Look for signs saying FKK if you want to find a nudist beach.

Further south in Kvarner, where the first official naturist centre was set up on Rab in 1934, naturism is still popular, with resorts also located on the islands of Cres, Mali Lošinj, Krk and Pag. The Northern Dalmatian cities of Zadar and Šibenik also have nearby naturist resorts, while the Dalmatian islands of Brač, Hvar and Korčula have all-nude beaches and resorts. Even Dubrovnik has its own naturist centre.

Areas without official naturist resorts will often reserve a section of beach for naturists. Look out for the FKK signs (an abbreviation taken from the German for Free Body Culture), indicating where nude sunbathing is allowed – usually away from family areas. These don't have the same facilities as the naturist resorts, but there is no entrance charge and you can just stop off if you are passing by. Some boat trips also revolve around naturist beaches – again look out for the FKK sign.

Today's naturists are a cosmopolitan bunch, coming mostly from Hungary, Germany and Austria, as well as Italy, the Netherlands and the Czech Republic. For more information on naturist holidays, for feedback from previous visitors, and for details of nudist sailing holidays, look up www.cronatur.com.

FESTIVALS

When it comes to celebrating, Croatians like to dress up – in the kind of costumes their forefathers wore, revealing how much their colourful folkloric traditions vary around the country.

Traditional costumes, folk music and dance have been extraordinarily enduring in Croatia, and seem to grow in genuine popularity. Many towns have a day on which to dress up in costumes that show exactly where the participants come from – fur and thick capes in the interior, beautiful embroidery in Slavonia and high lace hats on the island of Pag. Costumed groups come together at the annual International Folklore Festival in Zagreb in July, started in 1965, which attracts folk performers not just from Croatia and the Balkans, but from all over the world.

People don't need much excuse to dress up to celebrate their past – you can meet Diocletian, Marco Polo and Prince Branimir, while in June Opatija remembers the days when it was a favourite watering hole of the Austrian aristocracy, and people dress up in courtly style. The main pre-Lent carnival is in Rijeka, with many masked figures, and there is a big summer carnival in Pag. Since 1717, the Middle Ages have been evoked during the Sinjska Alka, a knights' tournament held in Sinj in the mountains north of Split.

One of the most famous folk dances is the Moreška, a ritualised sword dance representing the triumph of Christians over Turks, which takes place in Korčula on the feast of St Theodor on 27 July.

More modern tastes are celebrated too, as Croatia has seen the rapid growth of summertime music festivals such as Soundwave and Outlook. And Poreč has its new Poreč Open Air – Festival of Life (http://porecopenair.com), with numerous street performances and music nights, as well as cinema and theatre events staged from mid-June to mid-September throughout the town.

The 'Triestino' accordion is a popular instrument in Istria and an annual festival takes place in Roč.

Traditional embroidery and lace appear on costumes worn at the International Folklore Festival in Zagreb.

The vibraphone of Boško Petrovic, fusing jazz with traditional Croatian music, is a regular at the Libertas festival.

Dubrovnik Summer Festival performance at Rector's Palace.

Dubrovnik's Libertas

The hoisting of the Libertas, the flag of Ragusa, heralds the start of the renowned Libertas Festival on 10 July each year in Dubrovnik. Held since 1949, it attracts top artists, but there are no mass concerts in huge arenas; all performances are staged among 70 mostly open-air venues in the historic buildings of the old town. Perhaps the most dramatic setting is Lovrijenac Fort, the stone bastion on the edge of the old town, with the Adriatic lapping at its base. Daniel Day-Lewis is just one of several Hamlets to have stalked its ramparts. The Dubrovnik Symphony Orchestra and the Lindo Folk Dance Group are perennials.

Street performers fill the old town during the seven-week event, and, for much of the day, cafés are full of festival-goers soaking up the carnival atmosphere. For further information visit the Libertas website: www.dubrovnik-festival.hr or tel: 020 326100.

With the coats of arms of central Croatia, Dubrovnik, Dalmatia, Istria and Slavonia, the national flag is waved at every festival.

Christians and Turks do battle in the Moreška dance on the island of Korčula. This ritualised sword dance dates from the 15th century.

Watching Skream perform at Outlook Festival, held in an abandoned 19th-century fort near Pula.

THE CULTURAL SCENE

Tradition is central to all the arts, particularly music, in which Croatians excel. Luckily, there are many wonderful venues where you can see them perform.

Seasons in Croatia can be measured by their festivals of music, art, film, dance and drama, which fill the diaries of professional and amateur performers. These make the best use of some of the country's most beautiful buildings, from the dramatic castles and gilded theatres of Zagreb and Slavonia to the pretty churches of Istria and Dalmatia. What better place to attend a film festival than in the Roman amphitheatre at Pula, or to listen to a classical concert than in St Donat's in Zadar, or the Rector's Palace in Dubrovnik?

> Resorts in Istria, Kvarner and Dalmatia hold huge one-off outdoor dance parties all summer, usually attracting big-name DJs.

Croatian concert pianist Martina Filjak.

MAD ABOUT MUSIC

Of all the arts, however, music is the one that seems to course most easily through Croatian blood. In many towns and villages you may be walking down a street when the sounds of choirs in rehearsal, of instruments being blown, struck and plucked, drift out from behind closed doors. You may hear, too, the unique Croatian *ganga*, an exciting singing style in which a soloist is accompanied by a wailing chorus; or come across a group of boisterous a cappella *klapa* singers, particularly in the coastal regions.

In Varaždin in the north of Croatia, music seeps onto every pavement, from the School of Music, its 15 churches, its Baroque evenings and from a 10-day international music festival, Špancirfest, held every August. If you are visiting, you might also drop in at the workshop of Vladimir Proskurnjak, 'the Stradivarius of Varaždin', a master craftsman of violins and other stringed instruments, to see how they are made and hear how they sound.

Violins, violas, cellos, guitars – Croatians have a great ability to make strings sing. The Zagreb Soloists is a world-class chamber orchestra of more than a dozen string instrumentalists. Founded in 1954 and made up mostly of graduates from the capital's Music Academy, they play without a conductor and are great exponents of Croatian composers.

The guitar is also a popular instrument on which to play classical music in Croatia. You can hear it played by such talents as Zoran Dukić, one of the most prominent players today.

CROATIAN STARS

The international reputation is growing of a number of young stars such as Robert Belinić, who in 1991, at the age of eight, starred in *Story from Croatia*, the first film made in the newly independent nation. Piano soloists are highly accomplished, too. Martina Filjak, who debuted with the Zagreb Soloists at the age of 12, has gained an international reputation for her sensitive and imaginative performances.

Many towns have orchestras and choirs, some with reputations outside their own parish. Zvjezdice (Little Stars) is an all-girl choir from Zagreb that has gained accolades around the world, winning twice at the Llangollen Eisteddfod. One of the oldest amateur choirs is the Kolo singing society in Šibenik, which has been performing for more than a century, though its numbers are down on the 900 or so before the Homeland War. Šibenik, incidentally, has a beautiful 19th-century theatre, and any chance to watch a performance here is something to cherish.

FOLK MUSIC

Folk songs are at the root of all Croatian music. They were developed under the first kings in the 11th century and in the church music of the same period, involving Glagolitic song. Over the centuries, the many distinctive regions of the country developed their own folk songs, and most villages and towns produced colourful performers whose repertoires would include tragic stories of their history and lost love, as well as songs for local weddings and festivities.

⊘ PROMINENT COMPOSERS

In the sphere of classical music Croatia lays claim to the composer Franz Joseph Haydn, who was born in a Croatian enclave of Austria in 1732. Of those composers born within the present borders of Croatia, two of the earliest were Andrea Antico, who hailed from Istria in the 15th century, and his contemporary Franjo Bosanac. During the Renaissance Julije Skjavetić was a composer and the conductor at Šibenik's acoustically impressive cathedral. Further south, Luka Sorkočević rose to prominence in Dubrovnik in the 18th century. His two sisters became the first female composers in the country.

Their repertoire developed alongside traditional instruments. The *tamburica*, which has either three or five strings and offers a sound much like a mandolin, was brought to eastern Croatia in the 14th century by the Ottomans and was at first confined to the Slavonia region. Today it is the most recognised Croatian folk instrument, used by groups all over the country, and is the central instrument in the national kolo folk dance. Also common in the coastal areas and islands of Dalmatia and Kvarner are two variations of the bagpipe: the *gajde* and *dude*.

Kolo is a collective circular folk dance common in Croatia and Slovenia.

FINE ART

As in music, local traditions inform the most distinctive of Croatian art, naïve painting (see page 258). Under Austro-Hungarian rule, painters followed Western movements, evident in the modern galleries of the Museum of Arts and Crafts in Zagreb, where the pastoral and romantic paintings of artists such as Vlaho Bukovac (1855–1922) followed the fashion for painting en plein air. Communism required more revolutionary art, and a significant practitioner was Edo Murtić (1921–2005), whose work progressed fluently from figurative to abstract Expressionism.

The Museum of Contemporary Art in Zagreb, housed in a stunning modern building with a permanent collection of works dating from the early 20th century, brings the story up to date. The Split Museum of Fine Arts in its state-of-the-art premises in a converted hospital expands on Croatia's art history with works from the 14th century to the present day.

There are some excellent artists working today throughout Croatia, particularly on the coast where the Mediterranean light infuses their work with a great vibrancy. Paintings, prints and drawings can make lasting souvenirs. You might visit the inspirational artist communities in the hilltop

Participant in Ex Tempore, *an international art event in Grožnjan.*

villages of Grožnjan and Motovun in Istria, join the tourists browsing Rovinj's gallery-lined Grisia street, centre of an arts festival on a Sunday in August, or seek out the works of sunny artists such as Dubrovnik's Josip Pino Trostmann.

Ivan Meštrović (see page 179) is the country's best-known sculptor, and was considered by some as the finest since the Renaissance. In a different league but rather more fun is Nikola Bašić, who has been brightening up the seafront in Zadar. His *Sea Organ* is an award-winning sonic sculpture set in marble steps on the Riva seafront and powered by wind and waves that pass through its tubes and cavities. Nearby is Bašić's *Greetings to the Sun*, a 22-metre (72ft) circle containing 300

glass plates covering photovoltaic cells that produce a glittering light show at sundown.

LITERATURE

Contemporary Croatian literature is celebrated in *Croatian Nights*, a collection of contemporary short fiction by exciting and innovative writers from Croatia, many translated for the first time. Published in 2005, the book has given its name to a continuing part of the annual Festival of Alternative Literature (FAK) run by the playwright and novelist Borivoj Radaković, which brings together leading British and Croatian writers. As the critic Tibor Fischer says in the introduction to the book: '*Croatian Nights* was born out of a shared fondness for hard drinking and a contempt for regular employment.'

Drinking is one way of forgetting. The Rijeka-born journalist Slavenka Drakulić wrote about the abuse of women during the Homeland War in the fictionalised *As If I Am Not There*, which was made into a film in 2010 by the Irish director Juanita Wilson. Drakulić also chronicled the trials of war criminals in The Hague in *They Would Never Hurt a Fly*. Her other non-fiction works, *How We Survived Communism and Even Laughed* and *Café Europa: Life after Communism*, are brilliant insights into daily life in the country's recent history.

But Croatia's towering literary figure remains Ivo Andrić (1892–1975). The son of Croatian parents, he was born in Bosnia, and his stunning classic, *The Bridge over the Drina*, published in 1947, is still in print. This is an extraordinarily vivid account of life under successive rulers in the Balkans and it is no surprise that in 1961 he was made a Nobel Laureate.

⊘ KLAPA SINGING

The uplifting sounds of klapa singers can be found along the Dalmatian coast. It's usually a cappella, and the multipart harmonies celebrate the good things in life: love, the sea, wine. The group consists of a tenor, second tenor, baritone and bass, often with the parts doubled up, and it's rare that you'll find both sexes in one group. Professionals gather at klapa festivals, the most famous being the July festival in Omiš. The word klapa means group of friends, and it's something you'll hear friends do spontaneously. Klapa was recognised by Unesco in 2012 when it was added to the List of Intangible Cultural Heritage.

CINEMA

Croatia's history of cinema stretches back almost as far as the Lumière brothers. In fact, it was only months after the Frenchmen made their mark on Parisian society that the first moving pictures arrived in Zagreb in 1896. The 1956 thriller *Don't Turn Around, My Son,* set during World War II, made Dubrovnik-born director Branko Baur the leading figure in the fledgling Yugoslav film industry. It was around this time that Zagreb was developing its own school of animation, with one of its directors, Dušan Vukotić, winning an Oscar

Vlaho Bukovac depicted his wife and daughter in 'During Reading' (c.1905).

in 1963. These golden years of Croatian cinema ground to a halt during the Homeland War, but another golden age came with the beginning of the 21st century. In 2015, Dalibor Matanić won the Jury Prize at the 'Un Certain Regard' section of the Cannes Festival for his film *The High Sun*.

The country celebrates its film industry in several major festivals throughout the year, the oldest being the Pula Film Festival, which has been screening films in its Roman amphitheatre since 1954. The annual festival in Motovun celebrates small-scale independent productions, and this free-spirited attitude extends to the makeshift campsite outside the town that throngs with young people during the festival. Not to be outdone,

Zagreb holds two film festivals, including the acclaimed documentary festival ZagrebDox held in the winter. And Split invites experimental filmmakers to its annual summer festival to showcase the most creative multimedia productions.

THEATRE, OPERA AND BALLET

The Croatian National Theatre in Zagreb has been putting on theatre productions since 1860, with an opera company added 10 years later and a ballet troupe in 1876. In 1895, it was moved to its permanent home in Marshal Tito square, where its sumptuous red velvet and gold interior is enhanced even further by Ivan Meštrović's 1905 wall fountain The Source of Life.

The country has three other official state-funded national theatres: in Rijeka in Kvarner, Osijek in Eastern Croatia and Split, the last of which is one of Dalmatia's oldest surviving theatres. As with the national theatre in Zagreb, the regional outposts put on opera and ballet productions as well as stage plays. Osijek's theatre tradition stretches back to 1735, although it was formalised with the building of the national theatre in 1907. Rijeka's theatre has been entertaining audiences ever since a production of Verdi's Aida inaugurated proceedings back in 1885. Split's handsome theatre is one of the biggest in the Mediterranean, and has been going since 1893 despite wartime interruptions and a major fire.

Croatian playwrights figure as prominently in the theatres' repertoire as well-known operas, Shakespearean plays, concert performances and classical ballet.

⊘ CROATIAN POP

Ivo Robić (1923–2000) was a Croatian prodigy and pop singer who had a German hit in Europe and the US with the song 'Morgen'. He studied piano, clarinet, flute, sax and double bass at the Zagreb Music Conservatoire and was a guest star on many US TV shows, including The Ed Sullivan Show. His hit sold more than a million copies, hence his nickname 'Mr Morgen'. Other notable Croatian stars include pop singer Tereza Kesovija, the well-known singer and actress Dunja Rajter, and Radojka Šverko – one of the country's greatest female singers, known for her beautiful interpretations of Croatian songs.

Shellfish from Limski Kanal, a
sea channel that cuts into Istria.

FOOD AND DRINK

Whether you love the taste of fresh oysters and lobster or prefer to bite into rich schnitzels and strudels, you will find plenty of diverse dishes on the menu.

In a country with such a complex history, it comes as no surprise to learn that Croatia's cuisine is a smorgasbord of influences. The dishes of central and eastern Croatia have more in common with hearty Hungarian cooking, while Istria favours Italian-influenced seafood and sauce-rich pasta dishes. Dalmatian cuisine puts the emphasis on simply grilled fish and meat. Turkish influences also feature, particularly in the east.

Common to all areas is the abundance of fresh produce. Much of Croatia's food production is still small scale involving family-run farms and businesses, and though locally sourced produce may be played up in tourist areas, in many respects it is simply following tradition.

COASTAL CUISINE

When it comes to the differences between the regional cuisines, the major fault line is between inland and coastal cooking. While inland areas focus on meat dishes, broths and stews, as soon as the Adriatic Sea is within striking distance seafood dominates the menus and restaurant tables move outside.

Croatia's seafood is among the best in Europe, as this is one of the cleanest corners of the Mediterranean. Fish and shellfish, cooked simply in olive oil and fresh herbs, dominate the menus of the smallest and simplest restaurants; comprise the dish of the day in cheap and cheerful tourist restaurants; and come in all manner of delicious guises in the top-end establishments, such as Noštromo in Split and Villa Kaliopa on the island of Vis. In Southern Dalmatia the small town of Ston is a place of pilgrimage for gastronomes, who come just for the quality of its oysters.

Coastal menus tend to be similar to menus across the Adriatic in Italy, though prices are

Beachfront restaurant in Makarska, Dalmatia.

⊘ OLIVE OIL

Istria's microclimate has made it a natural habitat for the cultivation of olives, which produces a high-quality, slightly spicy olive oil that is much sought after by connoisseurs. It's still a small-scale, organic industry, although membership of the European Union has made it easier to export to new markets. Istrian producers are discovering the benefits of gastronomic tourism, with the growth of specialised tours exploring picturesque olive-oil routes all over the peninsula. More farmers are opening their cellars to offer tastings and direct sales of their own extra-virgin olive oil.

> *One of the tastiest ways of eating fish is to cook it on a rostilj (barbecue) and then serve it with blitva sa krumpirom (beetroot and potato smothered in olive oil and garlic).*

considerably lower. Menus follow a familiar pattern with a first course of seafood risotto *(rizot)*, *škampi na buzaru* (shrimps cooked in their own juice), octopus and spring onion salad or spa-

in Dalmatia. It consists of chunks of various types of fish that have been cooked slowly with parsley, garlic, bay leaves and tomato – all mopped up with polenta *(pura)*. Bakalar, the Croatian version of the salted cod dish found all over the Mediterranean, is traditionally served on Christmas Eve when no meat dishes are allowed.

INLAND INFLUENCES

Inland Dalmatia and the coastal areas of Kvarner and Istria have tasty meat dishes, including the traditional Dalmatian meat stew of pašticada.

Truffles on display in Grožnjan.

ghetti, followed by a main course of freshly grilled fish *(riba na žaru)* or grilled squid *(ligne)*. Variations on the risotto include *crni rizot*, a black risotto cooked in cuttlefish ink, and *škampi rizot*, made with shrimps' tails. In all cases, garlic and olive oil are used liberally. For a real feast, order a fish platter featuring the best of the local catch and available on almost every menu. Drizzle it with the olive oil that is usually on the table, and don't hesitate to ask the restaurant for its best oil.

Commonly caught fish include John Dory, sea bass, sardines, sole, hake, mackerel and sea bream. Oysters, crab, mussels and prawns are also abundant. A close relation of French *bouillabaisse* is the old peasant dish *brodetto* (also known as *brodet*), a fish stew served traditionally

Don't miss the wonderful *pršut*, smoked Dalmatian ham, which is often served as a starter with cheese (ideally from the island of Pag) or melon. At its best this salty full-flavoured ham is more than a match for Italian *prosciutto* and Spanish *jamón serrano*.

Roe from trout found in the rivers and lakes of the Lika region around Plitvice is sought after by gourmets, and soups from freshwater fish and crabs here are a speciality.

In central Croatia, as well as along the coast, spit-roasted lamb and pig can be seen slowly turning outside many restaurants. Head north into the Zagorje and the calories mount as Austrian and Hungarian influences begin to take over, with creamy, richly flavoured sauces

When in Croatia, you're bound to hear of peka or čirepnja. This is a traditional method of cooking meat (meso ispod peke) and vegetables beneath a cast-iron dome buried in glowing embers. It's also a delicious way of baking bread.

featuring strongly. Spicy *gulaš* is a mainstay of many menus.

Other specialities include *mlinci*, a rich pastry cooked with turkey, duck or goose, which is particularly popular in Varaždin.

Zagreb has its own signature meat dish, *Zagrebački schnitzel*, veal stuffed with ham and cheese and cooked in breadcrumbs, similar to the schnitzel that appears on menus all across the Croatian interior. In many ways the capital has the best of both worlds, with all the hearty meat dishes of the interior as well as good quality fish, and a wide variety of international and ethnic restaurants.

Perhaps the most distinctive regional cuisine originates from Slavonia in Eastern Croatia. Here fish makes a comeback with carp and pike, caught in the Drava and Danube rivers, meeting the influence of Hungary with delicious results, such as *fiš paprikaš*, a spicy fish stew. Slavonia is also home to the excellent *kulen* spicy sausage, flavoured with red peppers, garlic and salt. Not dissimilar to Spanish *chorizo*, it is perfect for picnics but also often incorporated into red meat and poultry stews. Slavonia is also a good place to sample more unusual meat dishes such as wild boar and various types of game.

The bountiful Dolac central market in Zagreb is the daily meeting place both of housewives and culinary stars. 'It is here,' they say, 'that we start cooking.'

CHEESE AND DESSERT

Croatia has some renowned cheeses. The Kvarner island of Pag is famous for *paški sir*, a sheep's cheese. The saltwater-blasted extremities of the island, on which the sheep graze, help produce a cheese with a unique flavour that visitors often grow to love. It goes well with *pršut*, olives or tomatoes, but is great just with bread.

Ice cream *(sladoled)* is especially good in Dalmatia and Istria where the Italian influence and expertise are at their strongest. Much of the ice cream that you will find along the coast more than matches Italian *gelati*. *Rožata*, similar to crème caramel, is also popular, as are *štrudle* filled with *jabuka* (apple), *trešnja* (cherry) or *sir* (cream cheese), and *palačinke* (crêpe-like pancakes) laden with creamy toppings that get more elaborate the further you head towards Austria and Hungary.

Equally calorific is *baklava*, filo pastry smothered in honey and nuts, introduced to the Balkans by the Turks.

The layered-pastry dish štrukli is comfort food from the Zagorje region.

FAST FOOD

Pizza is found everywhere. Usually this has a thin crust and some of the wood oven pizzas are every bit as good as you will find in Naples, though in Slavonia they tend to bulk up the base and overdo the toppings. Pizzas are very affordable and enjoyed as much by locals as visitors.

A number of international fast-food chains have moved into the big cities and towns, but take-away burgers and fries are nowhere near as popular as they are in Germany or the UK. The indigenous fast-food products include meat kebabs and snacks of Turkish origin common to all the countries in the region, such as *burek* (meat or cheese baked in filo pastry) and *štrukli*, a speciality of Zagorje, parcels of fresh pasta filled with curd cheese served with toasted or fried breadcrumbs.

If you can manage to pronounce *čevapčići* correctly you will be served with spicy meat rissoles.

WINE, BEER AND SPIRITS

Croatia produces good wines (see page 79) and excellent beers *(pivo)*. Perhaps the best of all Croatian beers is Karlovačko, a 5.2 percent lager beer with a full flavour and a pleasant aftertaste, perfect for a hot summer's day on the coast and equally at home in a cosy Zagreb

First course with the herb-flavoured aperitif Biska.

> Most Croatian beers are lager beers. One notable dark beer is the Zagreb-produced Tomislav, a hearty, yeasty brew that tempts the palate of many a visiting real ale drinker.

beer hall *(pivnica)* in winter. Its main rival is Ožujsko, a Zagreb-produced lager that is again very drinkable, though some connoisseurs complain of a slightly chemical aftertaste. In Istria, Favorit is a rather insipid beer hardly ever drunk by the locals, but Slavonia has its own enjoyable Osiječko.

The Croats are also a big nation of spirit drinkers, whether it be an aperitif or a fiery *grappa* to start or finish off a meal. In many restaurants a shot of Croatian grappa is offered with the compliments of the house, but beware, as it is a long way from the smooth variety that you find in Italy. The most popular spirit is šlivovica, a rather abrasive plum brandy, but others include maraschino, a cherry liqueur produced in Zadar, and Biska, a herb-flavoured aperitif from inland Istria.

A very good dessert wine, normally produced along the Dalmatian coastline and islands, is Prošek, which is the perfect accompaniment to the very sweet desserts. It is also a popular choice for an aperitif.

To end a meal, coffee is the preferred beverage, usually drunk very strong in tiny cups. Turkish coffee and cappuccino are sometimes available, along with herbal teas.

⊘ ISTRIA'S TRUFFLES

To connoisseurs, truffles are the ultimate gastronomic extravagance; to nervous first-timers, they usually smell disgusting and taste overpowering. Whether you like them or not there is no doubt that the white truffles found in inland Istria are considered as delectable as anything Italy or France have to offer. A whopping 1.3kg (nearly 3lb) white truffle was found in the Motovun woods in 1999, fetching $212,000.

Istrian truffles (*tartufi* in Croatian) were reputedly enjoyed by the Romans, who valued them as an effective aphrodisiac. However, they didn't really make much impact until after World War I, when, it is said, a sharp-nosed Italian soldier who had noticed the geographical

similarities between Istria and his native land went back in search of truffles. Today, the Istrian truffle harvest (from September to October) is a growing industry. Many of the truffles, unearthed by specially trained dogs in the inland forests, are harvested illegally, but a large-scale operator, Zigante (www.zigantetartufi.com), runs slick shops in Livade, Pula, Buje, Motovun, Grožnjan and Buzet, selling all manner of products, such as truffle oil and pasta sauce, slices of truffle and sheep's cheese infused with white truffle. The truffles, white or black, look nothing special, just hard lumps no bigger than a tennis ball, but their smell and taste are unmistakable.

WINE COUNTRY

Croatian wines aren't something you often find at home – but their variety and deep flavours have been impressing visitors since the times of the ancient Greeks.

The ideal conditions for viniculture in this region were recognised by the Greeks and Romans, who produced their wine often in the same places, and with similar types of grapes, as today's vineyards. Athenian writers in the 4th century BC praised white wines from the Dalmatian island of Vis, and rudimentary Greek and Roman wine-making equipment and goblets have been found during archaeological digs.

Today there is a healthy industry producing around 50 million bottles a year in 300 geographically identifiable regions, in Slavonia, Istria, Kvarner and Dalmatia. Two-thirds of the wine produced is white, with reds mainly coming from the coast. Champagne-method wines are also produced. Large commercial concerns make high-quality wines with international reputations, but there are also many small-scale producers. Croats like to drive out to the countryside at weekends and fill up containers with fresh, inexpensive wine – in Zagreb people head for the Samobor hills.

Most of Croatia's wine is produced near or along the coast. In the north, over 70 percent of Istria's production is white wine, with Muscatel and Malvazija the ones to look out for, while Teran is a reliable red. Check the local tourist office for details of wine roads and cellar open days. Further south in Dalmatia, Šibenik produces Plavina and Babić wines, as well as an acceptable rosé. Neighbouring Primošten makes its own excellent Babić.

The Pelješac peninsula, north of Dubrovnik, is rightly famous for its seafood, but it is also home to the Dingač, perhaps Croatia's finest wine, as well as its most expensive. High in alcohol content, this ruby-red wine holds its own against many French and New World competitors, although the export market is still very much at an embryonic stage. Pelješac is also home to the cheaper red Plavac, which can still be a quality tipple in the hands of the local producers.

Tours of the Pelješac wine makers, often just small farmers, are offered to Dubrovnik visitors, usually with a stop for a meal at Ston along the way. The Konavle wine district south of Cavtat, which produces the Dubrovnik Malvasia Blanc, can also be visited. On the end of the Pelješac peninsula is the island of Korčula, renowned for its Kaštelet, Pošip and the especially good Grk, all whites.

Wine production in Grožnjan.

Vis, the island mentioned by the Athenians, today has myriad small vineyards specialising in Viški Plavac and Vugava. On the Dalmatian island of Brač there is another version of Plavac, while Hvar has its Zlatan Plavac and Faros wines. Perhaps the best of all the island wines is Vrbnička Žlahtina. From the rich slopes around the town of Vrbnik, in the north of the Kvarner island of Krk, this straw-yellow wine is the perfect accompaniment to fish dishes.

Slavonia in eastern Croatia has some excellent wines, which, like the local food, are highly distinctive. Look out for the best of them all, Graševina and Kutjevo Chardonnay, both of which go well with the local fish dishes. The famous cellars at Ilok on the Danube can be visited. Slavonia also produces the oak to make wine barrels used in both Croatia and Italy.

Many Croatians choose to dilute their wine with a little plain water (a bevanda) or add a touch of sparkling mineral water (a gemišt), and Vrbnička Žlahtina works well with both of these.

Rock climbing in Paklenica
National Park.

THE GREAT OUTDOORS

Whether you want to cycle, climb, hike dive, fish or even ski, Croatia offers many exhilarating ways of enjoying the elements and getting close to its wild landscapes.

Croatia has a wide variety of flora and fauna, and much of the most interesting and wildly beautiful parts of the country have been well preserved. Conservation is taken seriously, for Croatians tend to have a great respect for outdoor living. The country's first national park at Paklenica was provisionally set up in the 1920s, and there are now eight official national parks dotted around the mainland and islands, as well as many smaller nature reserves and conservation areas. There are also 11 nature parks – areas that have an exceptional ecological, cultural or historical significance.

Five of the eight national parks are on the mainland, with Paklenica, Risnjak and Northern Velebit, Croatia's newest national park (set up in 1999), all covering harsh mountainous terrain. Velebit is a protected Unesco World Biosphere Reserve, the first such area in Croatia.

Eurasian brown bears at play.

> The Kornati Islands are perfect for canoeing – crystal-clear waters, numerous islands, consistently low winds and a real sense of getting away from it all.

Krka National Park in northern Dalmatia is a wetland area, while further north in central Croatia Plitvice Lakes National Park features numerous waterfalls within its forested wetlands.

The three island national parks are: Brijuni Islands in Istria, once Tito's private retreat; the Kornati Islands, a stark but beautiful archipelago in Northern Dalmatia; and lush Mljet in Southern Dalmatia.

FROM BEARS TO VULTURES

A number of rare species can be found on the Croatian mainland and islands. In Plitvice Lakes and Risnjak national parks, for example, there are brown bears, while Risnjak, Plitvice and Velebit are now home to lynx, which only recently returned to Croatia from across the border in the Slovenian mountains. Griffon vultures are thriving in their own sanctuary on the island of Cres, while further south on Mljet, rare monk seals, which were once prevalent throughout the Mediterranean, are often spotted, and have been sighted in several other places in recent years. Both the Krka and Plitvice national parks also support the threatened European otter.

ACTIVITY HOLIDAYS

Life in Croatia is lived outdoors, and there are always activities close at hand. The lakes, rivers and coast offer every kind of water-borne opportunity, from sailing, windsurfing, canoeing and scuba diving to fishing and rafting. The landscape is ever ready to take on rock climbers, hikers, cyclists, skiers and practi-

festival in Sutivan on the island of Brač (see page 184).

Further north, Risnjak National Park is a quieter alternative to Paklenica with fewer facilities, but equally stunning scenery and challenging climbing. Beware of the winter weather in both parks, as the fierce bura winds and heavy snow make conditions treacherous.

As Croatia is on a major bird migration route, birdwatchers have been heading to the tranquillity of the lakes and mountains to observe the seasonal flights. The Adriatic

Yachts moored in the harbour of Korčula's old town.

tioners of extreme sports. There are a number of 'adventure racing' events, combining various activities in different degrees of difficulty, organised around the country each year.

Croatia's rugged terrain makes it a popular destination for rock climbing. Among the best venues are the sheer limestone walls of the Paklenica National Park at the southern fringe of the Kvarner Gulf. At the entrance to the main gorge, a steep rock wall is used for practising, training and for showing first-timers the ropes. Some adventurous free climbers also use these walls, and they come together every July or August at the Vanka Regule (Without Rules) extreme sports

islands are an important wintering area for many species, too.

Fishing has been growing in popularity, particularly big-game fishing expeditions off the Adriatic coast. While some of the islands are protected, there are still areas where recreational angling and underwater spearfishing are allowed. A fishing permit is required, which costs 60 kuna per day.

> *Hunting – especially wild boar and deer – is growing in popularity and bringing more visitors to less well-known regions such as Slavonia.*

SAILING

With 1,246 islands, islets and reefs, Croatia is an ideal sailing destination. Throw in the favourable winds, the well over 50 marinas that are dotted up and down the coast and the often idyllic weather from May right through to September and it is no surprise that Croatia is a top sailing destination and a serious rival to Greece.

The marinas range from the resort of Umag in northern Istria right down south to the marina at Dubrovnik. The facilities of each marina do vary, but they all provide a safe place to moor for the night, the chance of a shower and somewhere to relax with a bite to eat and drink. State-owned Adriatic Croatia International (ACI; www.aci-marinas.com) is the biggest operator, managing 22 of the marinas. Some of the larger marinas are almost resorts in themselves with all the trappings that go with it, while others such as Trogir and Rab bring you right alongside the heart of the old town.

The main choice when organising a trip is whether to go 'bareboat' and just hire the boat or hire a skipper as well. For bareboat you will need at least one member of the party to be a qualified skipper who can use a VHF radio and you will also have to be prepared to do a lot of the legwork. If you choose the skippered option the cost goes up and you can take one fewer person in your party, but the toughest parts of sailing, such as navigation, will be taken out of your hands.

A number of companies run 'learn to sail' holidays in the waters of the Kornati Islands, with the chance to gain a 'competent crew' certificate, which essentially means you have shown you can be useful around the yacht and know the basics.

More experienced sailors might consider trying the indented and island-studded Dalmatian coast where local winds, such as the *bura*, *maestral* and *jugo*, can make life more interesting, as can sudden summer thunderstorms. The Dalmatian coastline is laden with historical towns and the islands are geared towards yachts arriving for lunch or evening stopovers.

The length of the Croatian coastline means there is a lot of ground to cover between the key attractions, so a good option is to arrange a one-way sail. A popular route is to head south from the central Dalmatian marinas at either Trogir or Split, via the islands of Hvar or Korčula, before making for Dubrovnik, which offers one of the most dramatic sea arrivals in Europe.

HIKING, CYCLING AND SKIING

Those looking for a gentler mountain experience will find many opportunities for hiking. Both Paklenica and Risnjak national parks have well-marked hiking trails and mountain huts. Further south the Biokovo mountain range offers

Cycling on Hvar island.

a multitude of hiking trails, many of which are accessible from the resorts along the Makarska Riviera. West of Zagreb are the Samobor Hills, where Tito first laced up his hiking boots; they remain a pleasing bucolic escape in the warmer months. The Gorski kotar range between Karlovac and Kvarner also has a network of trails and hiking opportunities, and overlooking the Kvarner Gulf is the Učka range, with trails that are easily accessible from the Opatija Riviera resorts. As yet facilities remain basic and the country is not set up for walks of more than one or two days, but that is likely to change as hiking becomes more developed.

Cycling also has great potential, particularly on the quieter islands where bikes are an excellent way of getting around. A lazy bike ride around the lakes of Mljet's two national parks is a great way to spend a day. There are several mountain bike routes, particularly in the Velebit area, and on the Kvarner island of Rab.

Croatia is not a significant ski destination. Skiers and snowboarders who happen to be in the country when conditions are right may want to venture on to the slopes. But there is little appeal in planning a whole skiing holiday in Croatia. Zagreb's Mt Medvednica has a num-

Paddling off the coast of Palmižana, one of the Pakleni islands near Hvar.

ber of runs, as does Mt Bjelolasica in the Gorski kotar region. There is also a modest ski slope at Snježnik in the Risnjak National Park.

HORSE RIDING

Riding is an enjoyable way to appreciate the countryside and there are equestrian clubs throughout the country, notably in the Cetina Valley, Velebit, Istria and on the plains around the rivers Sava, Drava and Danube. Croatia has a long equestrian tradition, developing a number of local breeds – the Tulipan in Slavonia, the Istrijanic in Istria, and the Posavina – descendants of Mongol horses. Even if you don't want to ride, you might like to visit the

Lipizzaner stud farm in Đakovo, Croatia's leading breeding farm and one of Europe's oldest, first mentioned in 1506.

WATER SPORTS

Whitewater rafting is possible in Croatia's southern uplands and also in the mountains of Dalmatia. The Kupa River, near the city of Karlovac, offers great rafting. In the Gorski Kotar of central Croatia, it is possible to arrange a rafting trip on the Dobra River. From the Dalmatian towns and resorts it is easy to get to the Cetina River, where there are regular whitewater rafting trips through spring and summer.

Croatia is not a big windsurfing destination, but there are a couple of worthwhile locations. The most renowned is at Bol on the island of Brač, a scenic spot close to Zlatni Rat beach in a channel that separates Brač from the neighbouring island of Hvar. Another recommended area lies further south around Orebić on the Pelješac peninsula, itself an attractive resort surrounded by a string of decent beaches, all within sight of the island of Korčula. Equipment is available for hire in the main resort; in summer there is a windsurfing school at Bol.

Keen canoeists will be at home in Croatia, especially if they prefer coastal kayaking to shooting river rapids. There are numerous opportunities for coastal kayaking all around Istria, the Kvarner Gulf and in Dalmatia, but the Kornati Islands provide an idyllic setting. You can also canoe the Dobra and Kupa rivers in central Croatia.

⊘ SAVE THE DOLPHINS

One of Croatia's most successful conservation initiatives is the Adriatic Dolphin Project, set up around the Kvarner islands of Cres and Lošinj in 1987 and strengthened with the establishment in 2006 of the Lošinj Dolphin Reserve. Today there are around 100 bottlenose dolphins in the area. The project takes on volunteers (www.blue-world.org); weather permitting, the time is spent out at sea recording, dating and tracking the creatures, and direct contact is common. Croatia's commitment to conservation was reinforced with an Animal Protection Act in 2007, which prevented a proposed dolphinarium from operating in Vodnjan.

DIVING

With visibility up to 40 metres (130ft), pleasant temperatures, fascinating wrecks, sheer drops and vast underwater caves, the waters of the Adriatic are a diver's delight.

Croatia is a major European dive destination and scuba enthusiasts flock from all over the continent to explore the warm, crystal-clear waters of the Croatian Adriatic, with its many shipwrecks and good dive facilities. Organised scuba diving in the country began in World War I when the first scuba course was offered on the Dalmatian island of Vis. Now it is a major sport, popular with locals and foreign visitors. There are official dive centres all the way from Umag in northern Istria, right down to the resort town of Cavtat in the extreme south, near the border with Montenegro. Some of the most popular are at Rovinj and Poreč in Istria; Mali Lošinj and Baška in the Kvarner Gulf; and Sali (Dugi otok), Murter, Vodice, Bol, Makarska and Trogir in Dalmatia.

Vis remains the top place to head for, with dive centres in both Vis Town and Komiža. As Vis was on the main trade routes during Roman and Venetian times (routes that were also busy during World War II and are still active today), there are more than half a dozen diveable wrecks within easy reach of the island. They include the *Brioni* (an Austrian cargo ship), the *Teti* (an Italian merchant vessel) and the *Vassilios* (a Greek commercial ship), as well as the remains of a World War II bomber and a sprinkling of Roman relics. Water clarity is good and the temperature balmy in summer, making for enjoyable diving conditions.

Just off Vis is the small island of Biševo, usually reached from the western Vis town of Komiža. In summer, Biševo's Blue Grotto offers a spectacular visual phenomenon as light bathes the cave in an eerie blue sheen. Experienced scuba divers get to appreciate it much more than the dry tourists on the bobbing boats in the bay. They can delve down the main channel into the central chamber of the cave itself before coming out through a second route.

Other top dive sites include the Kornati Islands, Mežanj Island near Dugi otok, Rovinj and, to the south, the shipwreck of the *Tottono*, which sank off the Dalmatian coast near Dubrovnik after being struck by a mine during World War II. The myriad dive operators know where all the best sites are and they offer a variety of day dives and night dives, as

The Kvarner region is known for its wall dives and coral reefs.

well as three-, five- and seven-night adventures, either on board or based at the centres themselves.

Scuba diving is strictly regulated and no one is allowed to dive without first obtaining a diving certificate. These cost 100 kuna, are valid for one year from the date of issue and allow qualified divers to dive in any permitted area, provided they pay any necessary fees that may apply, for example in areas of national parks where diving is allowed. The certificate allows divers to descend to a depth of 40 metres (130ft).

Some divers complain about the need for the certificate, but the Croatian Diving Association stresses that the funds raised are used to ensure the preservation of the dive sites for future generations. The certificate is available only to those with proof that they have already passed an internationally recognised dive course such as SSI, CMAS or PADI; these courses are run by many different dive centres. Safety is taken seriously in Croatia and there are decompression chambers at Pula and Split, which are ready around the clock to deal with any divers suffering difficulties.

📷 ARCHITECTURE

Many of Croatia's finest buildings tell the story of the country's past – and reveal the legacy of all those who have settled there over the centuries.

The history of Croatia is displayed in its architecture. Starting with the Roman grandeur of Pula's amphitheatre and Split's Diocletian Palace, it leads on to early Christian buildings such as the pre-Romanesque church of St Donat in Zadar. Byzantium brought the mosaic glister of the Euphrasian Basilica in Poreč, and the Renaissance – courtesy of the Venetians – helped produce the Cathedral of St James in Šibenik, the palaces of Dubrovnik and many fortresses and castles, as well as the sturdy walls of the one-time capital, Varaždin. The Franciscan and Dominican monastic orders brought in Gothic, which shaped Zagreb's cathedral, and with the Jesuits came Baroque, a popular style that invaded domestic architecture, created glittering Habsburg ballrooms and gave the pilgrimage churches of Vinagora and Belec the aesthetics of a candy store.

Zagreb saw the flowering of 19th-century Croatian aspirations in the palaces of Opatička Street. Most brilliant is No. 10, reconstructed by Izidor Kršnjavi in 1895, and decorated with painting and sculptures that turned its Golden Hall into a gallery of Croatian art.

Just as important is the country's home-grown architecture, from *kažuni* Neolithic stone huts to wooden buildings. The timber homes and farmsteads of central Croatia are particularly appealing. The Turopolje region southeast of Zagreb has fine wooden mansions called *kurija* and handsome wooden chapels, beautifully carved, such as the Chapel of St Barbara in Velika Mlaka, which dates from 1642.

Tkalčićeva Street in Zagreb shows the rich Baroque influence of the Habsburgs.

Stari Grad Fortress, Varaždin.

'Fisherman with Serpent', by Simeon Roksandić (1874–1943) in Jezuitski Square, Zagreb.

The Lion of St Mark, in Korčula: the Republic stamped its symbol along the coast.

The Venetian legacy

Venice did not own or conquer the entire Croatian coast, but through trade and agreements, treaties and example, it has left its mark from Rovinj to Dubrovnik. Sometimes this is evident in stone carvings of the Lion of St Mark, symbol of the Most Serene Republic, but most often it is through the buildings, which seem to belong more to the Italian peninsula than to Croatia.

Many towns and villages on the coast started life as offshore islands – a strip of sea acting as a moat to protect them from landward invaders – just as Venice itself had done. As trade among the communities prospered in the 11th century, an abundance of stone allowed a flowering of buildings and the start of some urban planning. By the 14th century, much of Venice was being built with Pietra d'Istria, a marble-like white limestone quarried in the village of Kirmenjak near Poreč. By the 15th century, Venice had all of Dalmatia, except the south, under its control and builders and sculptors worked and travelled freely between Croatia and Italy. It was known that the dazzling, durable Pietra d'Istria limestone actually increased in strength when exposed to the atmosphere and could be easily carved into attractive tracery, balustrades and decorative crenellations. And so, mini-Venices were built up and down the coast.

he Euphrasian Basilica in Poreč is one of the finest yzantine buildings in Europe.

Cloister of the Franciscan monastery in Dubrovnik.

Angel on Zagreb Cathedral by the Viennese sculptor Anton Dominik Fernkorn (1813–78).

Inside the city walls of Dubrovnik's old town.

Dive boat in the harbour of Omiš,
Dalmatia.

Vineyards around Motovun, an inland Istrian town.

INTRODUCTION

A detailed guide to the entire country, with principal sights clearly cross-referenced by number to the maps.

Pazin's castle on the edge of a gorge, Istria.

Scythe-shaped Croatia has the rich diversity of a country many times its size. Inland, lovely thick woods and limestone mountains drip with lakes and waterfalls; on the coast, myriad islands, from lush Hvar to the ethereal Kornatis, bask in warm, clear waters, capable of reviving even the most jaded traveller's spirits.

Zagreb is in many ways a typical Central European capital, with more than a whiff of Vienna or Budapest in its coffee houses and ancient architecture. In the Samobor Hills north of the capital, vineyards, castles and 19th-century spa towns are ideal for exploring by car.

In two weeks or so it is possible to sample all these different aspects of Croatia, but you could just as easily spend that time pottering about in Istria (think Tuscany-on-sea) or spend a month or more island-hopping in Dalmatia. Make sure to savour the Croatian cuisine – the seafood is some of the best in Europe – and try to catch one of the country's many festivals, which illustrate how the Croatians are defining their national identity.

But Croatia's varied natural beauty and lively traditions are not its only attractions. Over the centuries, invaders, traders and other migrants have left elegant imprints. Italian artists and architects were active in Dalmatia and Istria, and exquisite Gothic and Renaissance art and architecture are among the Adriatic coast's glories. The Austro-Hungarian Empire's splendour lives on in the Baroque civic

Monastery at Visovac in Krka National Park.

buildings of central and eastern Croatia – delightful, unexpected evidence of refinement in a mainly agricultural region.

Croatia's popularity grows steadily every year, especially in the fashionable Dalmatian hotspots of Hvar and Dubrovnik. But mass tourism has yet to spoil the country's charms, helped by the lack of widespread package holidays. Indeed, it's finding new ways of enticing the more discerning holidaymaker by emphasising its unique attractions.

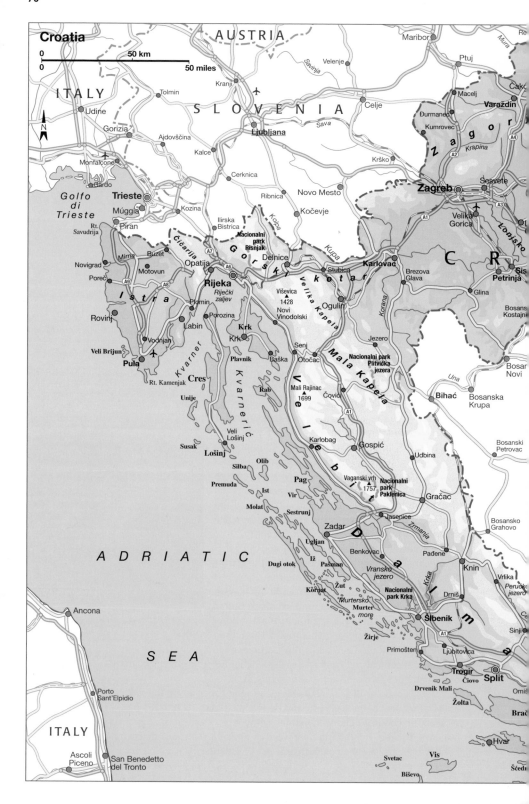

Croatia

0   50 km

0   50 miles

AUSTRIA

ITALY

SLOVENIA

Maribor

Re

Mura

Ptuj

Macelj

Čakċ

Varaždin

Velenje

Kranji

Tolmin

Celje

Đurmanec

Kumrovec

Z a g o r

Krapina

A4

Udine

Gorizia

Ajdovščina

Kalce

Ljubljana

Sava

Krško

A2

Monfalcone

Cerknica

Novo Mesto

Krško

Zagreb

Sesvete

Gardo

Golfo di Trieste

Trieste

Múggia

Piran

Kozina

Ribnica

Kočevje

A1

A3

Zagreb

Velika Gorica

Lonjsko

1

Rt. Savudrija

Ilirska Bistrica

Nacionalni park Risnjak

Kolpa

C   R

Novigrad

Mirna

Buzet

Č i č a r i j a

A7

G o r s k i

Delnice

Kupa

Karlovac

Brezova Glava

Šiš

Petrinja

Poreč

Motovun

Opatija

A6

k o t a r

Stubica

Glina

A9

A8

Rijeka

Riječki zaljev

Višęvica ▲ 1428

Ogulin

Bosna Kostajni

I s t r a

Plomin

Porozina

Novi Vinodolski

V e l i k a   K a p e l a

Jezero

Bosar Novi

Rovinj

Labin

Krk

Senj

Nacionalni park Plitvička jezera

Una

Vodnjan

K v a r n e r

Krk

Plavnik

Baška

Otočac

M a l a   K a p e l a

Bihać

Bosanska Krupa

Veli Brijun

Pula

Rt. Kamenjak

Cres

K v a r n e r i ć

Rab

Mali Rajinac ▲ 1699

Čović

A1

Bosanski Petrovac

Unije

V e l e

Karlobag

Gospić

Udbina

Susak

Veli Lošinj

Lošinj

Silba

Olib

Vaganski vrh ▲ 1757

Nacionalni park Paklenica

Gračac

Bosansko Grahovo

Premuda

Ist

b

i

t

Molat

Pag

Vir

Sestrunj

Jasenice

Zrmanja

A D R I A T I C

Zadar

D

Benkovac

Pađene

Knin

Vrlika

Peručko jezero

 C

Ancona

Dugi otok

Iž

Pašman

Uglian

Vransko jezero

a

Cc

Kornat

Žut

Murtersko more

Murter

Nacionalni park Krka

Krka

Drniš

l

Sinji

S E A

Žirje

Primošten

Ljubitovica

Šibenik

A1

m

Trogir

Čiovo

Split

Omi

Porto Sant'Elpidio

Drvenik Mali

Žolta

a

Brač

ITALY

Ascoli Piceno

San Benedetto del Tronto

Svetac

Vis

Hvar

Šćede

Biševo

Marcali
Tamási
Paks
Kiskunfélegyháza
Soltvadkert
Nagykanizsa
Kaposvár
Dombóvár
Szekszard
Kiskunhalas
Nagyatád
ica
Hlebine
Bátaszék
Baja
Szeged
rdevac
Barcs
Szigetvár
Pécs
Subotica
Kanjiža
Bjelovar
Mohács
Virovitica
Bezdan
Bajmok
Senta
Čazma
Bačka Topola
Ada
Veliki Zdenci
Slatina
Donji Miholjac
Bizovačke Toplice
Daruvar
Srbobran
T I A
Apatin
Drava
Osijek
Pakrac
Našice
Čepin
Odžaci
Novska
A5
Požega
Borovo
Vukovar
Bačka Palanka
Novi Sad
isenovac
Đakovo
Veternik
Petrovaradin
Nova Gradiška
Vinkovci
Mohovo
ka
A3
Ilok
Dunav (Danube)
Slavonski Brod
Irig
Bosanska Gradiška
Sava
Bosanski Brod
Županja
Šid
A3
Derventa
Bosanski Šamac
S N I A   A N D   H E R Z E G O V I N A
S E R B I A
Banja Luka

Makarska
Ljubuški
Plužine
Sava
etac
Hvar
Hvar
D a l m a c i j a
Nevetra
Obrenovac
Vis
Šćedro
Vela Luka
Pelješac
Capljina
BOSNIA AND HERZEGOVINA
Biševo
Orebić
Ploče
Metkovic
Ljubinje
Korčula
Korčula
Bilećko jez.
Sušac
Lastovo
Mljet
Trebinje
Dubrovnik
A D R I A T I C   S E A
Cavlat
MONTENEGRO
ivno
Zvekovica
uško zero
Herceg Novi
Požega
Bukovica
Trnovo
Goražde
Čajetina
Posušje
Drina
Priboj
Ivanjica
A1
Široki Brijeg
Foča
Ćeotina
Uvac
Župa
Mostar
Plužine
Pljevlja
Prijepolje
Ljubuški
Capljina
Đurđevića Tara
Duga Poljana
lješac
Metkovic
Pivsko Jezero
MONTENEGRO

The beautiful amphitheatre at Pula.

View from the tower of St Martin's church, Vrsar.

ISTRIA

Though geared to package tourism, Istria's resorts and towns have a distinctive Croatian-cum-Italian character, and in between the modern developments there are impressive archaeological sites.

The region of Istria is practically a country in itself, a sun-kissed peninsula given over to the demands of mass tourism for much of the year. Indeed, many locals often describe themselves as feeling more Istrian than Croatian, a sentiment that probably owes more to the amount of revenue generated by Istria's tourist industry for central government coffers in Zagreb than it does to any real desire for separatism.

With Istria capable of accommodating more than 200,000 visitors a night, it is by far Croatia's most developed and tourist-oriented enclave. The temptation to write it off as one big tourist resort, however, does not do justice to what is a visually dazzling corner of Croatia. The main tourist resorts – Rovinj and the granddaddy of them all, Poreč – are extensive, but they retain a Croatian character and historical interest. Many of Istria's most interesting sights, such as the amphitheatre in Pula and the Basilica of Euphrasius in Poreč, date from Roman times. Smaller coastal resorts such as Umag and Novigrad also have much to offer tourists.

The past two centuries have proven traumatic times for Istria, with the peninsula's ownership passing from the Austro-Hungarian Empire to Napoleonic France and back again, before Italy wrested sovereignty in 1918. This was followed by a brief stint under

Nazi Germany's grip, after which Istria was incorporated into Yugoslavia. It finally became part of the independent Republic of Croatia in the early 1990s. Istria escaped direct involvement in the conflict of those years thanks to its westerly location. The region's future has never looked brighter as tourists return to the coastal resorts and more adventurous visitors head inland on *agroturizam* programmes.

Italian influences abound. The peninsula was part of Italy for 25 years between 1918 and 1943, and although

⊙ Main Attractions
Pula
Rovinj
Poreč
Umag
Rabac
Pazin
Motovun
Vižinada
Grožnjan
Buje

Map on page 102

Arch of Sergius, Pula.

there was a large exodus of ethnic Italians (around 200,000 to 350,000) when it became part of Yugoslavia, thousands still live here. Most Istrians speak fluent Italian; Venetian-style architecture characterises the main towns; many signs are bilingual; and Istrians frequently slip between Italian and Croatian in the same sentence. Pasta, truffles, balsamic vinegar and prosciutto are on the menus and the pizzas are often as good as in Italy.

Italian yachts fill the many marinas, as they're a convenient place to moor before heading down the Dalmatian coast.

ANCIENT AND MODERN IN PULA

As the only city in Istria, with a smattering of industry and the working port that goes with it, **Pula** ❶ has gained something of an unwarranted reputation as the ugly sister to its more illustrious siblings further west. The sprawl of docks are an eyesore – although Pulans are generally proud of them – and the traffic can be infuriating, but Pula is Istria's oldest town with a captivating Roman history dating from 117 BC. As the Romans built roads, villas and settlements all over Istria, Pula was garrisoned as the main hub.

Latin remained the principal language even after the division of the Roman Empire, when Pula slipped under Byzantine control.

Pula also served as the Austro-Hungarian Empire's main naval base and it is Istria's largest port today. It is

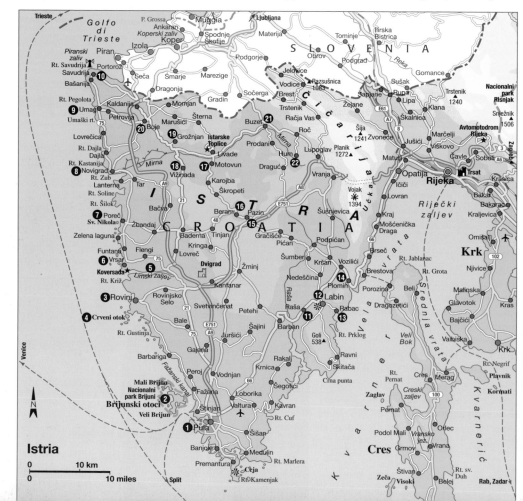

Istria

0   10 km
0   10 miles

home to Istria's only international airport, although Rijeka in neighbouring Kvarner also has international flights.

THE AMPHITHEATRE

The Roman legacy surfaces all over Pula. World War II Allied bombing raids actually helped uncover more of Pula's Roman heritage. The most impressive, and the most obvious point at which to begin a tour, is the 1st-century **amphitheatre** (amfiteatar; www.ami-pula.hr; daily Apr 8am–8pm, May–June and Sept 8am–9pm, July–Aug until midnight, Oct 9am–7pm, Nov–Mar 9am–5pm), set just back from the waterfront on a street rather aptly called Gladijatorska. The amphitheatre, also commonly known as the arena, is the world's sixth largest and the best for studying Roman building techniques; some 23,000 spectators attended gladiatorial contests, naval battles and other amusements during its heyday. After wandering around the outside, be sure to delve below ground into the old holding cells where prisoners were imprisoned whilst awaiting their gruesome fate. The wild animals were caged in the subterranean cellars.

The amphitheatre was built on a slope, partly to save money by reducing the number of stones needed, and so has three floors on the side facing the sea, two on the opposite side. Originally it had about 20 entrances and it employed a highly efficient network of tunnels to ensure spectators got to and from their seats quickly.

The amphitheatre itself has survived various assaults over the past 2,000 years. Over the centuries, whole limestone blocks, including much of the original seating, were removed to build local houses. In 1583, during Pula's stint as an outpost of the Venetian Republic, plans brewed to transport the whole structure across the Adriatic to Venice. The amphitheatre even suffered the ignominy of serving as a cattle market in the 5th century.

Today, the gladiators and lions may be long gone, but the amphitheatre regularly hosts plays, festivals,

Pula's Roman amphitheatre.

⊘ Tip

Since 1953, Pula has hosted its world-renowned Film Festival. Over two weeks in July, films from all around the world – along with concerts, exhibitions and children's events – are held in the magical setting of the amphitheatre.

classical concerts and, somewhat surreally, pop concerts by such artists as Elton John and Sting. The annual Pula Film Festival at the end of July is also staged here. A highlight of a visit to Pula is catching any kind of performance amongst the ghosts of this mighty testament to Istria's Roman heritage. It also houses a free exhibition of Roman amphorae salvaged from shipwrecks, and other equipment used for making and storing wine and olive oil.

A short walk south of the amphitheatre, past Pula's main tourist information centre, is the **Archaeological Museum of Istria** (Arheološki muzej Istre; closed for reconstruction at the time of writing). Exhibits date from the Histrian era to the Slavs' arrival in the 7th century. There is also a splendid sculpture garden.

Slightly further south is the **Triumphal Arch of Sergius** (Slavoluk obitelji Sergijevaca), dating from 27 BC, celebrating the powerful eponymous local family with a tribute etched into the stone. The arch was left looking rather forlorn when the original city walls were torn down in the 19th century. Continuing on through the arch and down Sergijevaca, you will come to the old **Roman forum**, once the hub of Roman society, home to a medley of temples and public buildings where the minutiae of life unfolded. Little of the original forum remains intact apart from the impressive **Temple of Augustus** (Augustov hram; www.ami-pula.hr; daily May–June and Sept 9am–9pm, July–Aug 9am–11pm, Apr and Oct 9am–7pm, rest of the year by appointment), built as a dedication to the eponymous emperor. The temple's construction took more than a decade, with a grand facade of four Corinthian columns giving it a solid appearance. Inside are just some of the Roman artefacts, such as portraits and bronze pieces, unearthed from a city where myriad treasures still lie buried beneath the streets.

Back towards the east is the **Historical and Maritime Museum of Istria** (Povijesni i pomorski muzej Istre; www.ppmi.hr; daily Apr–Sept 8am–9pm,

Temple of Augustus, Pula.

⊘ THE MUMMIES OF VODNJAN

There are few eerier sights in all of Croatia than the 'Mummies of Vodnjan'. The desiccated bodies of three saints and the relics of others are preserved in St Blaise's Church in what is an otherwise unassuming town. St Blaise's itself is notable for being the largest parish church on the Istrian peninsula and also for having its highest campanile, which at 60 metres (200ft) tall matches the height of St Mark's in Venice. However, most visitors travel the 10km (6 miles) north of Pula to see the mummies, which are tucked behind a shroud of curtains to the rear of the main altar.

On display in a remarkably well-preserved state are the corpses of St Nikolosa Bursa, St Giovanni Olini and St Leon Bembo. The last of these, also known as St Leon Bembo the Blessed, is said to have turned his back on the intrigues of Venetian diplomacy to take up the austere life of a monk and cultivate his skills as a faith healer. Some Croatians still believe that the mummies possess magical powers, citing as evidence the uncannily preserved bodies.

Public buses from Pula to Rovinj and Poreč stop off at Vodnjan, dropping passengers off just a short stroll from the church itself. The town is also notable for its large Italian-speaking community, which knows it simply as Dignano.

Oct–Mar 9am–5pm), inside a 17th-century Venetian fortress on the former site of the Roman Capitol. (The hilltop site is a hot hike in summer.)

Highlights include scale models of shipping vessels from various stages of Pula's maritime history, and displays relating to Italy's occupation of Istria during World War II, locally known as the 'People's War of Liberation in Istria'. The Romans chose the site well; it has good views across the city and also of the seaward approaches to Pula.

THE CATHEDRAL AND SOUTH

Back down the hill, just before Pula's sprawling docks, is the **Cathedral of St Mary** (Katedrala sv. Marija; high season daily, low season Mass only; free), showing the city offers more than just its Roman heritage. Built on the site of a former Roman temple, the cathedral is home to a 3rd-century sarcophagus said to contain the remains of an 11th-century Hungarian king. The cathedral is a melange of architectural designs with the Renaissance facade the most

memorable, though traces also remain of a 5th-century mosaic unearthed from beneath the cathedral's main body. Much of the 17th-century belfry recycles stone scavenged from the Roman amphitheatre.

South of the city centre is the green oasis of the **Verudela inlet**, where the city's busy marina is based. Austrian, British and German voices are an indication of the popularity of the yacht charters that use Pula as a base for exploring the spectacular coastlines and islands of Istria, Kvarner and Dalmatia. The tree-lined bay makes for a pleasant stroll away from the city bustle.

BRIJUNI ISLANDS

Set adrift in the Adriatic Sea just to the north of Pula are the **Brijuni Islands** ❷ (Brijunski otoci; www.np-brijuni.hr), once the private playground of yacht-loving Tito, who is said to have spent half his year on his favourite retreat. The 14 islands gained protected national park status in 1983 and public access to those without their own boats is

⊘ Tip

In summer, concerts take place in the sculpture garden of Pula's Archaeological Museum. Listening to classical music drifting past the statues on a warm evening is one of the best ways of experiencing the museum.

Sailing to the Brijuni Islands.

⊙ Fact

When Mussolini ruled Istria he attempted to wipe out the indigenous culture. The Croatian language was banned in public and Croatian surnames were outlawed.

allowed on only two of them, **Veliki Brijun** and **Mali Brijun**, and even then visitors must either be staying at one of the hotels or villas on Veliki Brijun or be part of an organised day tour.

Even before Tito brought the islands fame and entertained world leaders here, artists and writers such as James Joyce and Thomas Mann visited. Apart from the abundant wildlife, other attractions include the ruins of a Byzantine castle, a small museum dedicated to Tito, with photographs of the celebrities he entertained during his long stint as Yugoslav leader, and the strange apparition that is the **Brijuni Safari Park**. Most residents are gifts from the bevy of fawning world leaders who came to visit Tito in his island hideaway. A motley collection of confused animals, including giraffes, llamas and zebras, now idle away their days here.

Regular day tours leave from Fažana, Pula and Rovinj on the mainland, and it's recommended that you book a few days in advance. However, the experience is a shepherded and rushed one,

Pula's statue of James Joyce; the writer lived in the city for six months between 1903 and 1904.

with the island sightseeing conducted aboard a tourist train with an obligatory stop at a souvenir shop and restaurant. Those who really do want to explore the islands for themselves would do better to stay overnight. You are not allowed to bring your own bicycles, but there are cycle hire facilities.

NORTH TO ROVINJ

A short drive northwest up the E751 highway from Pula is **Rovinj** ❸, Istria's most attractive coastal resort and an excellent base for exploring the region. An island until connected to the mainland in the 18th century, Rovinj has flourished as a fishing port for centuries and you will still find a flotilla of colourful fishing boats bobbing in the harbour. Its main attraction is its Venetian-style architecture dating from the 14th to 18th centuries, when it was controlled by the Divine Republic. This Venetian connection was to cost Rovinj dearly as Venice's great rivals, the Genoans, frequently harassed the town when they were causing mischief in the Adriatic.

⊙ TITO AND BRIJUNI

Away from prying eyes of the vast majority of Yugoslav citizens, Tito ran the Brijuni islands as his private estate. In establishing Brijuni as his summer residence and luxury playground, he was in good company, as the remains of opulent villas built by Roman patricians attest. In the 19th century, an Austrian magnate, Paul Kupelwieser, bought the archipelago as an exotic retreat and built villas there for himself and his friends. After World War II, the Brijuni Islands became part of Yugoslavia, and in 1948 Tito made them his summer residence, renovating Kupelwieser's villas for himself and his guests. As the celebrity leader of the Non-Aligned Movement he hosted, with some extravagance, many world leaders such as Queen Elizabeth II, Emperor Haile Selassie, Indira Gandhi, Nasser and Nehru, as well as film stars including Sophia Loren, Elizabeth Taylor and Richard Burton. Tito's main palace was on the island of Vanga – currently off-limits to visitors without a special permit – while the larger island of Veli Brijun accommodated his guests. His Vanga palace also has historical importance as the place where Tito, Nasser and Nehru in 1956 formed the Non-Aligned Movement, a counterweight to the superpowers during the Cold War. Tito died in 1980 and the islands became a national park three years later. It is now popular with yachts that can afford the higher than average mooring fees.

Rovinj is home to Croatia's largest cigarette manufacturer, TDR – also the city's largest single employer. The tourist industry is becoming increasingly important both for mass tourism – Istria's traditional market – and more exclusive customers, for whom a luxury boutique hotel and niche shops cater. There are many places to stay in and around Rovinj, including Hotel Lone, the first hotel in Croatia to join the Design Hotels group. You'll also find all the tourist trappings, such as boat tours, multilingual menus and souvenir shops, yet somehow this ancient town manages to retain its character.

For many visitors, the highlight of visiting Rovinj is just wandering around the old town and exploring the narrow lanes. Old women sit in flower-shrouded windows and tiny bars fill with grappa-drinking locals. Rovinj's reputation as an enclave of artists and painters was rediscovered after World War II, when the government lured local artists into the old town with cheap rents. Myriad small galleries and workshops line the winding streets – follow **Grisia** as it tumbles seaward from St Euphemia's Church, a street lined with small galleries, jewellers and other shops showcasing Rovinj's bountiful artistic talent and creative spirit.

The atmospheric old town rambles around a small limestone peninsula, culminating in the voluminous **Church of St Euphemia** (Crkva sv. Eufemije), named after Rovinj's patron saint. The present building dates only from the 18th century, but it dominates Rovinj's skyline and has Istria's tallest bell tower, said to be modelled on the campanile in Venice. Look out also for the statue of St Euphemia rotating at the top. Local fishermen, who pray here for a good catch, have complained that since a renovation, using a helicopter to bring the statue down, she no longer gives such accurate weather forecasts. Today the church hosts classical performances during the Concerts in Euphrasiana festival in July and August, when musicians

One of the many great sunsets of Rovinj.

from Germany, Russia, Slovenia and elsewhere join domestic talent.

Many legends and myths haunt the church, including the particularly intriguing story of St Euphemia herself. She is said to have been thrown to the lions for her Christian beliefs at the order of Emperor Diocletian and her body later vanished from Constantinople before appearing off the Istrian coast aboard a ghostly transport in the 9th century. Local legend has it that moving her 6th-century sarcophagus from the shore to the lofty church seemed an impossible task until a local boy herding cattle received a divine calling and spirited the sarcophagus up the hillside.

The saint's heavily waxed remains are visible through a panel in the sarcophagus. A poignant addition is the wooden altar donated by refugees from Vukovar to thank the local people for their help during and after Serbia's siege of the city in 1991.

Rovinj's **Heritage Museum** (Zavičajni muzej grada Rovinja; www.muzej-rovinj.hr; daily 10am–6pm) is housed in a

Baroque creation. The eclectic exhibits range from paintings from the 15th and 16th centuries, including Pietro Mera's *Christ Crowned with Thorns* and works by Venetian artists, right through to the works of Rovinj's own painters. There are a number of traditional folk costumes on display, as well as various artefacts unearthed on digs in the surrounding region. Also in the museum are a few moderately interesting Etruscan pieces and some fine examples of antique furniture.

Back east over the channel that originally rendered Rovinj's old town an island, before it was paved over, is the **Franciscan Monastery** (Franjevački samostan; tel: 052 830390; visits by appointment), built at the beginning of the 18th century in Baroque style atop a hilly mound. The monastery contains an old library and a museum displaying18th- and 19th-century paintings, as well as ecclesiastical robes and religious artworks.

On the waterfront to the north, just outside the old town, is the **aquarium** (*akvarij*; July–Aug 9am–9pm, shorter

Rovinj.

hours rest of the year), part of the **Ruđer Bošković Centre for Maritime Research** (Institut Ruđer Bošković; www.irb.hr) and a good alternative for those unable to snorkel or dive in the clear waters around Rovinj. The aquarium dates from 1891 and houses a collage of colourful Istrian sea life, from sea-bed dwellers through to brightly coloured and poisonous fish. It may not be particularly hi-tech, but it is a useful distraction for younger visitors bored with churches and art galleries.

SVETI KATARINA

Rovinj's sunsets are justly famous, with the island of **Sveti Katarina** a particularly good place to watch the old town and the church of St Euphemia illuminated by an explosion of red and orange hues. Regular boats to and from Sveti Katarina leave from the jetty next to the Delfin Travel Agency. Back in town, the rocks at Valentino's Cocktail Bar are the best place from which to view the sunset. Cushions are dispensed on arrival and mellow music accompanies the sun's slow descent into the Adriatic.

After sundown the action moves on to the many bars, cafés, trattorias and pizzerias that line the waterfront, with the scene taking on a distinctly Italian feel.

CRVENI OTOK

A worthwhile day or half-day trip by boat from Rovinj is to **Crveni otok** , or Red Island, which is actually two islands connected by a causeway. One islet has two tourist hotels, while the other is home to a popular naturist resort. Both are heavily wooded and provide peaceful walks. The islands are also much better for swimming than Rovinj, which is often crowded. Boats leave regularly from Rovinj's waterfront in high season.

FROM ROVINJ TO POREČ

Limski zaljev  (also known as Limska Kanal and Lim Fjord), is a 9km (5-mile) -long flooded karst channel that looks unlike anywhere else in Istria, with its massive rock walls,

Climbing the bell tower in the Church of St Euphemia, Rovinj.

Look out for the Venetian Lion of St Mark on Istria's buildings.

⊘ VENETIAN INFLUENCES

The Venetian-style architecture that you see all over Istria is evidence of the peninsula's close ties with the Divine Republic arising from the Venetian conquest of the Adriatic coast in 1420 until its fall in 1797. Control of the coast was vital to securing the republic's all-important trade routes against the Genoans and the notorious pirates of Senj (see page 139). Istrian and Dalmatian ports were fortified with enclosing walls and lookout towers, and also beautified as they developed their own prosperous merchant class. Istria's quarries were a handy source of fine white stone, which was also used to construct many of the finest palaces in Venice.

Soon the Adriatic Sea was known as the 'Gulf of Venice', and from here the republic quickly pushed on to conquer Greece and Cyprus, as well as many territories in mainland Italy.

Venetian Gothic is the most visible style of architecture throughout Istria, most splendidly seen in the elegant piazzas of Rovinj and Poreč, but also in bell towers of quite small villages. Typical features include rose windows, ogival (pointed) arches, loggias and fine slender columns. Facades sometimes incorporate the traditional symbol of the Divine Republic, the winged Lion of St Mark holding a book inscribed with the word *Pax*.

emerald-green waters and unusual vegetation. Adriatic pirates used to plan ambushes from the sanctuary of this hidden world, but today the only signs of human activity are the seafood restaurants and the remains of the cave that was the hermetic home of St Romuald in the 11th century (closed at the time of writing). Those with their own transport who are planning to head from Rovinj to Poreč are well advised to avoid rejoining the fast inland road and instead curl around the old route passing the fjord. This diversion provides easy access to the seafood restaurants at the head of the fjord, which are ideal for a lazy lunch – specialities include the bountiful local oysters and mussels that thrive in the channel's peculiarly sweet waters. Fans of extreme sports venture to the northern side of the channel, where the cliffs are ideal for free climbing. From the waterside, the Poreč road climbs past a wooden viewing tower that opens up a cross-section of the forest-shrouded fjord as it snakes away seaward bound.

Just before the road reaches Poreč it comes to the small town of **Vrsar** ⑥, which is quieter and less brash than its larger neighbour. Vrsar's facilities include a small marina and the usual tourist hotels that line this stretch of coastline, but it has a pleasant character, with a church and bell tower presiding over its compact old town, a jumble of historic streets that lead down to a wide waterfront.

Just south of Vrsar, things are more relaxed still at pleasantly traffic-free **Koversada**, one of the world's largest and oldest naturist resorts – twice voted Croatia's best beach, which can handle the naked needs of more than 10,000 naturists at a time.

THE RESORT OF POREČ

For many people arriving in **Poreč** ⑦ alarm bells start ringing when they hear that this is the largest tourist resort in Croatia, the epicentre of one of the country's fastest expanding industries. The approach from the east takes one through the massive Zelena Laguna resort, almost a town in its own

Limska Kanal.

right. Since the 1960s, Poreč has been geared towards taking in thousands upon thousands of tourists from all over Europe, catering for them for one or two weeks, and then spitting them back out – admittedly with a friendly smile – at the end.

There may be only 16,000 residents in the town, but Poreč manages to accommodate more than 700,000 visitors annually with the two massive companies of Valamar Riviera and Plava Laguna soaking up most of the business. This all-too-obvious mass tourism can put people off visiting Poreč, but to avoid the town is to miss out on one of Croatia's most alluring attractions, the Basilica of Euphrasius, on Unesco's World Heritage List since 1997.

ST EUPHRASIUS

In almost any other European city, the 6th-century **Basilica of Euphrasius** (Eufrazijeva bazilika; daily June–Sept 9am–9pm, Oct–May 9am–6pm; basilica free), housing some of the Adriatic's finest Byzantine art, would draw long queues and charge a hefty admission fee, but in Poreč there are rarely queues and entry is free. Its highlights are the iridescent gold-laced frescoes, embellished with mother-of-pearl and precious and semi-precious stones, which adorn the main basilica's apse. The work of craftsmen from Constantinople and Ravenna, they include *Christ and the Apostles*, the *Virgin Enthroned with Child* and scenes of the Annunciation and Visitation. One interesting feature to look out for is Euphrasius himself, the bishop who commissioned the frescoes; he is depicted to the left of the largest fresco, holding a scale model of the church. In front of the apse, the 13th-century ciborium (canopy) is also decorated with mosaics. The wooden pews are a perfect place to sit and admire the intricate handiwork of the Byzantine artists and craftsmen.

The site's antiquity is further revealed in the mosaics on the floor on both sides of the entrance, originating from a previous church on the site, dating from the 4th century. The wooden

Church of St Euphemia, Rovinj.

Madonna and Child in the Basilica of Euphrasius, Poreč.

pews in the basilica are 15th century, as is the bell tower, which is accessible through the baptistry across the courtyard from the basilica. The steep and narrow climb up the bell tower is well rewarded with views out across Poreč and the Adriatic Sea; it is said that on a clear day you may even see Venice.

ROMAN POREČ

Just outside the basilica is **Eufrazijeva**, one of the two sturdy thoroughfares that, along with **Decumanus**, form the centre of Roman Poreč. When the Romans arrived this was little more than a sleepy Illyrian fishing village, but they transformed it beyond recognition. The town's ancient heritage is still very much alive, its old Roman thoroughfares lined with Venetian-style buildings in use as restaurants, cafés and shops.

Decumanus's southern fringe used to culminate in the Roman Forum, but little of the original buildings remain, bar the scattered ruins of two temples, the Temple of Neptune and another thought to pay homage to Mars. Little

reliable information is available on either, despite what the creative local guides may tell you.

Towards the southern end of Decumanus is the **Romanesque House**, dating from the 13th century. The unusual wooden balcony on the upper level would make a delightful vantage point for overlooking this stretch of the Decumanus and the orange-tiled roofs of Poreč, though at present this is not open to the public. The ground floor displays an ever-changing exhibition of the work of local artists and sculptors, with many of the exhibits on sale at reasonable prices.

In 2001, fresh Christian mosaics were uncovered in a courtyard behind the **Istrian Assembly Hall** (Istarska sabornica) and research is under way to find out more about them. The hall was built originally as a Franciscan church in the 13th century and its interior was revamped in Baroque style in the 18th century. In the 20th century, an Istrian assembly used to have its meetings here and today the local government still convenes in

the hall. During summer, classical concerts are held here, along with art exhibitions.

RESORT ACTIVITIES

Poreč's Roman history warrants at least a few days' exploration, but on longer stays you may want to take a break from mining Poreč's rich cultural seam. The many tourist-oriented facilities, including a number for families, are at their peak in high summer. The resort developments offer something for everyone, from all the usual water sports and the simple pleasures of sunbathing to more adrenalin-pumping activities such as paintball, paragliding and skydiving. The local tourist office also produces a series of leaflets on the network of paths for walking and cycling in the Poreč area. Nine inland routes range from 20km (12 miles) to a 56km (35-mile) ride through the Istrian countryside. More sedentary thrills include scenic flights over Istria's dramatic coastline and all the major west coast towns.

NORTH OF POREČ

While Poreč and Rovinj are the best-known Istrian resorts, there are another couple of historic resort towns on the coast curling northwest towards the border with Slovenia. A short drive north of Poreč is **Novigrad ❽**, a miniature Rovinj with its old town clinging to the shore and a bell tower rising above a smattering of orange-tiled roofs. Some of its former charm was sacrificed in the Communist-era drive to attract low-margin mass tourism, resulting in an untidy collection of hotel developments, but it is worth at least a day trip with lunch or dinner in one of its well-regarded fish restaurants. There is also an 11th-century church with a sarcophagus said to contain the little-known St Pelagius's remains.

Further north on the coastal road is **Umag ❾**, a compact town of 6,000 inhabitants and whose old centre is scenically located on a peninsula. Umag has a Roman heritage and an old town with a Venetian-style bell tower. Historical attractions that have survived its transformation from a

⊙ Fact

Since 1990, Umag has gained worldwide attention with its annual ATP Tour Croatia Open men-only tennis tournament in July. But the Umag Tennis Academy at Katoro Resort isn't just for pros: multilingual staff coach players of all ages and abilities during tennis holidays on the 25 clay courts.

View across the Adriatic from the bell tower of the Basilica of Euphrasius, Poreč.

modest Istrian town into a tourist resort include sections of the old town walls, the Church of Mary's Assumption and the **Town Museum** (July–Aug Mon–Sat 10am–noon and 7–10pm, Sun 10am–2pm, shorter hours May–June and Sept; free).

The Istrian west coast comes to an end at the small fishing village of **Savudrija** , a good spot for a simple meal of the fresh catch of the day. One tall village tale concerns its 36-metre (118ft) high lighthouse, the oldest on the Croatian coast. The story goes that Count Metternich fell head over heels in love with a Croatian woman at a ball in Vienna. His shyness prevented him from making a move and instead he decided to build a lighthouse in an attempt to win the heart of his love. Tragically, the object of his desire is said to have died on the very night his illuminated messages of love began beaming over the rocky Adriatic coastline.

ISTRIA'S EAST COAST

Istria's east coast is far less explored than the west and is not as saturated with tourists, though there is also no town that really has the appeal or facilities of Poreč, Pula or Rovinj. The landscape is dominated by wild, pine-covered mountains and a rambling, rugged coastline, though a number of power stations and industrial scars spoil the vistas across the Kvarner Gulf and towards the island of Cres. The coastal E751 road is a more inviting route to the Kvarner Gulf than that offered by the express toll road, which speeds through the interior, but expect delays because of roadworks.

The road northeast of Pula reaches the village of **Raša** after meandering through the Raška valley. This is the first of a number of villages offering clues to the region's main industry prior to tourism.

The east of Istria offers a rich seam of coal; in fact, this part of Croatia was first mined by the Italians in 1937. The neat rows of dwellings were built to house the coal workers during the Italian regime. Yugoslavia continued coal production after gaining control

Savudrija's rocky shore.

of Istria after World War II, but mining in the region finally ceased in 1989 and the village feels somewhat stranded in a time warp.

The most impressive building is **St Barbara's Church** (Crkva sv. Barbare) – look out for the bell tower sculpted to resemble a pithead.

LABIN

The largest and most interesting settlement on the east coast is **Labin** ⑫, consisting of an old town perched on a high hill and a newer settlement that has mushroomed over the past century. The town's original name, Albana, is said to be of Celtic origin, meaning simply 'town on a hill', but this aspect of the area's history has been little explored. Major subsidence problems caused by mining and careless planning put the old town in danger of collapse, and at one point it looked as though it would have to be abandoned altogether. Thankfully the subsidence was shored up, and the jumble of winding streets, tumble of church spires and sprinkling of

craft shops make it a pleasant place to visit.

The most impressive of Labin's churches is the **Church of the Birth of the Blessed Mary** (Rodenje Marijino), a fascinating place of worship built on 11th-century foundations, although the present structure dates from 1336. It incorporates both Renaissance and Gothic styles. Look out for the 17th-century Venetian lion above the Gothic rose window on the church's facade and the six sturdy marble altars inside.

Next door to the church, the town's eclectic history is explored in the **Town Museum** (Gradski muzej; July–Aug Mon–Sat 10am–1pm and 6–10pm, shorter hours May–June and Sept). The displays are housed in an 18th-century palace and range from traditional costumes and musical instruments through to an exhibit on the town's coal-mining days. One of the most intriguing coal-related stories concerns a period in 1921 when the local mine workers defied the Italian authorities and declared

Rustic items in the Ethnographic Museum of Istria, inside Pazin's castle.

Novigrad's old town and marina.

⦿ ECOTOURISM

Istria has not been slow to realise the increasing popularity of 'ecotourism', an environmentally friendly form of vacation offering holiday-makers the chance to spend time in a rustic setting very different from the kind of faceless tourist hotels often found in the built-up coastal resorts. They are usually much cheaper, too. The Istrian County Tourist Association's *Agroturizam* programme lists more than 100 cottages, farms, guesthouses and rural hotels dotted over the peninsula. It also has details of places where passing travellers can pop in for lunch if they book ahead.

All of the establishments listed in the programme offer the chance to sample the excellent food and drink of Istria. Specialities you can expect to savour include *pršut* (wind-dried ham), black and white truffles, blood sausages, honey and a range of cheeses. There are also many excellent Istrian wines such as Malvazija, Teran and Istrian Muscatel, as well as *Biska*, a fiery but very enjoyable mistletoe brandy. Some farms offer guests the chance to take part in various seasonal rituals: depending on the time of year, you can help with the grape harvest, go hunting for wild asparagus or spend a day in the woods learning about mushroom-picking.

Further details and information on the *Agroturizam* programme in Istria can be found at local tourist offices.

Istria's fish restaurants are among the best in Croatia.

Labin.

the 'Labin Republic' as they held a strike in protest at poor conditions. The helpful English-speaking staff at the museum are usually only too keen to fill visitors in on Labin's 15 minutes of fame.

RABAC

On sweltering Istrian summer days the coastal resort of **Rabac** 🔞 is a good escape, reached after a 30-minute walk or a 3km (2-mile) drive from Labin. The first settlers in Rabac were fishermen with a handful of boats operating out of the village.

The first hotel along the pretty bay was opened in 1889, but it did not develop as a proper resort until the Italian authorities promoted the village as the perfect getaway for the exhausted mine workers during the Italian occupation of Istria. Today's visitors tend to be holidaymakers seeking a quieter alternative to the west coast resorts, or young Croatian ravers looking for a party. In summer, Rabac hosts enormous dance parties with some of Europe's most celebrated DJs. The only

other real attraction as such is a sculpture park.

PLOMIN

The last settlement of note on the E751 before the Kvarner Gulf is the village of **Plomin** 🔞, set on a high forested ridge. You are unlikely to find any other tourists in this hill village, and very few locals for that matter. The small settlement may have a sense of foreboding and decay, and the fishing bay nestling below has long since silted up, but its narrow streets and relaxed atmosphere warrant a quick stop. The Church of St George has a fine early example of Glagolitic script.

Superb views from Plomin take in a wide sweep of the Kvarner Gulf and the beautiful Adriatic island of Cres. The village provides an atmospheric last stop in Istria.

INLAND ISTRIA

Often overlooked by the tourists on Istria's coast, the attractions of inland Istria – rolling vine-clad hills and perched villages – are making

it a successful centre for rural tourism. Given the millions of tourists who descend on the Istrian coastline every year it is surprising that so few think about heading into the region's rural hinterland. Travel professionals have often described it as the new Tuscany or Umbria, and its rolling green hills, sweeping vineyards and idyllic hill towns certainly bring Italy to mind.

Getting into Istria's hinterland could not be easier. In high season plenty of day trips operate from Poreč, Rovinj and other resorts, and there is also a passable public transport system with rail and bus connections. However, if you really want to explore the region in some detail, rather than just dipping in for a taste, it is advisable to hire a car and spend a few nights in at least one of the hill towns. Just a short journey north of Poreč is Istria's humble regional capital, Pazin, which year round makes a good base and starting point. Nearby is Motovun, one of the most delightful of all the hill towns and perhaps the most visited.

One of the real joys of exploring inland is driving aimlessly around, stopping off whenever you feel like it. There are many pleasant surprises, such as the village of Vižinada, where you are almost guaranteed not to find any other tourists, and few inhabitants either. As with many of the hill towns it suffered serious depopulation during and after World War II, with about two-thirds of all ethnic Italians leaving.

One of the upsides of the population drift away from the hill towns has been the availability of homes for local artists. The enlightened local authorities have opened up many of the towns' deserted houses on low-rent or even rent-free schemes to attract colonies of artists, sculptors and craftspeople. The shining example of the success of this programme is Grožnjan, in itself a scenery-rich hill town, where dozens of artists work in the rambling old stone buildings. It is easy to spend a whole day in Grožnjan browsing through the galleries and studios and picking up some interesting art.

Rabac's harbour.

St Stephen's Church, Motovun.

Since independence, the Istria County Tourist Association has been very proactive in pushing the attractions of inland Istria. It has set up a wine trail, published a guide to the region's gastronomic highlights and initiated the *Agroturizam* programme, which encourages local people to open up their farms and homes to fee-paying guests from abroad. Its emphasis is on meeting local people and sampling the fine wines and foods that the region has supplied in such abundance since Roman times.

PAZIN

A 35km (22-mile) drive north of Poreč is Istria's rather unlikely regional capital, **Pazin** ⑮. While Pula is the *de facto* capital of the peninsula because of its size, the post-war Communist authorities designated this modest inland town the official seat of the regional government as they attempted to wrest power away from Pula and Poreč. First mentioned in historical records by Emperor Otto II, the town today is largely unappealing, modern and

A house in Pazin.

industrial. The old town and its austere castle teeter on the brink of a dramatic limestone gorge that drops over 100 metres (330ft) below and was said to have been the inspiration for Jules Verne when he hurled the protagonist of his novel *Mathias Sandorf* over the abyss. Some Pazin residents insist that the vertigo-inducing gorge was also the inspiration for Dante's *Inferno*.

Pazin's castle, a utilitarian 9th-century fortress that overlooks the Fjoba stream, is Istria's largest and best preserved. Fifteenth-century additions include the sturdy defensive walls. Cross the drawbridge into the castle itself to visit the **Ethnographic Museum of Istria** (Etnografskog muzej Istre; www.emi.hr; daily 10am–6pm). It displays a selection of historical costumes from the surrounding region and an array of jewellery, and documents the history of the fishing and agricultural industries in Istria. Look out also for the collection of bells, some dating back as far as the 14th century, and finds from local archaeological digs. The museum's atmospheric galleries

⊘ ACROSS TO SLOVENIA

Slovenia declared independence on the same day as Croatia in 1991, but since then their paths have gone in markedly different directions. While Croatia was dragged into the bitter conflict with Yugoslavia, Slovenia got on with modernising its economy and building ties with its neighbours, Austria and Italy. Popping into Slovenia for a few days is well worthwhile. The 'Slovenian Riviera' is not on the scale of Croatia's meandering coastline, but this patch of the Adriatic, tucked between Istria and the Italian city of Trieste, has plenty of attractions. Close to the border crossing is the resort of Portorož, but a better option is to continue on to Piran, a dreamy Venetian Gothic town set on a narrow peninsula, offering views west to Trieste and east to Istria, with the spires of Venice visible on the horizon on a clear day. Koper, 17km (10 miles) to the north of Piran, has a rambling old town that was built by the Venetians in the 15th and 16th centuries. Its main square has a Renaissance loggia and there are concrete beaches. Koper is connected by regular buses to Trieste and north to the Slovenian capital, Ljubljana, a small city with a blend of Austro-Hungarian and Italian architecture that is enlivened by a large student population.

Bear in mind that if you plan to drive on any motorways in Slovenia, you will have to buy a vignette, or toll sticker. The minimum is a weekly sticker for €15, and these can be bought at service stations.

also house a number of temporary exhibitions. If you are looking for an unusual activity, the museum runs weaving workshops on request. The town museum (mid-Apr–June Tue–Sun 10am–6pm, July–mid-Sept daily 10am–6pm, shorter hours rest of the year), at the same location, displays items from the castle's history. In the castle's courtyard is a water cistern that was installed to provide fresh water in the event of a siege, an ever-present danger in Pazin for centuries.

Pazin also has a couple of interesting churches. The **Church of St Nicholas** (Župna crkva sv. Nikole) on the town's southern perimeter was built in 1266 in austere Romanesque style, with the bell tower an 18th-century afterthought. The rather plain exterior gives way to a more elaborate interior with three naves and a series of Gothic frescoes from the 15th century, depicting scenes from the Bible and the life of St Nicholas. A Gothic sanctuary and vault were also added in the 15th century – look out for the coat of arms of Pazin, the oldest surviving in

the town. Meanwhile, the Franciscan monastery and attached church were built between 1463 and 1477 with a late Gothic presbytery from the same period. According to tradition, anyone who visits it on 2 August will be absolved of their sins.

Another good time to visit Pazin is the first Tuesday of the month, when it runs a traditional market. Honey is a particularly good buy.

FINE FRESCOES AROUND PAZIN

The main attraction in the area surrounding Pazin is the bucolic little village of **Beram** ⑯ 5km (3 miles) to the northwest. It is renowned for its cemetery church of St Mary (Crkva sv. Marije na Škrilinah), containing a fine collection of 15th-century frescoes. Getting access to see the frescoes can be problematic as the church is not often left open. Either ask locally for the key or plan ahead and make enquiries at the tourist office in Pazin, which may be able to point you in the right direction. It is well worth the effort.

⊙ Tip

Started in 1999, Motovun's film festival (www.motovunfilmfestival.com) is exclusively for films, documentaries and other works by small independent producers. Held in late July, it attracts 50,000 visitors, many of them staying at a free eco-campsite in an idyllic setting. Special buses run from Pazin throughout the festival. If you are camping, it is a good idea to arrive early.

Pazin sits right on the edge of a limestone gorge.

Depicted on the medieval frescoes are scenes from the lives of Mary and the saints, with Adam and Eve also featuring on one. Look out for the signature of the man who crafted them, Vincent of Kastav. Perhaps the most dramatic of all the works is the vividly portrayed *Dance of Death* in which a procession of citizens headed by the Pope is attended by scythe-wielding skeletons. Unfortunately, some of the frescoes were damaged when new windows were added to the church and also when they were covered up by mortar, not to be rediscovered until just before the start of World War I. The church is a small, mainly Gothic structure, but in the 18th century the entrance was widened and a wooden roof built to shore up the building.

MOTOVUN

Motovun ⑰, 20km (12 miles) from Pazin, home to one of Croatia's most popular film festivals, is perhaps the archetypal inland Istrian town and the best place to head if you are short of time and want a quick taste of what the region has to offer. Its chocolate-box beauty unfolds atop a rocky 280-metre (920ft) high outcrop, which rears seemingly from nowhere amidst the rolling green fields and vineyards of the Mirna River valley. Getting up to Motovun is fun in itself; the winding road meanders up the green slopes, seemingly in search of a way through the Venetian stone walls. The forests surrounding the town are renowned for the excellent truffles that are unearthed here in autumn, and make up the world's largest natural habitat for the prized product. The forest once covered a massive area, but the Venetians cut down large parts, floating the trees downstream to the Adriatic where they used them for shipbuilding. A small section of the original forest is now protected by conservation laws.

Venice's influence is apparent as you enter the town, in the trademark Venetian lion casting a watchful eye over all new arrivals, and palatial homes dating from the 15th and 16th centuries. Motovun has some of the best-preserved defensive walls in the

Frescoes in St Mary's church, Beram.

region, with a single line encircling the historic core and two smaller semicircles aiding defence. The best way to get an understanding of the place is to climb on to the town's walls and walk around, taking in the views of Motovun and the Istrian countryside stretching away into the distance. Look out for the rich collage of architecture that Motovun embraces. Gothic, Venetian and Romanesque buildings are squeezed into a town that today has fewer than 600 inhabitants.

St Stephen's Church (Crkva sv. Stjepana; daily; free) is Motovun's only real must-see sight, a Renaissance parish church with a lofty campanile built in the 17th century by the Venetian architect Andrea Palladio, while the marble statues on the altar of St Laurence and St Stephen were sculpted by another Venetian artist. When the bell tower is open (times vary depending on staffing levels), head up the stairs of the campanile for an unforgettable view of the town and the Istrian landscape, which is even more impressive than that from the town walls.

For an unusual perspective of Motovun, attempt to climb the 1,052 steps that lead up to the old town from the valley floor, a feat that is practically impossible in the height of summer.

Apart from truffles, it would be rude to visit Motovun without sampling the renowned local Malvazija and Teran wine varieties. The second goes especially well with *pršut* (prosciutto).

VIŽINADA

Southwest of Motovun, the small village of **Vižinada** ⑱ is a real find and well worth a stop. There are only a few small agrotourism places in town to stay or eat at, but Vižinada has all of the best bits of inland Istria without many tourists: unspoilt countryside, panoramic views, impressive old churches and the historical relics of the various civilisations that have influenced the region through the centuries. Its tiny old town covers the hillside away from the main road. Crowded around the small central square are a jumble of old churches, Roman remains and the foundations of a Venetian-era loggia, while all around

Artist's workshop in Grožnjan.

⊘ THE WINE TRAIL

All over inland Istria you will see vineyards and signs pointing to small local outlets where families sell their own wine from the cellars of their homes. Driving out to the vineyards to stock up on supplies is tremendously popular among Istrians themselves.

To help foreign visitors join in the fun, the Istria County Tourist Association has put together a *Guide to the Wine Roads of Istria*. It identifies three wine routes (Buje, Buzet and Poreč) and recommends specific vineyards and cellars where you can taste and buy. In addition, a Wine Day takes place on the first Sunday in May in Buje, Buzet and Vodnjan, when around 60 cellars open for wine tasting. The majority of the production is based in the western portion of inland Istria in the fertile land between Rovinj, Poreč and Buje, while to the east there is a much smaller district around Labin. You will also find local wines served by the jug in Istria's *konoba* (taverns), accompanied by hearty rustic fare.

Istrian wines vary greatly in price, ranging from just 20 kuna for a cheap litre bottle of the dry white Malvazija to around 80 or 90 kuna for a 75cl bottle of red Teran and more for a good vintage. In winter in Istria, look out for *supa*, made from red wine mulled with sugar, olive oil and pepper and scooped up with toasted bread.

are sweeping views of the peninsula's countryside. There is nothing much to do but congratulate yourself on finding this little hidden-away slice of inland Istria. In summer, outdoor classical concerts brighten up the main square.

From Vižinada you can take a 27km (17 miles) bike trail that brings you back to where you started via some impressive views, an old wine railway track and the village of Kaštelir. Details of the route are available from the small mountain bike information office on the main road through Vižinada.

GROŽNJAN

To the north of Vižinada, towards the mountains that mark the border with Slovenia, is the hill town of **Grožnjan** ⑲. Since Croatian independence, the local authorities have breathed new life into it, with many public buildings revamped and the infrastructure restored from its dilapidated state. Wandering along the cobbles of its well-preserved medieval centre is a joy. With Communism gone, a number of young people have moved back and set up small businesses and

the population has been boosted by fresh young blood. Grožnjan also has the distinction of being the only locality in Croatia with an Italian majority – 51 percent at last count.

Since World War II, Grožnjan has also become an oasis for artists and writers, as the enlightened local authorities offered them the empty homes that had been left by fleeing Italians and young people heading to find jobs in nearby cities. The result is an artists' colony that has become a tourist attraction. It offers the opportunity to buy a broad range of paintings, sculptures and ceramics, along with the chance to talk to the artists.

Strolling around the various studios and workshops, having a nose into any that look interesting – doors are left open for passing visitors – is the main pleasure in the town. A group of musicians have formed the International Centre for the Young Musicians of Croatia in previously uninhabited buildings, and the sound of their music often wafts through the narrow stone streets, adding to the artistic ambience.

Grožnjan.

In summer, students from many other European countries come to work with the Croatian students, giving the town's cafés a cosmopolitan air.

GROŽNJAN EVENTS

There are myriad cultural events with exhibitions, concerts and workshops taking place daily in rejuvenated venues such as the Fonticus Gallery and the Kastel Concert Hall. Grožnjan hosts an award-winning jazz festival that runs over three weeks from late July into early August.

Apart from the main town gate, the Venetian walls have been pulled down, leaving uninterrupted views of the rolling countryside and over a dozen surrounding villages. When the visibility is especially good, the naked eye can see as far as the Julian Alps in Slovenia and east to the rugged outline of Mt Učka, on the edge of the Kvarner Gulf. There are few historic sights apart from the 18th-century **Church of St Mary** (Crkva sv. Marije). It is worth peeking inside to see the Baroque altars and the wooden choir stalls that were added in Renaissance style. The Venetians left a fine loggia in the centre of the old town. Built around four sturdy columns in the 16th century, it houses four Roman tombs, relics of the days when Grožnjan was garrisoned as a hill fort by the Roman rulers. The Italians returned in the 20th century and many locals are still bilingual; a large portion of everyday speech is in a local adaptation of a Venetian dialect.

VENETIAN-STYLE BUJE

Even farther northwest towards the Slovenian border is the hill town of **Buje** ⑳, still only 34km (21 miles) as the crow flies from Poreč, in the heart of Istria's leading wine-growing area. Buje's old town has a solid feel to it and it is less touristy than either Motovun or Grožnjan. It was fortified in the Middle Ages by a succession of Istrian counts, before the Venetians shipped in and took most of the fortifications down. A wealth of Venetian-style architecture survives, including the town loggia, a classic of Venetian Gothic design with an elegant facade.

Motovun.

From the post-Venetian town walls, the views from Buje are amongst the finest in the whole of Istria. The town spreads below, a picturesque collage of terracotta roofs, while in the background lush fields run into a patchwork of vineyards and rolling hills. Framing the scene is the crumple of peaks marking the backbone of the Slovenian border and the Adriatic Sea, with a sprinkling of the Istrian coastal resorts also visible on a clear day.

Buje's **Church of St Servulus** (Crkva sv. Servola) is worth entering. It has undergone many modifications since a Roman temple stood on the site, the current building owing much to an 18th-century face-lift. Look out for the organ, which has survived on the site since it was installed in 1791. If the facade of the church looks a little ramshackle, do not be too surprised as it was never actually finished. Nearby, the **Church of St Mary** (Crkva sv. Marije) dates from the 15th century, though the bell tower was added a century later. The distinctive Lion of St Mark on the belfry once again emphasises the Venetian connection that crops up throughout Istria.

THE HILL TOWN OF BUZET

Heading back east across the northern portion of inland Istria, you come to the town of **Buzet** ㉑, a larger settlement than most and an option if you would prefer to be based in the interior rather than in one of the coastal resorts. If you are planning on heading from coastal Istria to Kvarner, with a few days exploring inland Istria in between, Buzet is also handy, as it is around 50km (30 miles) from both Poreč and Rijeka.

Buzet is a typical Istrian hill town, with green slopes rising to an old town core, overlooking a verdant valley with the ubiquitous River Mirna running through it. Settlement in Buzet dates back to before the arrival of the Romans, who knew it as Pinguentum. A number of major archaeological finds have been made in and around Buzet, some of which are on display in the **Buzet Region Museum** (Zavičajni muzej; July–Aug Mon–Fri 9am–3pm and 5–8pm, Sat–Sun

Hum's bell tower.

10am–1pm, rest of the year Mon–Fri 10am–3pm, weekends by arrangement), inside a 17th-century palace. The museum's highlights include pagan carvings depicting sacrificial altars and gravestones, as well as pagan gods. The Roman period is also well covered, as is World War II, which dwells on the heroic deeds of the local people. There is also a colourful collection of traditional Croatian folk costumes.

Buzet is not known as the 'Truffle City' for nothing, as it is at the centre of one of Istria's most bountiful truffle areas. The delectable fungi are harvested in the fields and woods surrounding the town in September and October, and are celebrated by an annual truffle festival in September, in which the locals prepare a truffle omelette in the town square. One of the highlights of visiting is eating in the local restaurants, which all feature truffles on their menus.

GLAGOLITIC ALLEY

Blink and you will miss the tiny town of **Hum** ㉒, which is signposted just below the town of Roč. It lies at the head of a road known as **Glagolitic Alley** (Aleja glagoljaša), a kind of sculpture trail created in the 1970s to celebrate the Glagolitic script (see page 143), the precursor of Cyrillic. The 11 works include copies of important Glagolitic documents.

Hum claims to be the smallest town in the world, which may have some validity, as its 2017 population was just 28 inhabitants. It is certainly the smallest town in Istria, although it still manages somehow to pack in a couple of churches, a restaurant and a set of town walls.

ISTARSKE TOPLICE

The health spa **Istarske Toplice,** 10km (6 miles) outside Buzet on the road to Poreč, has been famous since Roman times. It is renowned for its beneficial effects on aching backs, arthritis and skin conditions, especially acne, but as yet it offers no cure for an insatiable addiction to truffles. The sulphur-infused waters stay at around a constant 30 to 35°C (86–95°F) all year.

Eat

If you are thinking of visiting Buzet, consider timing your visit either for the Truffle Festival in September or for the Town Festival in December, when a programme of concerts livens up the town.

Mending a roof in Buzet.

 **BIRDS**

Of all the wildlife in Croatia, birds are the most visible – and the most rewarding – with rare species breeding in many of the nature reserves found around the country.

There are birds to see in every season in Croatia. Spring brings migrating flocks from Africa, and martins and swallows are busy in their nests beneath the eves. In summer, towns are filled with the shrill cries of swifts careening around bell towers and rooftops, and in early autumn, brilliant blue kingfishers flit through rocky coves. Raptors soar over the islands; woodpeckers tap away in the forests that conceal owls and tits; and warblers, buntings and wheatears flit over more open ground. Croatia, with its great variety of habitats, has a rich roll call of birds, so it is not surprising that a number of companies offer birdwatching holidays. Many bird species will be unfamiliar. You might not recognise the pale grey olive-tree warbler or sombre tit, but a blue nuthatch, red-rumped swallow, black-eared wheatear, bee-eater and rock partridge are more easily identified.

July and August are not the best times, as birds are on the whole inactive in summer. (Nature compensates for this in Croatia by providing a wide variety of butterflies.) But when on a boat trip or wandering through meadowlands, there is still usually something to see. Spring and autumn bring the large migrations: more than 350 varieties have been recorded in the country. In winter, water birds collect in their thousands around Lake Vrana and the Kopačevo marshes.

It can take a trained eye to know one songbird from another, a gull from a tern, and to sort out the difference between birds of prey, and this is a good place to start learning.

White-backed woodpeckers, which breed in Paklenica National Park.

Swifts swoop around the streets and squares of coastal towns such as Split.

The great white pelican, one of the world's largest birds, is a visitor to the coast.

Pack the binoculars.

Along the coast

The coast presents three distinct types of habitat.

Mountains: choughs and larks and other mountain species head for the Velebit Mountains in Paklenica National Park, which is also a breeding ground for capercaillie and white-backed woodpeckers. Biokovo Nature Park is where the ortolan bunting breeds, while the Dinaric mountains possess the only breeding population of shore larks. Eagles and falcons can usually be seen in the high ground above Trogir.

Rivers and lakes: the freshwater lakes and deltas are breeding grounds for herons and coots, plovers, curlews and terns. The largest delta belongs to the River Neretva, scene of great spring and autumn migrations, and more than 100 species nest here. Lake Vrana and the Krka and Zrmanja rivers are important too.

The islands: terns, shearwaters, shags and gulls all nest among the islands. The endangered griffon vulture is helped with a rehabilitation centre on the island of Cres, and the only nesting areas for Eleanora's falcons are on the islands of Vis, Biševo, Jabuka, St Andrija, Brusnik and Palagruža, where Cory's shearwaters also breed.

wood warbler, more colourful than the grey olive-tree arbler, snacks on a ripening olive.

he unmistakable bee-eater, which catches insects only hen they are in flight.

A rescued griffon vulture at the Eco Centre on Cres island, founded to protect the species.

Rab town.

Opatija Riviera.

KVARNER

This enormous bay has a long history of high-class tourism. The Opatija Riviera was popular in Austro-Hungarian times, while islands such as Krk and Rab are among Croatia's most beautiful.

The vast, island-studded Kvarner Gulf (Kvarnerski zaljev) connects the Istrian peninsula in the north with the Dalmatian regions to the south. To the rear its coastal strip is backed by the hulking sweep of the Velebit Mountains, Croatia's largest range, cutting off coastal towns and villages from the interior and necessitating long trips along the Adriatic Highway (or *Magistrala*), which runs south all the way from Rijeka to Dalmatia. Tourism here began in the 19th century when rich citizens of Vienna and Budapest, many leaving for health reasons, fled their own harsh winters and sought refuge in the relatively balmy climes of the Opatija Riviera, running along the eastern flank of the Istrian peninsula. The area lies under the protective shadow of Mt Učka, which is actually in Istria but is more accessible from Kvarner. Its peak keeps away the worst of the wind and chill and offers good opportunities for hiking in summer, with spectacular views across the whole expanse of the Kvarner Gulf.

Tourism is flourishing, both in the Opatija Riviera resorts of Lovran, Volosko and Opatija and on the islands in the gulf, including Krk and Cres, the two largest Croatian islands, and Rab, home to one of

the most attractive towns in Croatia. The Kvarner marks the transition between Istria and Dalmatia, with islands such as Lošinj, which is dotted with interesting towns, beaches and lush landscapes. The eerie landscape of Pag, in which humans have struggled to survive for centuries, offers a taste of things to come further south in Dalmatia.

Back on the mainland, the only city in Kvarner is Rijeka, Croatia's third-largest city, which is interesting enough to detain the tourists passing through its

⊘ Main Attractions
Opatija
Lovran
Mt Učka
Rijeka
Paklenica National Park
Krk
Rab
Pag
Cres
Lošinj

Map on page 134

The maiden with the seagull statue is one of the symbols of Opatija.

port for a few nights. It receives nothing like the attention of Split or Pula, but it is worth exploring nonetheless. Elsewhere on the mainland there is little to stop off for on the route south, bar the Risnjak National Park, a mountain paradise, and the town of Senj, famous for its 16th-century Uskok warriors.

A highlight in the extreme south is the Paklenica National Park, with its many opportunities for walking and hiking, and spectacular views of Kvarner and its myriad islands.

OPATIJA RIVIERA

The **Opatija Riviera** (Opatijska rivijera) stretches for over 40km (25 miles) along the shores of Kvarner, enjoying a unique microclimate that ensures year-round balmy temperatures and evergreen vegetation. It owes this to the hulking presence of Mt Učka and other lofty mountains, which stretch high above the coastal flatlands and protect them from the worst of the winds and rain. With such agreeable weather, the Riviera has been popular since the 19th century, when the wealthy classes of the Austro-Hungarian Empire, particularly those with respiratory problems, came to enjoy the climate. Its 2,200 hours of sunshine a year and an ever-present cooling breeze ensure that summer temperatures average a very pleasant 22°C (72°F).

Opatija ❶ is still the main resort on this stretch of coastline. Until the end of the 19th century it was little more than a few houses that clustered around the 15th-century abbey (*opatija* in Croatian). All that changed, largely thanks to one man and a railway. The man was Iginio Scarpa, a nature-loving patrician from nearby Rijeka, who built his Villa Angiolina – named after his late wife – in Opatija in 1844. He filled his garden with plants brought from South America, Australia, the Far East and other parts of the world, including the Japanese camellia, which later became the symbol of Opatija. Within a few decades, distinguished visitors to the villa had been so impressed that many

Opatija's promenade.

bought property there and Opatija's first hotel, the Quarnero, now the Kvarner Hotel opened its doors in 1885. Several sanatoria opened soon afterwards. The rail line from Vienna to Trieste was also in the process of being built and, when it reached the Adriatic at Rijeka in 1873, Opatija's tourist industry blossomed. By the 1910s, Opatija was the most visited resort in the Austro-Hungarian Empire after Karlsbad (Karlovy Vary).

With the growth of tourism and the opening of yet more hotels and sanatoria, Opatija began to expand and its waterfront was landscaped with a promenade, the *lungomare*. It stretches for 12km (7.5 miles), all the way from the town of Volosko in the north to Lovran to the south of Opatija. Ornately planned gardens also flourished, as Opatija became a sort of Vienna-on-Sea for Austrian holidaymakers. Famous people queued up to see and be seen in Opatija. They included such diverse luminaries as Mahler, Chekhov, Puccini and various European royals, aristocrats and politicians.

The best place to start a tour of Opatija is where it all started – at the Villa Angiolina. This stylish neoclassical creation is in the leafy Opatija Park, close to the Adriatic, which is full of exotic plants from all over the world brought by Scarpa's varied friends. As a landmark in the history of tourism, the villa is a fitting co-host for the **Museum of Croatian Tourism** (Hrvatski muzej turizma; www.hrmt.hr; daily July–Aug 10am–10pm, Apr–June and Sept–Oct 10am–8pm, Nov–Mar 10am–6pm), housing several permanent collections including one exploring the history of Croatian Tourism. The other venue, the Juraj Šporer arts pavilion next to the church of St James (Crkva sv. Jakova), hosts temporary exhibitions.

From the garden, the *lungomare* (seafront) is just a short stroll away. This boulevard circles the resort's rocky outcrops and small coves in an explosion of pavement cafés, concrete swimming pools and shady cypress, oak and palm trees. In summer it fills with splashing children

Volosko.

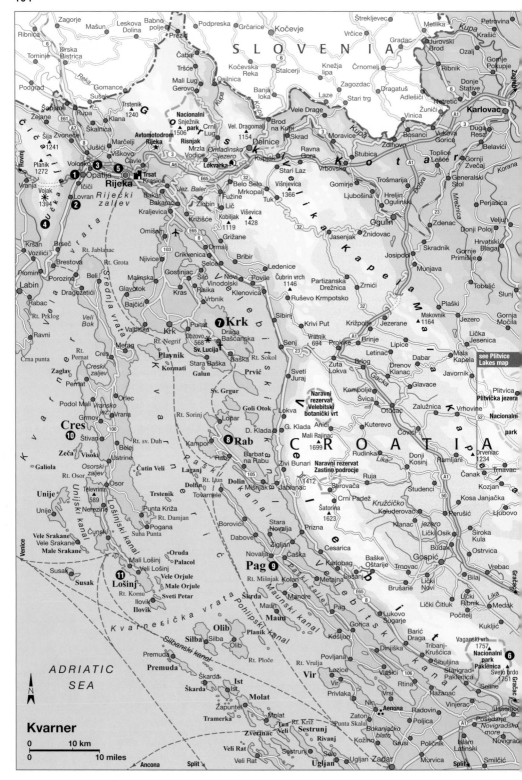

Kvarner

0   10 km

0   10 miles

and bronzed bodies topping up their tans, giving some credence to Opatija's nickname, the 'Nice of the Adriatic', while in winter it is the venue for bracing walks.

The **Church of St Mary** (Crkva sv. Marije) was built on the site of the abbey at the start of the 20th century, designed by the German architect Gabriel Seidl. Neither its exterior nor interior arouses paroxysms of visual ecstasy, but for a glimpse into Opatija's history it warrants a quick look.

LOVRAN

Just 6km (4 miles) south of Opatija, easily reached by local bus or along the *lungomare*, the resort town of **Lovran** ② is a sort of mini-Opatija clustered on the peninsula. Like its more illustrious neighbour, there was nothing much to Lovran until the 19th century when a road was opened through to Rijeka in 1885. Then a sprinkling of hotels arrived to cater for wintering Austro-Hungarians convalescing on the riviera from various ailments, mostly respiratory. Lovran's stretch of the *lungomare* is lined with parks of evergreen vegetation and chestnut trees.

To the rear of Lovran is **Gorica Hill** (Grešna gorica), which in turn is part of the Čićarija mountain range that includes Mt Učka. With the major exception of tourism, Lovran's history is more gripping than Opatija's as it saw battles between Uskok (fugitive) pirates (see page 144), who were based in the Kvarner town of Senj, and the Venetian Republic, confrontations which ensured that little of Lovran's old architecture has survived. One remnant is the Church of St George (Crkva sv. Jurja), rebuilt in Gothic style in the 14th century with a vault that dates from 1470. Look out also for the ceiling frescoes that are not dissimilar to those found in Beram in Istria. Lovran's frescoes were the work of Croatian artists in the 15th century.

Instead of heading south from Opatija to Lovran, it is also worth walking a few kilometres north to the old fishing village of **Volosko** ③. The halcyon days of Volosko, when the small harbour used to be alive with the frantic hollering and bustle of tuna fishermen, are long gone, but the old stone buildings crowded around the harbour are alluring. Compared with increasingly slick Opatija there is not much to do in Volosko, but wandering around the narrow alleyways and reclining in the modest seafood restaurants are pleasant ways of spending a few hours.

OPPORTUNITIES FOR HIKING

Keen hikers may find spending time in the shadow of **Mt Učka** ④ tempting. The rugged limestone hills are not as impenetrable as they may appear, even for less experienced walkers. The 20km (12-mile) range is easily accessible from towns and villages along the coast between the Poklon Pass in the north and Plomin Bay

Seafront at Lovran.

Entrance to the fortress of Trsat, the best place to begin a tour of Rijeka.

Classic architecture along Rijeka's seafront.

(Plominski zaljev) in the south. The main peaks are Plas (1,285 metres/4,216ft), Brgud (907 metres/2,975ft), Sisol (835 metres/2,739ft), Kremenjak (827 metres/2,713ft), Suhi vrh (1,333 metres/4,373ft) and, the highest of them all, Vojak, which rises 1,394 metres (4,596ft) above the Kvarner Gulf. Sweeping views from the top of Vojak take in everything from the Bay of Trieste to the north through to the island of Dugi otok on the edge of the Kornati Islands to the south.

Facilities along the Mt Učka massif are not extensive, but you will find a few mountain lodges and stone cottages that can house hikers. There is also a pension and restaurant at Poklon and a viewpoint tower on the peak of Vojak. For those wanting to take Vojak head on, the best bet is to climb through Lovran's old town and follow the steps that break off up the hillside to the village of Liganj and on to the small settlements of Dindici and Ivulici, where all traces of civilisation are left behind as the ascent begins through the evergreen forests.

Usually it is possible to manage the whole climb in less than four hours, but allow for time at the top and for the descent. Climbers should take plenty of water and provisions, as there are few places to procure anything en route. The Croatian National Tourist Board website (www.croatia.hr) has details of Mt Učka walks.

THE PORT CITY OF RIJEKA

Rijeka ❺, Croatia's busiest port, is by far the largest settlement in Kvarner, with around 130,000 inhabitants. It's a working port city that is often overlooked by those heading to the gulf's celebrated islands, but it has much to recommend it for those prepared to delve past the industrial scars and untidy port district. Locals take great pride in their shipbuilding tradition; today Rijeka's shipyards specialise in ships for transporting cars.

Rijeka came to prominence at the end of the 19th century when it benefited from the new rail links to both Vienna and Budapest, and from its increasingly busy port; the majority

of its impressive architecture dates from this period. These days the city has a spring in its step once again. Public works of art brighten up its old streets, cultural events are blossoming and there is a buzz about the waterfront, the Riva, in summer. It may not be as pretty as Split, but if you are catching a ferry or passing through it merits a night or two, especially if you have been on an outlying island without any of the conveniences that Rijeka offers in abundance.

A TOUR OF RIJEKA

A good place to begin a tour of Rijeka is the fortress of **Trsat**, set spectacularly above the city and offering panoramic views of the gulf. For those who would have liked to enjoy the sweeping views from Mt Učka, but were unprepared to do the legwork, Trsat, accessible by public bus from Rijeka city centre, offers a good alternative. For Učka veterans, the 561 steps connecting the city below to Trsat are still something of a test.

Trsat's fortifications date back to pre-Illyrian times, and the Romans are among those who have exploited the site's strategic importance over the centuries. Today's fortress owes its design to the 13th-century Frankopan kings, who came from the Kvarner island of Krk. Defences were strengthened over the next few centuries, but once the Ottoman threat had receded and military technology had moved on, the castle was less strategically vital and fell into disrepair. It is now being restored and in summer hosts outdoor concerts. The on-site restaurant enjoys commanding views.

Just across from Trsat's castle is the **Church of Our Lady of Trsat** (crkva Gospe Trsatske), associated with several legends. Devout residents of Rijeka claim this was where the House of Mary and Joseph came to rest after fleeing Nazareth on its way to Italy. The house is said to have remained on this spot for three years before continuing on its unusual journey west. The church contains tributes and messages

◑ Tip

It is worth timing a visit to Rijeka to coincide with the Rijeka Carnival, the largest in Croatia, which runs from mid-January through February. Events include balls, parades and various cultural events.

The 19th-century Croatian National Theatre, Rijeka.

RISNJAK NATIONAL PARK

Despite its proximity to Rijeka, and its rich flora and fauna, this haven for mountaineers, hikers and botanists remains largely unknown to travellers in Kvarner.

Compared with the Plitvice Lakes and the Kornati Islands, Risnjak National Park, 18km (11 miles) north of Rijeka, is far less visited. It became a national park in 1953 and commercial development has been strictly limited. It was extended in 1997 to encompass the Kupa area, bringing the total land mass to 64 sq km (25 sq miles) and making it a paradise for walkers, mountaineers and botanists.

The park is made up of the Snježnik and Risnjak massifs, which are part of the larger sweep of the Dinaric range. This rugged limestone and sandstone landscape separates the heavily wooded Gorski Kotar inland region from the Kvarner Gulf coast and comprises tree-shrouded slopes and karstic features such as caves, precipitous drops, sinkholes and disappearing streams. Various species of flora and fauna inhabit the park at different heights, but only

Mountain hut on Veliki Risnjak.

the hardiest survive on the upper slopes, where bitter winds and heavy snowfalls are common. At lower altitudes, tree species include sycamore, maple, wych elm, fir, birch and, on the upper stretches, mountain spruce and juniper. As the area has never been heavily logged, much of it is virginal forest. Many parts of the park are off limits to visitors.

The fauna is also interesting. The lynx, which disappeared from Risnjak for more than a century before its return from across the Slovenian border in 1974, is flourishing; indeed, the park takes its name from *ris*, the Croatian for lynx. Wolves and wild boar are among the residents, alongside red and roe deer, brown bears, pine and stone marten, chamois, poisonous horned vipers and wild cats. The 51 native bird species include capercaillie, woodpecker, hedge sparrow, lesser whitethroat and black redstart, as well as eight species of birds of prey. During winter, rangers have to leave food out to help the most desperate animals stay alive. Hunting and fishing are permitted but strictly licensed. Hunters can organise trips in search of chamois, deer, wild boar and capercaillie; anglers can fish for trout and grayling.

One of the best times to visit the park is in late June and early July when a multitude of wild flowers bloom. Highlights are the edelweiss, mountain milfoil, alpine clematis, violet, alpine snowbell, alpine rockrose and the orange lily. This is also a good time for hiking. (Hiking is inadvisable in winter or early spring, as there are more than 100 days of snow on average a year and layers of snow reach 4 metres/13ft deep.)

The highest peak is Veliki Risnjak (1,528 metres/ 5,952ft), which has a mountain lodge, but perhaps the most appealing peak is Snježnik (1,506 metres/ 4,940ft; also with a modest lodge). A good base for accessing both is Bijela Voda, close to the little highland village of Crni Lug, where there is a small hotel and restaurant. There is also a shelter in the village of Kupari. Another good base is Platak, a 26km (16-mile) bus ride from Rijeka, with special buses in summer laid on for hikers. In winter it is possible to access the Snježnik ski field.

Visitors to the park need to buy a ticket. There are various restrictions on visits. For further information about the park, visit http://np-risnjak.hr or tel: 051-836 133.

of thanks, in various languages, from those who believe their prayers have saved loved ones from a litany of disasters. Among the petitions and messages are many from local fishermen, recounting the dangers they have faced. Donated in the 14th century, the supposedly miracle-working icon of the Virgin Mary – whose cult in Croatia is massive – is said to have been the work of St Luke.

The 16th-century steps lead down from Trsat to the regal **Hotel Continental**, a good place to stop off for a refreshing drink or a bite to eat.

Just across from the hotel is the **Mrtvi kanal**, which accompanies the sleepy Rječina river on its final run towards the Adriatic. Head south and you will come to the metal bridge across the channel that takes you from the suburb of Sušak into the city centre. Under Italian occupation Sušak was part of Yugoslavia, while the Italians controlled Rijeka's western flank. These days the local tourist office is trying to promote the merits of Sušak, but in reality there is little to see and do and you are far better off spending the lion's share of your time in the city centre.

Directly across the canal is the **Croatian National Theatre** (Hrvatsko narodno kazalište), an elegant neoclassical concoction with a pale yellow facade and decorative pillars beneath its green-tinged dome. It was designed by the Austrian architects Fellner and Helmer at the end of the 19th century, and a major renovation in the 1980s brought it back to something approaching its former glory. The interior is spectacular, with a fabulous rococo ceiling. Acoustically it is one of Croatia's most impressive venues and it attracts international as well as domestic artistes. Its first performance was Verdi's Aida back in 1885. Look out for the statue of Croatian composer Ivan Zajc outside the theatre.

Just across the square from the theatre is the **Main Market** (Velika tržnica), dating from 1880 and lined with cheap and cheerful eateries and beer terraces. The interior

The Main Market's facade.

Korzo is Rijeka's main boulevard.

⊘ PIRATES OF SENJ

Today, the sleepy Kvarner Gulf town of Senj is somewhere that most visitors glimpse fleetingly as they zoom past on the Adriatic Highway between Rijeka and Northern Dalmatia. The town's history, though, is steeped in the exotic tales of the 16th-century Uskoks, piratical warrior oarsmen.

Refugees kicked out of the hinterland by the advance of the Ottoman Empire, the belligerent Uskoks bore a grudge against the Turks that the Austro-Hungarian rulers of the Kvarner Gulf were only too happy to exploit. Their numbers expanded even further with more refugees from Serbia, Bosnia and other parts of Croatia. With the tacit support of Vienna, they built their Nehaj Fortress overlooking the town and used the forested cove of Senjska Draga to launch surprise attacks on Ottoman vessels plying the lucrative trade routes to Venice. Their attacks were so successful and savage that they triggered a war between Venice and the Austro-Hungarians in 1615, culminating in the Treaty of Madrid two years later. The Uskoks were forced inland, and the Austro-Hungarian navy sank many of their ships.

Today, the legacy of the Uskok pirates is resurrected during Senj's August carnival and is recorded in exhibits in the forbidding Nehaj Fortress. From the hillside ramparts you can see the stretch of the Adriatic that the Uskoks had brutally made their own.

The City Tower in Rijeka.

is an architectural free-for-all that has evolved over the ages, but the facade retains its Austro-Hungarian elegance, with a grand arch welcoming customers. Construction of the superstructure by the architect Izidor Vauchning was a pioneering effort in the use of metal and glass, reflecting the period's changing architectural ideas. The market is a good place to get a snapshot of Rijeka life, with lashings of local colour, especially in the Liberty-style fish market.

RIJEKA'S KORZO

From the theatre, walk northwest to the **Korzo**, an elegant boulevard running through the heart of Rijeka. It is flanked by Austro-Hungarian-era buildings evoking more a provincial Austrian city than an Adriatic port. It encompasses the stretch of land between the canal and the main railway station, but the most interesting section is just behind the waterfront north of the Riva. Its basic design and many of its buildings owe much to Trieste-based architect Anton Gnamb, who

Nehaj Fortress in Senj.

arrived in Rijeka in 1773 and worked in the city until his death in 1806. Even the fast-food outlets and tacky shops cannot impair the air of elegance. Several stately cafés offer the chance to take in the ambience and watch local people flitting by or enjoying their evening promenades, and the quality of the shops is rapidly improving.

Roughly halfway along the Korzo on its north side is the **City Tower** (Gradski toranj) with four clocks, which was built on top of the old medieval gateway into Rijeka and was one of the few buildings to survive Rijeka's 1750 earthquake. The 18th-century Baroque design incorporates an ostentatious Austro-Hungarian eagle over the entrance to remind the citizens of just who was in control.

Look out for the busts of the emperors Charles IV and Leopold I. The former first designated Rijeka a free port, leading to a rush of prosperity that funded the construction of much of the city centre and enriched the local merchants. In the 1980s, the tower underwent extensive restoration work, which shored up its superstructure but left it a rather unsettling shade of lime green. Today, the City Tower marks the fault line between the order and harmony of the Austro-Hungarian section of the city and the more shambolic **Old Town** (Stari grad) beyond the arch. The rambling streets are still fairly shabby, but there have been a few attempts at restoration and the introduction of modern street sculptures.

The main square in the old town is **Trg Ivana Koblera**. One interesting feature is the Stari kolodrob fountain, the work of Croatian architect Igor Emili. Two large concrete wheels sit atop the spouting water, forming an arresting sight that manages to divert attention from the square's ugliest post-World War II buildings. Close by, a 4th-century **Roman Arch** (Stara vrata) is the oldest standing structure in the city.

Farther to the north is the **Cathedral of St Vitus** (Katedrala sv. Vida), one of Rijeka's most impressive churches, dedicated to the city's patron saint. The 17th-century cylindrical design is unusual. Its construction dragged on for more than 100 years and was never really finished, as the two bell towers that were part of the original design were ditched. The most noteworthy part of the interior is the Gothic crucifix above the main altar. Local legend has it that a blasphemer once hurled a stone at the crucifix, whereupon it began to bleed and the ground beneath the assailant opened up and swallowed him.

Further north is the green expanse of the **Park Nikole Hosta**, containing the Rijeka City Museum and the Historical and Maritime Museum. In Communist times, the modern building housing the **City Museum** (Muzej grada Rijeke; June–Sept Mon–Sat 10am–8pm, Sun 10am–3pm, Oct–May Mon–Sat 10am–6pm, Sun 10am–3pm) used to be the Museum of National Revolution and it has been a little slow to find its feet in its new role. Its highlights tend to be

the temporary exhibitions that occasionally pass through.

The **Historical and Maritime Museum of the Croatian Littoral** (Pomorski i povijesni muzej Hrvatskog primorja; http://ppmhp.hr; Mon 9am–4pm, Tue–Sat 9am–8pm, Sun 4–8pm) occupies a far grander building next door, which used to house Rijeka's governor. You can walk along the arcade from the City Museum, passing some outdoor sculptures on the way. Inside, the highlights of the maritime exhibits include replicas of Rijeka-built tankers, paintings of old sea dogs, stuffed sharks and replicas of the sailing ships that once used the city's port. Other displays include weapons, traditional folk costumes and assorted finds from local archaeological digs. Look out for two torpedo-firing cannons – torpedoes are said to have been invented by Croatian pioneer Ivan Lupis (Baron von Rammer) in Rijeka in 1878.

SOUTH TO PAKLENICA NATIONAL PARK

If you head south along the *Magistrala* towards the Paklenica National Park,

Cathedral of St Vitus, Rijeka.

Island-hopping from Krk to Cres.

Gateway to Paklenica National Park.

Rock climbing is popular near the park's entrance.

there are few reasons to stop off, as the towns of Bakar, Kraljevica, Crikvenica, Karlobag and Jablanac have little to recommend them. Senj was the base of the piratical Uskoks (see page 144), but there is not much to see apart from a small castle once used by the pirates. As the 145km (90-mile) Velebit range reaches its final flourish, this sheer karst fortress concedes a brace of gorges that cut deep into the massif, opening up a wild landscape where four types of eagle and honey and mouse buzzards wheel overhead and bears roam. This spectacular corner of Croatia has been protected as the **Paklenica National Park ❻** (Nacionalni park Paklenica) since 1949, with hunting and hotels banned within its confines and all visitors paying an admission charge to help cover conservation costs. The best base for exploring the national park is Starigrad, increasingly referred to as Starigrad Paklenica. It's more a gaggle of pensions, grill restaurants and campsites littered along the coastline rather than a real town. Be sure to secure a room with a view

of the Velebit for unforgettable multi-hued mountain sunsets.

Paklenica National Park itself is divided into two main gorges: Mala Paklenica and Velika Paklenica, literally 'small' and 'big' Paklenica. The former has been preserved as much as possible in its original condition, with no amenities and loosely marked trails that deter day-trippers. Being well prepared with good local advice and accurate maps for exploring this part of the park is essential. Velika Paklenica is more user-friendly, with drinking fountains and a well-marked main trail that snakes up in a two-hour walk from the car park to a mountain hostel, where more serious hikers and climbers spend the night before starting early ascents of the park's lofty peaks.

As you enter the park, you will usually see rock climbers tackling the faces of the sheer rock walls. Organised mountaineering excursions are possible, if booked seven days ahead: see www.np-paklenica.hr for details. Look out for a small door on the left

that leads into a secret bunker (opening hours change monthly) used by the Yugoslav Army until 1990. On the way up to the mountain hostel, two paths break away from the main artery to the peak of Anica kuk, a steep but straightforward scramble that most reasonably fit people can manage. To the left of the main path, a trail leads to the Manita peć, a cave with a fine array of stalactites and stalagmites.

The main path has plenty of interest, with voluminous rock skyscrapers rising hundreds of metres above and a section running alongside a gurgling stream surrounded by alpine trees and vegetation. From the mountain hostel, those with the necessary equipment can tackle various climbs and hikes depending on their level of expertise. Croatian climbers conquered the highest peaks in the 1940s, and today mountaineers from all over Europe come to pit themselves against peaks and ridges ranging from easy to extreme, with some routes having an X+ rating for free climbing.

Do not underestimate the weather; even on a bright day in summer, a violent thunderstorm can quickly whip up and crash over Velebit. Whether you are just dipping in for an afternoon walk or embarking on a week-long assault of the most challenging peaks, Paklenica is a highlight of Kvarner.

KRK

Krk ❼ vies with neighbouring Cres for the title of the largest island in Croatia. It is the most easily accessible of the Kvarner islands, as you can drive over the bridge from the Croatian littoral. The island also has its own international airstrip, which functions as Rijeka's airport. As it is so close to the major road arteries to Zagreb, Istria and Slovenia, the island is maddeningly popular with tourists in summer and many of the island's 68 settlements struggle under the strain of thousands of Slovenes, Austrians, Germans and citizens of the former Soviet Bloc states. In fact, tourism on Krk dates back to at least 1866, when the island's first postcards were produced.

⊘ Tip

There are numerous caves within the boundaries of Paklenica National Park. One of the most impressive is Manita peć, which is more than 170 metres (560ft) long and contains a number of large underground chambers.

⊘ GLAGOLITIC SCRIPT

Until well into the Middle Ages, the Croatian language was usually written down using a unique alphabet known as the Glagolitic script, introduced by the monks Cyril and Methodius in the 9th century, and a precursor of Cyrillic. But as Renaissance influences grew stronger in Croatia, the Roman alphabet overtook Glagolitic and gradually the languages of the Serbs and Croats began to merge. After World War I and the establishment of the Kingdom of Serbs, Croats and Slovenes, this similarity was officially recognised as Serbo-Croatian, which came to be the chief language of Tito's Yugoslavia. Opposition to this merger, and the consequent relegation of pure Croatian to a local dialect, became a rallying point for nationalist feelings following the break-up of Yugoslavia.

Today, Croatians take enormous pride in surviving examples of Glagolitic text, and 'Glagolitic Alley', as the road to Hum in Central Istria is called (see page 125), celebrates this unique heritage with a series of sculptures based on Glagolitic characters. Look for examples of the real thing in some of the country's museums, usually inscribed in stone. The oldest and longest example is the 12th-century stone tablet known as the Baška Ploča, which records a gift to the church from King Zvonimir.

On the beach at Baška.

Krk Town's marina.

The most attractive and historically interesting settlement on Krk is **Krk town** (Grad Krk) itself. Its rambling old town is complemented by an attractive modern section that reclines by the sea in a collage of villas and stone cottages.

It is more than an hour's drive from the mainland bridge to Krk town, but in high season there is little appeal in stopping off in the congested resorts of Omišalj, Njivice and Malinska on the way south. In summer, it is essential to book accommodation in Krk town.

The town's sturdy defensive walls date from Roman times, though the Venetians added parts in the 15th and 16th centuries. The highlight of the old town is the Romanesque **Cathedral of the Assumption** (Katedrala Uznesenja), constructed over the foundations of a 6th-century church. Particularly interesting are the nave and the 15th-century Frankopan chapel, as well as the graves of local bishops dating from the 16th century.

In an adjoining gallery there is a collection of works by Italian 16th- and 17th-century masters. One of the most interesting is an earlier work, a rare painting by the 14th-century Venetian artist Paolo Veneziano.

Other attractions in Krk town include the **Canon's House** (Kanonička kuća), with its Croatian Glagolitic script, the Romanesque basilica of the Church of Our Lady of Health (Crkva Majke Božje od zdravlja) and the Decumanus Art Gallery (Galerija Decumanus), showcasing the work of some modern Croatian artists, particularly those from in and around Krk. The town's castle has also been reinvented and now stages a varied summer-long programme of cultural performances.

BAŠKA TO VRBNIK

The most dramatically located resort on Krk, and the one with the best beach, is **Baška**, on the island's southern tip, with the lofty ridge of the Velebit mountains rising like a wall out of the Adriatic in the distance. Baška is no secret and is very popular in summer, but its 2km (1-mile) sweep of beach (a European Blue Flag winner since

1999) is impressive, its restaurants fairly good and its old town full of cosy pensions with a splash of personality missing in the large resorts that cover Krk. If you are looking for a few days of seaside relaxation with all the facilities that you need before heading south or north, then Baška is a recommended stop. The town is also within easy reach of the village of Jurandvor, where St Lucy's Church (Crkva sv. Lucija) houses a replica of the 12th-century Baška Tablet (Bašćanska ploča) that was found here. The tablet is the oldest existent example of Glagolitic script and also includes the first mention of the Croatian kings who presided over Croatia a millennium ago. The original tablet is at the Academy of Sciences and Arts in Zagreb.

If you have more than a couple of days on Krk and have fallen in love with Croatian wine, then head for the north coast town of **Vrbnik**. This scenic town, set atop rugged cliffs with views back to the sweeping mountains of the mainland, is renowned for its first-rate white wines, especially Vrbnička žlahtina. In Croatian *žlahtina* means 'noble', and this straw-coloured wine impresses most visitors who savour it in the old town's wine cellars and restaurants.

RAB

From Baška regular ferries make the short and enjoyable crossing over to the town of Lopar on the northern tip of **Rab island** ❽ (otok Rab). Rab's north coast is much less developed than Krk's, but it is hard to find much reason to hang around in sleepy **Lopar** for long when **Rab town** (Grad Rab), one of the most beautiful towns in Croatia, is less than an hour's drive south. Rab town is quite simply dazzling, a medieval oasis stretched out in a riot of church spires and winding streets on a narrow peninsula surrounded by crystal-clear water. Whether you prefer exploring the churches or just swimming in the pine-shrouded beaches, it is hard not to fall in love with the town. A feature of Rab, captured on many a postcard, is the lovely silhouette of bell towers on the skyline. A good place to start a walking tour of the churches to which they

> **Tip**
The Krk Summer Festival is the pick of the Kvarner island festivals. Krk town's old quarter is the main venue for classical concerts and folk music, but there are events all around the islands from late July until late August.

It is essential to book car ferries in summer.

Church of St Anthony, Rab.

Taking cover from the sun on Rab.

belong is Trg svetog Kristofora, where you can climb the steps into the old quarter of Rab town. Take a quick diversion up the short section of the medieval walls that are open to the public to gain a good overview of the town's layout. The Church of St John the Evangelist (Crkva sv. Ivana Evanđelista) is just a short walk along Gornja ulica. In the 19th century, much of the 6th-century original was scavenged for building materials, but the crumbling remains retain plenty of charm.

A little further along Gornja ulica is St Justine's Church (Crkva sv. Justine), with its 16th-century bell tower, today home to the **Museum of Sacred Art** (Muzej sakralne umjetnosti). Its collection includes a painting by the 14th-century Venetian painter Paolo Veneziano and a 12th-century reliquary containing the skull of St Christopher, with scenes of his martyrdom worked into the design along the sides. The last of the churches on Gornja ulica is St Andrew's (Crkva sv. Andrija), a 12th-century construction topped by a Romanesque bell tower.

RAB TOWN CHURCHES

The most magnificent campanile in Rab town belongs to the 11th-century **Cathedral of the Holy Virgin Mary's Assumption** (Katedrala Uznesenja Blažene Djevice Marije), tucked towards the end of the peninsula. Actually it lost its cathedral status in the 19th century but everyone still calls it one. You can climb the 25-metre (82ft) -high bell tower for a sweeping view of Rab town and the surrounding area, but it is also worth taking time to savour the calm simplicity of the interior. In particular, look out on the left wall for the relief of Christ, originally belonging to a 7th-century church on this site. Also look out for the fine *Pietà* by Petar, an artist from the Dalmatian town of Trogir, which was positioned over the main altar in the 15th century. Behind the cathedral, on the tip of the peninsula, is the Church of St Anthony (Crkva sv. Antuna Malog), which has a wooden sculpture of the saint said to date from the 12th century.

St Marinus, who founded the world's oldest surviving republic, San Marino,

in AD 301, was born on Rab and the two places have a twinning agreement.

Away from its churches, Rab town is perfect for aimless wandering. Its tight warren of medieval streets is enlivened by small bars and boutiques and opens out to café-strewn squares, with glimpses of the sparkling Adriatic waters around every corner. Even at the height of summer, the old town is quiet during the day as its many tourists are either at the beaches on the peninsula or on one of the boats lined up along Rab town's wide waterfront every morning, offering a huge selection of day tours. At night in high season things are a different proposition altogether, as thousands of visitors crowd the streets and a number of discos thump on into the small hours.

THE FRKANJ PENINSULA

The rugged Frkanj peninsula just west of Rab was one of Croatia's oldest naturist resorts. In August 1936, it was visited by Britain's Edward VIII and his American future wife Wallis Simpson, who obtained special permission from the town authorities to go skinny-dipping there. However, there are records of naturism on Rab going back more than a century (see page 67).

Rab also has the distinction of having more sandy beaches than are usually found along Croatia's Adriatic coast. The Lopar peninsula to the north of the island has several sandy beaches, ranging from the popular and busy Paradise to the quiet naturist beach at Sahara.

From 1942 to 1943, Italy ran a concentration camp near the village of Kampor, 5km (3 miles) northeast of Rab town by road. Most of the prisoners were Slovenian, with smaller numbers of Croats and Jews. After Italy signed the armistice in 1943, Italy allowed most of the surviving Jews to flee to the Italian mainland, although some who were too sick to travel remained and were deported to Auschwitz when the Germans took over the camp. After the war, a memorial complex and cemetery were built on the site.

⊙ Tip

Rab Musical Evenings is a very popular festival that takes over Rab town from June through to the end of August. One of the main venues is the Church of the Holy Cross. Also look out for the Rab Tournament in August, with jousting and other medieval sports and games.

View over the small resort of Baška on the island of Krk.

⊘ **Fact**

The Adriatic coast has a long history of salt mining, going back at least to Roman times. Croatia's leading salt producer is on Pag Island and the superior taste of the island's lamb is attributed to the saline soil.

PAG

The last Kvarner island before the rump of Dalmatia is **Pag ❾**, a barren place with far fewer facilities than the other main gulf islands.

However, its reputation as Croatia's party island has grown thanks to its bars and clubs around **Zrće beach**, near Novalja on the south coast. Summer dance festivals with international DJs draw partygoers to thronging beach clubs such as Papaya and Aquarius.

Away from the hedonism of the beach, Pag is celebrated for its epony-mous hard and salty-tasting sheep's cheese *(paški sir)*, served with *pršut* (a Croatian version of prosciutto) in res-taurants all over the country. Its other renowned product is the intricate lace *(paška čipka)* that local women have been crafting for centuries. You can see these lace-makers selling their wares in the centre of captivating Pag town. The old town rises above the water-front and is home to a small cathe-dral, a couple of churches, the Ducal Palace (Kneževa palača), an unfinished bishop's palace and a museum dedi-cated to lace production.

CRES

Within sight of the Opatija Riviera and the inshore islands is the long, thin stretch of **Cres ❿**, sometimes con-fused with the island of Lošinj as only a very narrow 11-metre (36ft) -wide channel separates the two. This is supposedly where Jason and the Argo-nauts came in search of the Golden Fleece. It is easy to reach the island by ferry from either mainland Istria or Valbiska on Krk. If you are coming on foot your best bet is the catamaran from Rijeka.

Cres town (Grad Cres) crowds around Cres Bay in the verdant north-ern half of the island, which offers a sharp contrast to the dry south. The town still owes much of its livelihood to fishing, and its restaurants are a treat. Choose between the fresh sea-food catch and the delicious lamb for which Cres is renowned (which is also a speciality on Pag). Cres town's high-lights include the **Church of St Mary of**

The marina at Lošinj.

Snow (Crkva sv. Marije Snježne), with its 15th-century relief of the Madonna and Child, a Venetian loggia, a Franciscan monastery (Franjevački samostan) and a museum in the old town with many Roman artefacts – legacies of the time when Cres lay on one of the main Roman trade routes.

Farther north, the town of **Beli** is known for its population of rare griffon vultures *(bjeloglavi sup)*, which are as fond of the local lamb as the tourists are. Today the vultures are a protected species and survive along the cliffs near the town. Beli also has the **Caput Insulae Ecology Centre** (Eko-Centar Caput Insulae), set up as part of the conservation effort.

LOŠINJ

Across the channel, **Lošinj** ⓫ first came to the attention of tourists in the 19th century when elderly Austrians came to spend the winter. Today tourism is the main industry, and Mali Lošinj is a fully fledged resort town. In the summer, stalls around the harbour sell all types of souvenirs, while bobbing boats also offer fresh fruit and vegetables in a colourful scene. There are plenty of pavement cafés dotted around the bay where you can relax and enjoy the action. Mali Lošinj's other attractions include a couple of art galleries, the 15th-century Church of St Martin (Crkva sv. Martina) and the Baroque Church of the Nativity of the Virgin (Crkva Rođenja Blažene Djevice Marije).

Veli Lošinj is much quieter than its bright sibling, and its fishing industry still manages to hold its own against the demands of tourism. The pedestrianised old town is an atmospheric place for aimless wandering, interrupted by visits to the many cosy cafés and inexpensive restaurants serving excellent seafood. The steep streets do not really house many tourist attractions as such, bar the 18th-century Church of St Anthony (Crkva sv. Antuna) and a Venetian defensive tower built at the height of the Uskok threat, when the notorious marauders of Senj (see page 144) were at their peak.

(see page 144)

> ⊙ **Fact**
>
> The aptly named Goli otok (Barren Island), an uninhabited dot midway between Rab and the Croatian mainland, was from 1949 the site of a little-known gulag where political prisoners had to carry out hard labour in a stone quarry. The subject of many books, it closed in 1988 and is now falling into ruin.

Ringing the church bell, Lošinj.

Skradinski buk waterfall, Krka
National Park.

ZADAR, ŠIBENIK AND ISLANDS

This region has Venetian-style ports and Roman remains, but the highlights are its natural attractions – the lakes and waterfalls of Krka National Park and the Kornati archipelago.

Crossing the Maslenica Bridge from Kvarner transports travellers into the long, sinewy rump of Dalmatia, a slice of Croatia that stretches all the way around the belly of Bosnia to the Republic of Montenegro in the extreme south. Northern Dalmatia may not have the renowned cities and resorts of Central or Southern Dalmatia, but it does offer a wealth of history, superb coastal scenery and two of the most impressive natural parks in Europe.

During the 1990s war, the region was one of the worst affected parts of Croatia as rebel Serbs from nearby Knin and the Yugoslav army conspired to establish a sturdy front line and mount major attacks on the cities of Šibenik and, especially, Zadar, as well as terrorise and ethnically cleanse smaller towns and villages around the region. The Serbs blew up the Maslenica Bridge and it was not until the Croatian offensive of 1995 that the threat was lifted.

Although much of the heavy industry that used to power the economy is in the doldrums, tourism is growing faster than ever in the region, helped by an international airport in Zadar. Lovers of dance music can argue that the Garden Festival, which started near Zadar in 2005, led the way for other dance festivals that have sprung up in the meantime all along Croatia's coastline. After seven years being held in the

small fishing village of Petrčane north of Zadar, the Garden Festival moved 60km (37 miles) south in 2012 to the resort of Tisno where 2,000 people descend every July.

NORTHERN DALMATIA HIGHLIGHTS

While the cities of Northern Dalmatia are not as well known as those further south, they have much to recommend them. The old centre of Zadar is dramatically situated along a peninsula and has a wealth of Roman architecture. Old

◎ Main Attractions

Nin
Zadar
Lake Vrana
Šibenik
Krka National Park
Primošten
Kornati Islands
Zadar Islands

Map on page 156

Church of St Nicholas, Nin.

⊙ Tip

For those looking to get away from it all, there is a string of idyllic sand bars a few kilometres north and east of Nin, though they have little in the way of tourist facilities.

sits comfortably with the new in Zadar in the form of innovative public art. Visitors are mesmerised by the glowing lights of *Greeting to the Sun*, Nikola Bašić's work of art set into the marble seafront. Its companion piece is the Sea Organ, an underwater art installation that entrances with its haunting sounds as water seeps in and out of its tubes. Šibenik is perhaps the most 'Croatian' city on the whole coastline, largely devoid of Roman and Venetian embellishments. Smaller towns and resorts such as Vodice and Primošten are pleasant oases in which to spend a few days, enjoying the fresh local seafood and good Dalmatian wines. Nin is one of the most historically important towns in Croatia, but neglected by most foreign visitors who are more interested in reaching resorts farther south.

The non-urban highlights are the Krka National Park, the Kornati Islands and Lake Vrana (Vransko Jezero). Krka, in many ways every bit as impressive as Plitvice National Park in Central Croatia, is a breathtaking limestone landscape of plunging waterfalls, broad lakes and rugged ravines. The Kornati Islands are unique in the Mediterranean, an uninhabited and barren but beautiful playground for day-trippers and yachtsmen that is gaining a reputation as one of the most popular sailing destinations in Europe. To the north of the Kornati group is the large and rugged Dugi otok, where the main activity is taking it easy and enjoying the fact that there are no crowds or tour buses. It offers good food, plenty of low-key places to stay, and has a beautiful setting; in many ways it encapsulates the attractions of Northern Dalmatia island life. Halfway between Zadar and Šibenik is the largest natural lake in Croatia, Lake Vrana, a nature park whose unusual biodiversity attracts rare water birds.

NIN

The small town of **Nin** ❶ is something of a sleepy backwater, far from any major resort and relatively untouched by tourism. From the 7th to the 13th centuries, it was a major hub for the Croatian bishops and kings – seven of

Holy Cross Cathedral, Nin.

whom were crowned here – though the Venetians practically levelled it in 1570 when they feared it would fall into Ottoman hands, and so little of its original grandeur remains.

The old town occupies an islet only 500 metres/yds in diameter, surrounded by a lagoon and linked to the mainland by a 16th-century stone bridge. The most significant building left standing is the **Holy Cross Cathedral** (Crkva sv. Križ), whose claims to be the smallest cathedral in the world may indeed be valid. The stark stone structure was built in the shape of a domed cross in the 9th century, with an inscription carved above its entrance that is thought to be the oldest inscription surviving from the age of the Croatian kings. In recent years, there has been some debate over whether the irregular lines and angles of the superstructure were the result of shoddy design and workmanship, as some outside scholars have suggested, or a more calculated attempt to use the cathedral not only as a religious building, but also as a timepiece and calendar, an idea proposed by the late Dubrovnik-born artist Mladen Pejaković.

A short distance southwest of town on the Prahulje hill, another important monument is the 12th-century **Church of St Nicholas** (Crkva sv. Nikole), a rare surviving example of the early Romanesque style, and where the Croatian kings had vowed to defend their nation.

On the coast on the outskirts of Nin are extensive mud plains. The mud is said to have curative properties, and in the summer an outpatient programme allows visitors to sample one of the rejuvenating mud treatments. The set-up is not as slick as in most spa-type centres in other parts of Europe, but the treatments are not necessarily any worse for that.

ZADAR

Take a 17km (10-mile) drive south of Nin and you will come to **Zadar** ❷,

Northern Dalmatia's most populous settlement, and once Dalmatia's largest town. Although Split may now have overtaken it in terms of size, it remains a lively city whose citizens overcame the trauma of devastating Allied bombing raids in World War II only to be subjected to a three-month Serbian siege in 1991. Then followed what the international community described as 'low level warfare' (random artillery barrages and rocket attacks) up until 1995. Today, Zadar is back on its feet and most of the damage has been repaired. The city is wooing back the tourist business that its Roman heritage and dramatic old town so well deserve.

The centre of Zadar occupies a narrow peninsula overlooking the Zadar Channel (Zadarski kanal), with the old Roman town hemmed in by sturdy walls and a wide seaside promenade circling the fortifications. The most dramatic entrance to the old quarter is the **Mainland Gate** (Kopnena vrata), accessible from the small harbour at Foša, the only surviving portion of Zadar's protective moat system. On the right as

⊙ Tip

Surrounded by a lagoon and with a strong north wind and long sandy beach, Sabunike, a short walk from Nin, is a popular spot for windsurfing and kitesurfing for all levels. Equipment and training are both available.

Watching the sunset at Zadar's 'Greeting to the Sun' installation.

you approach the gate is a citadel that functioned as an active garrison from Venetian times until the 18th century; it lies over earlier, Roman fortifications.

Once inside the Mainland Gate, turn right and three blocks in is Široka ulica, an arrow-straight Roman road dissecting the old town, passing many of the main sights on its way west to the sea. Its old churches, squares and museums have been painstakingly restored, but they are interspersed with large areas of modern buildings, resulting in some odd juxtapositions.

On the way west, the first church you come to is **St Simeon's** (Crkva sv. Šimuna), rebuilt in the 17th century in Baroque style, though there are elements of Renaissance and Gothic architecture, as well as evidence of a 5th-century church on the same site. The main attraction is St Simeon's gold sarcophagus, moved here from its original home in the Church of St Mary the Great when that was knocked down during the building of the city walls. The work of the Milanese goldsmith Francesco di Antonio da Sesto,

it is covered with reliefs depicting the life of the saint and the rescue of his relics from the Venetians by Louis I of Anjou. According to a local legend, Queen Elizabeth of Hungary commissioned the church to atone for her attempt to chop off and keep the finger of St Simeon.

A short distance down the street is **Narodni trg**, one of the city's busiest squares. The 16th-century town watchtower presides over outdoor cafés, invariably packed with ice-cream-licking locals, while the eastern side of the square is home to a Venetian-style **loggia** (loža; Mon–Sat 8am–8pm, Sun 9am–1pm), which is now an art gallery housing temporary exhibitions. Its modern, glass-fronted design harmonises with the older building. Along with the modern exhibits, look out for a stone table dating from 1600.

Narodni trg was Zadar's main public space in the Middle Ages. The **Forum**, a short walk further west, was the city's original hub. Little remains of the Roman buildings apart from a few columns, but an information board gives

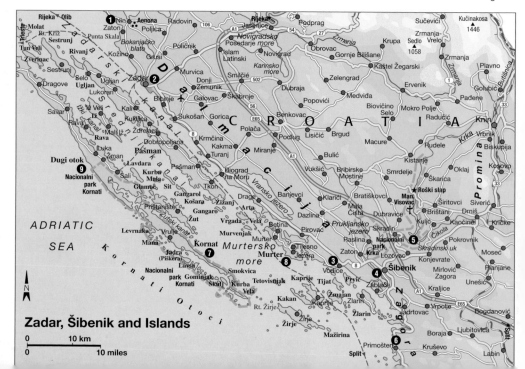

Zadar, Šibenik and Islands

0   10 km
0   10 miles

some idea of the scale of the once-mighty colonnades. A couple of cafés – Zadar is renowned for its vibrant café culture – spill out into the Forum, where you can sip a cappuccino or a cold beer on the very spot where the Romans once went about their business. Look out for the chains in one of the largest Roman pillars: these were used to shackle miscreants in Venetian times.

ST DONAT'S CHURCH

The most impressive building in the square is undoubtedly the 9th-century **St Donat's Church** (Crkva sv. Donata; daily Apr–May and Sept–Oct 9am–5pm, June until 9pm, July–Aug until 10pm), for many years the symbol of Zadar but no longer functioning as a church. This Byzantine monolith was commissioned by the Irish saint and built using stones from the Forum. Look closely and you may be able to make out jumbled snatches of Latin script on the stone walls and columns. The church is reputed to bear a similarity to the court chapel in Aachen, and in fact Bishop Donat visited Aachen during his mission to Charlemagne before commissioning the church. The severe exterior encloses a stark interior, whose acoustics are perfect for the classical concerts performed here in summer.

Nearby is the **Archaeological Museum** (Arheoloski muzej; daily Apr–May and Oct 9am–3pm, June and Sept until 9pm, July–Aug until 10pm, Nov–Mar Mon–Fri 9am–2pm, Sat 9am–1pm), the oldest museum of its kind in Croatia. It is best to start on the upper floors, which house Neolithic and Liburnian artefacts that predate the Roman collection on the first floor. The Liburnian materials are some of the most interesting, with jewellery and weapons over 2,000 years old. The collection culminates with exhibits from the Middle Ages and the time of the first Croatian kings. Look out also for artefacts preserved from Zadar cathedral.

Just off the Forum is the **Cathedral of St Anastasia** (Katedrala sv. Stošije), a vast Romanesque structure that was substantially rebuilt after World War II bombing and Serbian shelling in the 1990s, not to mention an attempt to destroy it by 13th-century crusaders. The original was consecrated in 1177 by Pope Alexander III. Although it blends in well, the bell tower was added in the late 19th century by an English architect, who may have been inspired by the bell towers on the Adriatic island of Rab further north.

The cathedral's ornate facade has three portals leading into a vast interior with three apses. Look out for the frescoes of John the Baptist, Christ and St Anastasia dating from the 13th century. You should also seek out the marble sarcophagus of St Anastasia, located in the left aisle. A six-sided baptistry used to stand on the southern wall, but it was destroyed by bombing during World War II. Look, too, for a marble plaque commemorating Pope Alexander III's visit, which has remained intact since 1177 and has

⊙ Tip

Zadar boatmen – the Zadarski Barkajoli – have been rowing their small boats across Zadar's harbour for more than 800 years. If you want to save yourself a long walk around the harbour, catch a lift with one of the boatmen for only a few kuna.

The Sea Organ, Zadar.

⊙ Drink

Zadar's local liqueur, maraska, is a strong cherry brandy made from the sour maraschino cherries found in the Zadar region. It's one of the fruit brandies made by the manufacturer Maraska, which also produces pear and plum varieties.

St Donat's Church behind an archaeological site, Zadar.

survived the various travails of the cathedral.

In the 19th-century Cosmacendi Palace, overlooking the Jazine harbour, the **Museum of Ancient Glass** (Muzej antičkog stakla; June–mid-Oct daily 9am–9pm, late-Oct–May Mon–Sat 9am–4pm) has a superb collection from Roman times and one of the best souvenir shops in town, selling replicas from the exhibition.

ZADAR'S SERBIAN COMMUNITY

The Orthodox heritage of local Serbians, something that few Zadar residents are interested in today, surfaces behind the cathedral in Zadar's Serbian **Church of St Elijah** (Crkva sv. Ilija). Built in 1563 and originally consecrated by the Greek Orthodox Church, it passed into the hands of the local Serb community in the 18th century. It contains a small collection of Orthodox icons. Architecturally it is not the most fascinating church in Zadar, but coupled with the knot of streets around it that makes up the small Serbian community, it is a reminder that the two

communities had co-existed peacefully before the disintegration of Yugoslavia.

EXCURSIONS AND LOCAL BEACHES

At the northern end of the Zadar peninsula, regular ferries leave for Ancona in Italy. To the right, you will find a confusing array of local ferries and tourist boats, where a gaggle of operators tout day tours to the Kornati Islands. These are not bad value, but it is worth shopping around as business is highly competitive and a subtle haggle out of earshot of the other operators is often well rewarded.

It's at this end of the seafront where you see and hear Nikola Bašić's art installations *Greeting to the Sun* and the Sea Organ. People of all ages never tire of the moving along to the flashing lights of the former, and sitting on the marble steps on the edge of the seafront listening to the sounds of the latter.

An interesting walk, particularly when sunset is approaching, is to head left away from the boats and stroll back around the tongue-twistingly named

Obala kralja Petra Krešimira IV to Foša. The walk takes you along a breezy boulevard with sweeping views south across the Zadar Channel to the island of Ugljan; these views are particularly enchanting at sunset. There is a sprinkling of cafés and restaurants where you can savour the view and the expansive seafront; like the rest of this underrated city, they are never too crowded with tourists.

Zadar's beaches are spread out both north and south of the historical centre. While many are rocky – where it would be a good idea to wear swimming shoes – there are some sandy stretches as well as gravel. Borik to the north combines sandy areas with gravel; carry on further a few hundred metres and you reach quieter Diklo. South of the old town is one of the most popular beaches, Kolovare, where again it's a mixture of sand, gravel and paved areas. Children are well catered for in all the beaches, with plenty of play areas and facilities.

SOUTH OF ZADAR

About 11km (7 miles) southeast of Zadar is **Sukošan,** home to Marina Dalmacija, the largest marina in Croatia. It's not just the sailing fraternity that likes to flop on Sukošan's beaches that sit in a protected bay; the long gravel stretch of Dječji Raj is a magnet for families – so much so that the meaning of the beach's name (Children's Paradise) can be a bit misleading at the height of summer. But you can escape the crowds at the quieter beaches at Tustica and Makarska, even if the facilities are few and far between, and naturists can head to the beach at Punta.

A further 20km (12 miles) further south along the coast brings you to Biograd na Moru, the former capital of the medieval Croatian kingdom. The Venetians sacked the city in 1125, destroying its medieval splendour. But the Venetians got their comeuppance, in a way, when one of their ships sank in the canal facing Biograd in the 16th century; the contents of the ship form part of the archaeological and cultural collection in the Homeland Museum (Zavičajni muzej Grada Biograda na Moru; Mon–Fri 8am–2pm and 7–10pm, Sat 9am–noon and 7–10pm). The city sits on a peninsula surrounded by inviting coves, including one of Croatia's Blue Flag beaches, Dražica. Pine forests back Dražica's 300 metres/yds of pebbly beach, which not only has extensive water sports, including a giant water slide for children, but has also been adapted for people with disabilities. Soline beach is partly sandy and has a long, shallow stretch, and naturists are catered for in the deep bay at Crvena Luka.

Just a few kilometres beyond Biograd are the deep blue waters of Lake Vrana, the largest natural lake in Croatia. Officially declared a nature park in 1999, Lake Vrana's 57 sq km (22 sq miles) provide a unique habitat for 249 different bird species, seven of which are on the endangered list. Fishing is allowed on the lake away from the area that has been designated an

Statue of the medieval Croatian sculptor and architect Giorgio da Sebenico (Juraj Dalmatinac in Croatian) in the square Trg Republike Hrvatske in Šibenik.

Some of the stone heads at the Cathedral of St James.

ornithological reserve, and cyclists can make use of the 50km (30 miles) of bike routes around the lake. While the coast buzzes all summer in the resorts, herons, cormorants and egrets flit in peace in this green haven.

Less than an hour's drive south of Zadar is the resort town of **Vodice** ❸. Vodice may be the most popular beach resort on the Northern Dalmatian coastline, but many of its beaches are made of concrete and there is little of historical interest. The town grew as a bulwark against the Ottoman Empire in the 14th century and by the 16th it had its own protective walls, but the only remnant of these today is the three-storey **Ćorić tower** (Ćorića kula).

Mass tourism came to Vodice with a vengeance in the 1960s, leaving a number of bland hotels and a sprinkling of tourist-related facilities. But there has been an attempt in the past few years to move away from the large modernist hotels towards smaller and more intimate accommodation that shows a bit more architectural style. The town also has

a well-equipped marina with nearly 300 berths. In high season, however, when the crowds descend, you might want to head out of Vodice on one of the ferries to the nearby islands of **Logorun, Tijat, Zlarin** or **Prvić**, which has a naturist beach.

Another dreamy spot is the nearby town of Tribunj, with its long pebbly Bristak beach a short walk from the marina. The other beach, Zamalin, is backed by pine forests to keep things cool. Both are well served by restaurants, bars and water sports centres. Olive growing is still an important part of the local economy, as is wine making, and the quiet hinterland above the town is covered in a picturesque landscape of vineyards and olive groves. Walkers and cyclists head up to the hilltop vantage points of Sv Nikola or Križine, where sweeping views of the Adriatic and the Kornati Islands are the reward for the trek.

ŠIBENIK

Just another 11km (7 miles) south down the E65 from Vodice is the city

Šibenik.

of **Šibenik** ❹. Until 1991, Šibenik was the chrome- and aluminium-producing capital of Croatia, a wealthy city known for having one of the finest cathedrals on the Adriatic coast. The Serbian shelling that followed the break-up of Yugoslavia, though, dented its prosperity and now it is one of the most economically depressed cities in the nation. There is little sign of the heavy industry coming back and the local authorities are pinning their hopes on tourism. This is growing, as the war-damaged old town has been patched up and a string of restaurants and cafés revive some of the city's former lustre. The city's geographical position made it a natural home for Croatia's first marina for superyachts, D-Marin Mandalina, which opened in 2012. It is also a convenient base for visiting **Krka National Park** ❺, one of Croatia's most spectacular landscapes (see page 163).

Unlike most of Croatia's coastal cities, Šibenik has no Roman heritage, built as it was 1,000 years ago during the reign of the Croatian kings. This Croat ancestry gives it a unique feel, with winding, narrow streets and small buildings instead of wide Roman thoroughfares and spacious houses. The best way into the old core is through the public gardens on the east of the old town, with their trickling fountains. The garden benches are a good place to sit and read up on the city before you delve in.

The **Franciscan Church and Monastery** (Franjevački samostan i crkva) at the southern end of the gardens was built in Gothic style in the 14th century, but it is relatively plain and simple. The ceiling was embellished later in the 17th century with various depictions of the life of St Francis. Hiding away in the treasury is the *Šibenska molitva*, or 'Šibenik Prayer', said to be the oldest manuscript using the Croatian language in Latin script.

Just a few metres away is the waterfront, offering fine views out towards the narrow channel leading from the city's protected harbour to the open sea. A string of cafés and restaurants hug the seafront as it meanders round to the **Town Museum** (Muzej grada Šibenika; Mon–Fri 8am–8pm, Sat–Sun 10am–8pm), a small venue for temporary exhibitions with Croatian themes. There is also a permanent collection recounting the history of the city from prehistoric times through to the present day.

Shortly after the museum, steps lead up to Trg Republike Hrvatske, the city's imposing main square. The 15th-century **St James's Cathedral** (Katedrala sv. Jakova), a Unesco World Heritage Site, dominates the scene. The cathedral took over a century to build; the bulk of it is the work of Zadar-born Juraj Dalmatinac, who came over from Venice. The cathedral is a cocktail of architectural styles, as the original relatively modest Gothic plans were repeatedly revised, becoming ever more elaborate as ambitions grew.

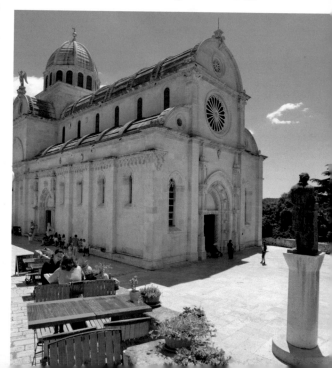

Cathedral of St James, Šibenik.

> **Tip**

For those who do not have their own transport, regular tours to the Krka National Park operate from Zadar, Šibenik and other coastal resorts in the region.

The upper sections of the exterior were constructed in the Renaissance style; the interior is a visually pleasing blend of Gothic and Renaissance forms.

The interior is dominated by the dome, inspired by Brunelleschi's dome in the Duomo in Florence, which is supported by four immense columns. Crowded around the cupola are the statues of various saints, the work of Dalmatinac, though he never lived to see his masterpiece finished. (His son was among those who completed the work.) Look out for the sarcophagus of St James to whom the cathedral is dedicated.

Among the most striking features of the exterior are 70-odd stone heads depicting local luminaries of the day – they hang like Christmas decorations from the apse. The best place to appreciate the beauty and scale of the cathedral is from the seafood restaurant Gradska vijećnica, which has outdoor tables huddled under the old loggia on the opposite side of the square. The square, with its old, polished stones, is an agreeable spot, where children

play in the day and Šibenik's citizens go for their evening strolls, a far cry from 1991 when Serbian shells hit the square, damaging the cathedral, although it was soon repaired. Look out for patches of bright white stone on the cathedral's walls, indicating where they have been patched up.

Farther west still, the waterfront is packed with café-bars, which get busy in the evenings. The buzz lasts until around midnight, after which the crowds dissipate, the hardy heading off to Vodice or Primošten in search of their resort nightlife.

Inland, the old town's streets run higgledy-piggledy in a confusing pattern, but wherever you go you will probably end up climbing to **St Nicholas Fortress** (Tvrđava sv. Nikola), built during Venetian times to keep the Ottomans at bay. Most of the original fortress has fallen into ruin, but its sturdy cliff-top ramparts offer panoramic views of the city and out towards the Šibenik Channel and the Adriatic islands. There are three other fortresses inland, the medieval Fort of St Anne (Tvrđava sv. Ana), the 17th-century Šubićevac Fort (Tvrđava Šubićevac) and the 15th-century Fort of St John (Tvrđava sv. Ivan).

For more than 50 years, Šibenik has been hosting its celebrated International Children's Festival in late June/early July. For two weeks, a lively programme of children's theatre, concerts, puppet shows, open-air screenings of film and television and workshops in art and music takes over the city, attracting youngsters from all over the country.

THE RESORT OF PRIMOŠTEN

Southeast of Krka National Park and 30km (18 miles) south of Šibenik on the E65 is the pleasant coastal resort of **Primošten** ⑥. The best approach is from the sea, from where you can appreciate its position on a jutting peninsula. At first sight there are echoes

Restaurant on Trg Republike Hrvatske, Šibenik.

of Rovinj, further north on the Istrian coast.

The dramatic setting and the sheer brilliance of the local light, which gives the waters deep-blue hues, help to hide the fact that much of Primošten is a 20th-century construction, partly due to devastating bombing during World War II and partly because of the tourist boom in the 1960s, when concrete monoliths sprang up.

Many of Primošten's main tourist hotels have limited allure, but there are plenty of good spots for swimming and relaxing. Primošten works best as a place in which to lie back and recover from the nearby cities as there is little actually to do apart from sunbathe and enjoy eating in the many local restaurants overlooking the sea. The local Babić dry red wine is also likely to enhance a stay, as are plates of spiny lobster served in the seaside restaurants – a speciality here. For those looking for a different kind of relaxation there are also popular naturist beaches on the nearby island of Smokvica – take

your own provisions – and 3km (2 miles) south of Primošten at Marina Lucica. Smokvica is accessible by taxi boat.

KORNATI ISLANDS

George Bernard Shaw summed up the ethereal charm of the **Kornati Islands** (Kornatski otoci) best when he first sighted them: 'On the last day of the Creation God desired to crown his work, and thus created the Kornati Islands out of tears, stars and breath.' This lofty praise is well deserved as there is nowhere else in Europe quite like this string of stark white islands strung out like a necklace in calm, balmy waters. For centuries locals dismissed the Kornati Islands as an arid, infertile wasteland, but to today's tourists and yachtsmen they are as near to paradise on earth as many can imagine getting. Local legend has it that when God threw the white hulks of rock into the sea, intending to sculpt them into fertile land, he was so taken by their perfect beauty that he chose to leave them as they were.

> **⊙ Tip**
>
> In Dubrava, 8km (5 miles) inland from Šibenik, is Croatia's only centre for falconry. The Sokolarksi Centar also cares for injured birds of prey including peregrine falcons, kestrels, owls and vultures.

⊙ KRKA NATIONAL PARK

Northern Dalmatia's most striking natural mainland attraction is the **Krka National Park** (Nacionalni park Krka; www.np-krka.hr). The Krka river forges its way through 72km (45 miles) of countryside from its lofty source in the Dinaric Alps to its effluence at Šibenik. Since 1985, the area south of Knin as far as Skradin has been protected as a national park. Some Dalmatians reckon that the lakes, rivers, gorges and waterfalls at Krka are even more impressive than those at Plitvice Lakes National Park in Central Croatia.

To access the park you can take a car to Lozovac and park at the entrance, where a free bus will pick you up. (In winter visitors can drive the extra 4km/2.5 miles on their own.) There are also daily buses from Šibenik. But a more popular way of accessing it is by boat from the pretty little village of Skradin, from where boats leave regularly for **Skradinski buk**, the area's most impressive waterfall. The basic cruise to the waterfall is included in the entrance charge. Forming one huge mass of pumping water and solid rock is a spectacular array of 17 waterfalls; wooden

walkways help visitors to navigate the site. There is a third entrance at Roški slap (see below).

Additional cruises from both Skradin and Roški slap explore the wetlands further upstream. They stop off at the little island of **Visovac**, where a monastery is in dramatic isolation in the midst of the Visovačko lake. The monastery was built in 1445 by Franciscans fleeing the Ottomans, and inside is preserved a beautifully illustrated copy of *Aesop's Fables*, said to be one of only three of its kind in the world. Another sacred building, in the middle of the Krka River canyon, is the Serbian Orthodox Monastery of the Holy Archangel, dating from the 15th century or earlier.

The cruises also cover the early Croatian fortresses of Trošenj and Nečven and **Roški slap**, another impressive cascade of water. It is also possible to visit the remains of a Roman military camp, **Burnum** (daily Apr–Oct). It is best to check on the latest park opening times and boat schedules before visiting. There is no accommodation in the park itself but there are a couple of small hotels in nearby Skradin.

View over Vransko jezero (Lake Vrana), which lies within the protected Biokovo nature park, between Zadar and Šibenik.

The Kornatis form the largest archipelago in the Adriatic, with a total of 147 islands, many of them completely uninhabited and others abandoned outside the summer. The archipelago stretches 35km (22 miles) south to the island of **Žirje**, which helps to form the natural barrier against the open sea that makes the region so enjoyable for yachting and boating. As there are no sources of fresh water anywhere on the islands, populating the area has always been difficult.

Roughly speaking, the islands fall into four strips running north to south towards Žirje, with the two closest to the coast known as Gornji Kornat. The two outer strings make up the **Kornati National Park** (Nacionalni park Kornati; www.np-kornati.hr), comprising more than 100 islands in total, three-quarters of which are no more than 1 hectare (2.5 acres) in size. The park's main island, **Kornat ❼**, which is around 25km (15 miles) long and 2.5km (1.5 miles) wide, is the largest uninhabited island in the Adriatic.

Attempts are being made to promote Kornati as an ecotourism destination, where man has done little to change or damage the environment. This is somewhat ironic, as man has already wrought havoc on the environment by burning down the indigenous oak trees for firewood, while sheep introduced by local farmers have destroyed much of the original vegetation. Only tough grass and wild herbs such as sage survive amidst the crumbling old stone dykes that used to pen in the sheep.

Thankfully the very barrenness of the area and the logistical difficulties of setting up large-scale tourism have stopped real development, and the establishment of the national park in 1980 has also helped to keep the developers at bay. Although in summer there are plenty of yachts and boat day trips, the sheer size of the archipelago means that things seldom feel too crowded. Facilities are low key – almost non-existent outside high season – and rustic, with many sailors just choosing to moor in one of the many tempting bays rather than looking for a proper harbour. The restaurants that exist on some of the islands are informal and small scale, serving simply cooked seafood. Accommodation tends to be in characterful old stone cottages and small houses, rather than in hotels. Camping is permitted only at the Levrnaka and Ravni Zakan campsites.

The most convenient marina for accessing the islands is on **Murter ❽**, an island just off the Northern Dalmatian coast, connected to the mainland by a bridge some 25km (15 miles) south of Biograd. Murter has hotel accommodation, restaurants, shops, supermarkets, travel agencies and all of the necessary facilities for setting out on a sailing expedition. The experience of sailing around the archipelago is exhilarating, but sailors must have proper navigation tools, as there are many dangerous shallows and rocks around the various islands. The best time for sailing is May or June, when a pleasant breeze is present; July and

August can be a little too calm unless you use a motor. Novice sailors will be safer joining one of the organised day trips; regular boat tours of the Kornatis leave from Murter, Šibenik and Zadar.

THE ZADAR ISLANDS

Dugi otok ❾ (Long Island), north of the Kornati Islands, stretches for more than 50km (30 miles) and is the largest of the so-called Zadar archipelago, which consists of some 300 islands. It is home to around 2,500 inhabitants and characterised by the same haunting beauty that pervades the Kornatis, as, like its neighbours, it has no natural fresh water supply. The rocky land undulates through a series of rocky ridges, coves and bays, with the highest point the limestone crest of Vela straža, which reaches a height of 338 metres (1,110ft).

The main settlement on Dugi otok is **Sali**, which is a thriving fishing port. It also has a reasonable supply of accommodation and a sprinkling of pavement cafés and restaurants. Boat tours leave from Sali in high season for **Telašćica**, which is frequently cited as one of the most beautiful bays in Croatia. The sweeping bay is usually littered with yachts in summer, but there are no cruise liners, ferries or hotels to clog up the view. As elsewhere on the Dalmatian islands, the main pleasure is relaxing and enjoying the clean seawater and the natural beauty. If you are visiting on a yacht, it is well worth heading ashore to walk around to **Lake Mir**, a lagoon separated from the sea by a narrow band of rocks.

The other inhabited islands of the archipelago – Ugljan, Pašman, Premuda, Olib and Molat – are similar in character, with isolated churches, the occasional monastery, small farms and, on Ugljan and Pašman (which are linked by a bridge), second homes. Ugljan is one of the greenest islands in the region, its interior smothered in olive groves, vineyards and pine forests. Its rugged western side is sparsely inhabited, as most life centres on the eastern side where you find the island's villages and best beaches. Its economy still revolves around fishing and wine and olive oil production, but there are still hotels and restaurants catering for visitors. Its peaceful hinterland is crisscrossed with nature and bike trails for all levels of cyclists.

Cross the bridge at the island's southernmost point and you enter Pašman, whose waters are said to be the cleanest in the Adriatic because the current changes direction every six hours. Like Ugljan, the island is covered in rich green vegetation and has a rocky western side that is indented with coves. The island's villages dot the eastern side, facing Biograd on the coast across the channel, while up in the hills are a 12th-century Benedictine monastery and its Franciscan counterpart from the 14th century. Hotels are small and family run, and many of the farmers and fishermen who supply the island's restaurants also offer private rooms to rent.

Primošten's beach.

📷 BEACHES AND BOAT TRIPS

With a long, dazzling coastline and more than 1,000 islands, there is so much to explore – and the choice becomes dizzying if you decide to travel by boat.

It has been estimated that, if you count the islands and reefs, there are 5,385km (3,625 miles) of coastline in Croatia. It's a country just made for blissing out on the beach. Most beaches are pebbly or rocky and not very wide, and though this might seem a hindrance, it does help to keep the waters of the coast wonderfully clear, as very little sand is churned up by the waves. A lack of tides, which never rise beyond a metre, also means that debris is not continually washed up. Around 100 beaches have earned a EU Blue Flag for cleanliness.

There are, however, some spectacular sandy beaches, both on the mainland and, more often, on the islands, some reached only by boat. Beaches are universally safe, with few currents or undertows, and the water is warm from May to October. Facilities vary, depending on how remote the beaches are, but the main resorts are fully kitted out for windsurfing, sea kayaking and other water-borne activities.

If you are swimming in rocky areas, forget your image and put on plastic shoes – there are often sea urchins with nasty spines. Apart from any influx of jellyfish, these are the only nasties to worry about. Speedboats and jet skis are the only real hazards, though the larger beaches have designated areas.

As to etiquette, topless is normal, and there are always nudist beaches nearby. In high summer, keep out of the sun in the middle of the day. Local people descend on the beach in the late afternoon for a swim and a touch of sun – not a bad habit to follow.

Sheltered cove in the rocky shoreline of Krk island.

Paradise Beach in sandy Crnika Bay in the Lopar peninsu Rab island, is very shallow and ideal for children.

The shore at Orebić, a family holiday resort in a town that was once known for its sea captains.

Swap a motorboat for a traditional sailing boat to travel between the island idylls.

Boat trips

Croatia has some of the best sailing waters in the world, and you should not visit the coast without taking a boat trip, particularly in Kvarner and on the Dalmatian coast. To the people of this region, water transport is a way of life, but for visitors it is still something special. Small boats in towns and resorts everywhere will ferry you to island villages and beaches, to hidden coves and special sites, often offering a fish lunch on the way, with perhaps some local brandy.

Take a trip from Zadar or Šibenik to Murter and the Kornati archipelago, or make a round trip from Dubrovnik to Koločep, Lopud and Šipan. As you sail among the islands, around headlands and through channels, you will get closer to feeling what it is like to be not just a Croatian fisherman, but to have been an adventurer in ancient times, a Greek explorer, a Roman soldier, a Venetian merchant – a timeless traveller in the ancient sea.

Some excursion boats have on-board fish meals included in the price of the ticket.

Tree-fringed Paradise Beach.

Though an island, Pag is only just off-shore, reached by a causeway from Zadar. It has one of the longest shores, stretching 270km (170 miles). Packed with bays, coves, capes and beaches, it offers limitless opportunities for water activities.

Trogir's waterfront.

SPLIT AND ISLANDS

With its rich culture, stunning coast and myriad islands, Central Dalmatia is hard to beat. Its main city is Split, whose inhabitants have a reputation for being cosmopolitan, hedonistic and chic.

Central Dalmatia is one of the most popular regions to visit in Croatia and it is not difficult to see why. It is easy to spend a month, never mind a week, here, exploring its intriguing historical towns and cities, and relaxing on its many rugged islands with their pristine beaches and warm breezes scented with wild lavender and rosemary.

The region largely escaped the 1990s war. While the Serbs failed to make a real breakthrough, previous invaders such as the Romans, Venetians and Austro-Hungarians were more successful and their legacy is evident in the rich collage of architectural styles in the main ports.

Mercifully, Central Dalmatia was also largely spared the hotel building boom that changed the face of Istria in the 1970s and 1980s and as a result it has far fewer large, anonymous-looking hotels. Tourism is emerging as the main industry and many tourist developments are pleasantly small-scale with family-run restaurants and *pensions* offering a cheap and atmospheric alternative to impersonal eating places and large hotels.

The region has also been discovered by the extremely wealthy international yachting community, and you will see plenty of multimillion-dollar yachts in the marinas. Indeed, sailing is a

great way to explore the islands and coast; the marinas are well equipped and there are far fewer boats than in the Greek Islands. Add the first-rate seafood, the relaxed pace of life, the openness of the local people and the quality of the scuba diving, and Central Dalmatia is hard to beat as a summer holiday destination.

TROGIR

Less than an hour's drive south of Šibenik (see page 160) is the picturesque town of **Trogir** ❶, set on a

◉ Main Attractions
Trogir
Split
Salona
Biokovo Mountains
Makarska
Ploče
Brač
Hvar
Vis

◉ Maps on pages
172, 176

Kamerlengo Fortress, Trogir.

St John's Chapel and sarcophagus inside the Cathedral of St Lawrence.

narrow island that is linked by bridge to the mainland on one side and by another bridge to the island of Čiovo across the Trogir Channel on the other. Trogir has been inhabited for around 4,000 years. Some 3,000 people live in the old town, which they like to refer to as the 'town museum', in acknowledgement of the rich range of architectural influences – medieval fortifications, Renaissance palaces and Venetian Gothic mansions meet on narrow medieval lanes and wide waterside boulevards. Unesco placed the town on its World Heritage List in 1997.

A good place to get acquainted with the layout of the town is from the ramparts of the **Kamerlengo Fortress** (Tvrđava Kamerlengo), originally built by the Venetians in 1420 to fend off Turkish attacks. The ramparts offer good views across the old town's spires and rooftops and out to sea, with the suburbs of Split visible in the distance. During summer, film screenings and other open-air events take place in the courtyard.

THE RIVA

From the fortress, head east along the **Riva**, Trogir's main boulevard, which in summer is lined by expensive yachts, tour boats and crowded pavement cafés. This emphasis on leisure and tourism has resulted in the loss of some of the old town's traditional features; during a face-lift of the area, for instance, the characterful fish market that used to occupy a 16th-century loggia at the boulevard's eastern end was evicted and relocated on the mainland. Rearing up behind the loggia is the best-preserved stretch of old town walls, now home to the immensely popular Padre Café and Big Daddy Bar.

Head through the late 16th-century South or Sea Gate (Južna vrata) and you come on to **Gradska**, the old town's main artery. Many of the town's key attractions are on this narrow street, which runs the length of the island and culminates in the Land Gate (Sjeverna gradska vrata), where a sculpture of St John, Trogir's patron saint, overlooks proceedings.

At the southern end of Gradska, just inside the South Gate, the 11th-century Benedictine **Convent of St Nicholas** (Samostan sv. Nikole; opening times erratic and limited) is inhabited by just two priests and three nuns. The original building dates from the 11th century with the interior constructed in the Baroque style. Highlights include a 13th-century Romanesque painting of the Madonna and Child and Croatia's finest example of Greek art (the Greeks arrived in Trogir from Issa, now the Croatian island of Vis): the 3rd-century reliefs of Kairos that were unearthed in the 1920s.

CATHEDRAL OF ST LAWRENCE

Further along Gradska the narrow street opens out upon **Trg Ivana Pavla II** (John Paul II Square, honouring the pontiff who made three episcopal visits to Croatia), which has a number of pavement cafés that are busy by day but fairly quiet by night. Looking across the square, the eye is drawn to the **Cathedral of St Lawrence** (Katedrala

sv. Lovre; June Mon–Sat 8am–7pm, Sun noon–6pm, July–Aug Mon–Sat 8am–8pm, Sun noon–6pm, shorter hours rest of the year).

The interior of the cathedral is breathtaking in its level of adornment. Enter from the side door of the three-nave building rather than the main portal and you will face the superb **St John's Chapel** (Kapela sv. Ivana). This ornate work by Nikola Firentinac just manages to stay on the right side of overblown, with more than 160 sculpted heads of angels, cherubim and saints surrounding the figure of God. Look out for the flower-embellished torches that are Firentinac's signature (also visible in a relief in the loggia across Trg Ivana Pavla II). St John's sarcophagus lies in the centre, a focus of devotion for many devout citizens of Trogir.

Leave the cathedral via the **West Portal** (Portal zapadnih), a 13th-century Romanesque masterpiece by the sculptor Radovan, with assistance from his many talented protégés. The upper section depicts scenes from the

☉ Tip

Taking place in various indoor and open-air venues, the Trogir Summer Festival (Trogirskog ljeta) is a 10-week celebration of classical, choral and folk music in July, August and September. For more information visit www.tztrogir.hr.

The South Gate, Trogir.

life of Christ and also scenes of local Dalmatian life, with hunting and fishing featuring strongly. The lower sections depict large figures of Adam and Eve hiding their modesty atop a couple of lions and, reflecting the politics of the time, exhausted Jewish and Ottoman figures bearing the weight of the door on their shoulders. The portal merits detailed viewing; make sure you come early in the day before the tour groups descend en masse.

TROGIR'S LOGGIA

Also on Trg Ivana Pavla II is Trogir's 15th-century **loggia** (loža), formerly the city court, which is topped by a clock tower. On the inside wall there is a slightly incongruous Meštrović relief of Petar Berislavić astride a rather strange-looking steed, while on the other wall is another Firentinac relief, which used to hang above the judge's chair when the loggia was used as a court. More interesting in some ways than what is still there is what is not: the sculpture of a Venetian lion that was destroyed by Croats opposed to Italian expansion in Dalmatia in the 1930s, something that the local guides claim to know nothing about. At the western end of the loggia there is a small shrine to the victims of the 1991–5 war and three Roman sarcophagi. At the other end of the loggia, a door leads to the **Museum of Sacred Art** (Muzej sakralne umjetnosti; June–Sept daily 8am–7pm), which houses a small but valuable collection of sacred art from the 13th to 16th centuries, including a 13th-century polyptych of the Virgin and Child with Saints from the main altar of the cathedral. Another branch on the other side of the road (same hours), next door to the tourist office, houses a small collection of medieval stone masonry.

From the square continue north along Gradska to Trogir's Town Museum (Gradski muzej; July–Aug daily 10am–1pm and 6–9pm, June and Sept Mon–Sat 10am–1pm and 5–8pm, Oct–May 9am–2pm), which is housed in an old Venetian palace. The family that built the villa kept a private library that was the largest in Trogir, with more

Trogir's 15th-century loggia on Trg Ivana Pavla II.

than 5,000 books, many of which are still on display today. The main exhibition consists of stone artefacts, some Roman and others attributed to the Dalmatian sculptors Ivan Duknović and Nikola Firentinac. There is also an art gallery showcasing the work of local painter Cata Dujšin-Ribar (1897–1994).

Any sightseeing tour should finish up on the Riva, perhaps after a stroll west around the island, past the Kamerlengo Fortress. By evening the Riva is packed with tourists, and teenagers from Split, who scream aboard a fleet of scooters as night falls. The bars, cafés and waterfront restaurants stay open late; when they close, hardcore revellers continue on to clubs in nearby Primošten and Split.

For relaxation in the sun, cross the bridge from Trogir on to the island of Čiovo, where pebbly beaches at the villages of Arbanija and Slatine dot the eastern coastline. On the island's western side, choose from the beaches at Okrug Donji and Okrug Gornji, where there are also scuba-diving schools and jet skis for hire. To visit one of the region's few sandy beaches, take a boat ride west of Trogir to the tiny island of Drvenik Mali and its peaceful olive groves. Its bigger neighbour, Drvenik Veli, has quiet coves with pebbly beaches tucked around its coast.

Back on the Dalmatian mainland, the gulf between Trogir and Split is marked by the seven towns that make up Kaštela. Strung out along a 20km (12-mile) stretch of coast are these enchanting little ports with fortified castles built by rich Split families as defences against the Ottoman Turks.

STYLISH SPLIT

Split ❷ is one of the Adriatic's liveliest and most alluring cities, and it often manages to seduce visitors initially planning on passing through to stay for months or even years. Croatia's second city is a proud place; the local Splićani cultivate a fierce rivalry with Zagrebians, a rivalry that reaches fever pitch on the football field when Hajduk Split lock horns with Dinamo Zagreb. The Splićani like to see themselves as infinitely more stylish and glamorous

Split.

⊙ Tip

The Split Card gives holders free or reduced entrance to the city's museums, discounts at some hotels, on excursions and at the theatre. Valid for 72 hours and costing around €10, it offers excellent value. The card is available from the Tourist Information Centre in the Peristyle and other authorised outlets. For more information see www.visitsplit.com.

than their inland brethren, a view that the proliferation of fashionable shops and nightclubs and the local passion for people-watching support.

But Split has its problems, with high unemployment due to the decline of the city's traditional industries such as shipbuilding, high levels of crime in the housing developments that radiate from the centre, and suburbs blighted by the scars of heavy industry. But there is no denying the city's dramatic setting, with sheer karst mountains on one side and the Adriatic on the other. Arriving in Split on an early ferry and catching sight of its old town shimmering in the morning light create a wonderful first impression. It's one that many people experience, given that the city is an important hub for island-hopping, with its ferry harbour conveniently located right next to the train and bus stations.

DIOCLETIAN'S PALACE

The centre of Split life still focuses upon Diocletian's Palace (Dioklecijanova palača), built on the waterfront

by the Roman emperor Diocletian as a retirement home between AD 295 and 305. It was later inhabited by the citizens of the neighbouring Roman city of Salona after invading Avars and Slavs destroyed their homes in the 7th century. Over the centuries, Split's citizens chose to build into and around the palace structure rather than demolish it, offering today's visitors the unique chance to eat, sleep and drink in the footsteps of a Roman emperor. Unesco listed the complex in 1979. Two reasons for the remarkably well-preserved state of the ground floor are the high quality of limestone used – brought in from the island of Brač – and the fact that townspeople filled it with rubble from building works above.

The palm-fringed waterfront **Riva** Ⓐ is the most obvious place to begin a walking tour of the palace area. Its pavement cafés, cheap restaurants and waterside benches, all built around the grand facade of the palace, make it a natural focus. The waterside scene is all the more alluring because the Riva is pedestrianised.

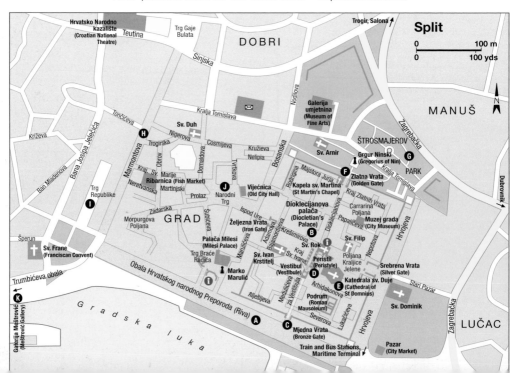

From the waterfront you can delve straight into **Diocletian's Palace** through the **Bronze Gate** , which used to be right on the water's edge and only accessible by boat. The gate leads up through a tunnel to the Peristyle, where the Cardo joins the Decumanus, a simple layout that makes navigating the palace area very easy.

Diocletian was born in Dioclea, near Salona in AD 245, the son of former slaves, and rose to emperor through a distinguished career in the army. His retirement palace, which he began about halfway through his 21-year reign, was conceived on a grand scale and completed in AD 305 – the year he abdicated, the only Roman emperor to do so – and six years before his death. More than 200 buildings remain inside the original dimensions: his old chambers and garrisons have been converted over the centuries into shops, bars, cafés, hotels and homes, with more than 3,000 people still living where refugees from nearby Salona originally moved in. As you enter the Bronze Gate look out for the entrance

to the subterranean museum, with artefacts from Roman times laid out in the emperor's old living quarters.

Once you are back above ground, continue through the tunnel, which is lined with souvenir stalls, and at its end some steep stairs bring you up into the **Peristyle** (Peristil). This remarkable Roman set piece features a sunken square, which houses a couple of cafés, while to the right are a line of Roman columns and the octagonal **Cathedral of St Domnius** (Katedrala sv. Duje; hours vary; free), whose lofty bell tower, one of the symbols of the city, was a later addition. Head past the Egyptian sphinx, once the guardian of Diocletian's tomb, and into the octagonal cathedral.

It is somewhat ironic that the last resting place of a man notorious for his persecution of Christians, and who was present at the beheading of St Domnius, the first bishop of Salona, should have been converted into a Christian cathedral – albeit one of the world's smallest – and that the nearby Roman temple has become a baptistry. Look

⊘ **Eat**

Split's City Market (Pazar; daily usually 6am–lunchtime) offers a chaotic array of seasonal fruit and vegetables, salamis, honey and home-made cheeses. If you are planning a picnic, stock up here.

Café in the Peristyle.

out for the intricately carved reliefs of scenes from the life of Christ on the entrance doors.

Inside, the highlights include a portrait of Diocletian with his wife Prisca, which somehow survived the post-Roman makeover; the main altar, with paintings by Croatian artist Matija Pončun; and the north altar, sculpted in the 18th century by the Venetian Giovan Maria Morlaiter.

Other eye-catching things to look out for are the sacristy, dating from the beginning of the 17th century, and the ornately decorated 13th-century Romanesque choir stalls.

GOLDEN GATE

From the Peristyle continue north past the tourist information office on Dioklecijanova towards the Golden Gate and the minuscule **St Martin's Chapel** (Kapela sv. Martina), occupying an old Roman guardhouse and probably built in the 5th or 6th century. Today it caters to a Dominican nunnery next door. Most of Diocletian's garrison was housed in the northern portion of the palace. It is worth seeing the memorial to St Domnius. The **Golden Gate ❼** (Zlatna vrata), which led to the Roman town of Salona, used to sport a figure of Diocletian amongst other statues, but these have long gone.

Pass through the Golden Gate and you will be struck by the massive sculpture of **Grgur Ninski**, the 9th-century bishop who challenged Rome by advocating that the Croatian Church use the Slavic tongue and Glagolitic script rather than Latin. The toe much rubbed for luck, this is one of Ivan Meštrović's best-known works, though perhaps not among his best. The sculpture stood by the Peristyle inside the palace complex until the occupying Italian authorities moved it out, fearing its symbolic importance to Croatian national consciousness.

Near the statue, at ulica kralja Tomislava 15, the **Museum of Fine Arts** (Galerija umjetnina; www.galum.hr; Tue–Sun 10m–9pm) spans the 14th to 20th centuries. Some of the most valuable works are three pieces by Meštrović.

Statue of Grgur Ninski.

Built in the early 16th century and catering to a 100-strong community, Split's **synagogue** (sinagoga; Mon–Fri 10am–2pm; donations requested) on Židovski prolav (Jewish Passage) inside Diocletian's Palace is one of only a handful still functioning as such in Croatia. It is the third oldest in Europe in continuous use. Visitors are welcome. Under Nazi occupation this street formed part of the Jewish ghetto but most Jews were interned on Rab. In 1942, Italian Fascists took most of the synagogue's ritual objects and religious books and made a bonfire in the main square, but local people rescued some and returned them to the Jewish community. Jews have lived on the Dalmatian coast since Roman times. There is also an old Jewish cemetery on the eastern slope of Mt Marjan above Split. Although the Jewish community took over the site in 1573, plots were initially recycled and the oldest surviving tomb dates from 1717. The cemetery's neighbouring café, Vidilica, offers one of the loveliest views of the city below.

THE REST OF SPLIT

From the palace area, walk west through **Štrosmajerov Park G** and follow the outline of the city walls that were added as Split outgrew the original confines of Diocletian's Palace. Eventually you will come to **Trg Gaje Bulata**, home to the grand Croatian National Theatre. Its impressive facade was restored after a devastating fire in the 1970s.

Stroll south back towards the sea and down **Marmontova H** and you will see the shiny, modern face of Split. The locals descend on this polished promenade every evening to browse in the fancy designer shops and to see and be seen. The street shows how seriously the Splićani take their fashion, as prices are not much cheaper than in London or Paris in spite of the much lower local wages.

As Marmontova approaches the sea, turn right on to **Trg Republike I**. After the throngs of people and general vibrancy of Diocletian's Palace, this sombre Austro-Hungarian imperial square is a marked contrast. As

The bell tower of the Cathedral of St Domnius, Split.

Ⓞ IVAN MEŠTROVIĆ

An apprenticeship as a stone-cutter in Split at the age of 15 set Ivan Meštrović (1883–1962) on the path to becoming one of the most highly regarded sculptors of the 20th century. The classical remains in his home city are said to have inspired the unschooled artist and he soon attracted the attention of benefactors. With their help, he went on to study at the Academy of Art in Vienna during the heyday of Secessionism. He worked first in Paris, where he won the admiration of Rodin, and then Rome, where he achieved first prize for the Serbian pavilion at the International Exhibition of 1911 for a series of bronzes commemorating heroic Serbians warriors fighting the Ottomans at the Battle of Kosovo.

Meštrović was intensely nationalistic, and much of his work was inspired by his desire to shake off the shackles of first the Austro-Hungarians and later the Italians. His politics took up almost as much time as his art. Believing that the way forward was for Croatia to forge a union with Serbia, he was a founding member of the Yugoslav Committee. However, he was bitterly disillusioned by the first Yugoslavia created after World War I, in which Croatia was subordinate to Serbia, and refused to live in Tito's Yugoslavia after World War II. In 1954, he became a citizen of the United States. His later themes tended to be religious rather than political.

Another of Split's main attractions is its nightlife.

In the Meštrović Gallery.

the crowds pass by on Marmontova a few metres away, this elongated square with its attractive colonnades and buildings and view towards the Adriatic lies forgotten, with only the Bellevue Hotel providing any life. But increasingly the annual Split Summer Festival is bringing live music to the Trg Republike, so it may not be too long before the square finds itself on the tourist map.

To find the most impressive Venetian portion of Split, walk back along the Riva to **Narodni Trg ❿** (People's Square). This graceful space looks as if it has been transported from the Divine Republic, a little corner of Venice on the edge of Diocletian's Palace. In the 15th century, as the city expanded beyond the confines of the palace, this square took on the mantle of the most important in the city. A legacy of those glory days is the Town Hall, dominating the square on the northern flank, and several palaces, the most impressive of which is the Renaissance Karapić Palace. Pop around the corner to Trg Preporoda, home to another Meštrović

work, this time a striking sculpture of the 15th-century writer Marko Marulić, one of Split's greatest literary sons and the author of the play *Judita*, one of the first secular works of Croatian literature.

If the Meštrović sculptures around town have sparked an interest in the controversial Croatian sculptor then consider venturing to the **Meštrović Gallery ⓚ** (Galerija Meštrović; 46 Šetalište Ivan Meštrovica; May–Sept Tue–Sun 9am–7pm, Oct–Apr Tue–Sat 9am–4pm, Sun 10am–3pm). Housed in what he intended to be his retirement home, before his decision to emigrate to the United States, this is the largest collection of his work – in bronze, wood, stone and marble. Standout sculptures include *Distant Accords, Vestal, The Madonna and Child* and his bronze of Job. The entrance fee includes admission to Kaštelet (same hours), at No. 39 in the same street, devoted to his series of wood carvings portraying the life of Christ.

To the east of the port and the marina is the city's main beach, Bačvice, a busy strip within a protective bay. Carry on further east and you soon reach the Zenta Marina complex in Firule, the tennis club where Goran Ivanišević first learned how to play tennis. For views of the city and the sea, hike up the steps that lead to the 123-metre (403ft) summit of Marjan Hill to the west of the centre.

SPLIT BY NIGHT

One of the most alluring aspects of Split is its vibrant nightlife. As the sun comes down over the Adriatic, people gather in the cafés along the Riva. As the night progresses, the wealthier, trendier participants move on to Diocletian's Palace, where several chic bars hide away on the upper level. (Take the stairs by the Hotel Slavija.) Suitably attired and discreet visitors are welcome, but anyone bearing a camera or guidebook may not even get

served at these trendy haunts. They offer the unusual experience of sipping a cocktail by candlelight right in the heart of the 2,000-year-old Roman palace. Nights in Split, especially in summer, are long and sultry; activity later moves on to the seafront south of the centre, where bars and clubs cater for various different crowds.

ROMAN SALONA

Outside Split itself the old Roman city of **Salona** ❸ (Solin in Croatian) is well worth discovering. The No. 1 bus stops near its main entrance. Salona's ruins are extensive, and it is best to arrange a guide through the local tourist office. The story of its destruction in the 7th century and the panic that accompanied the citizens' flight to Split is gripping.

The Romans first established Salona in the 1st century BC, under the Emperor Augustus' rule. It quickly prospered on the local salt industry (*sal* in Latin) and Diocletian liked it so much – he was born near Salona – that he chose to build his retirement home on the waterfront to the southeast in modern-day Split. Salona later fell under the control of the Eastern Roman Empire, but in the 7th century Avars and Slavs descended to rout and sack the city. Those lucky enough to escape with their lives fled to Split and never looked back.

You can easily cover the 156-hectare (385-acre) site on foot. There is a modest museum at the main entrance and a café for those needing a drink to counter the baking heat of a summer's day. You can still make out some of the old city walls, as well as the ruins of a 5th-century cathedral, a 2nd-century amphitheatre able to accommodate 18,000 spectators and a medieval fortress. Look out, too, for the remains of the aqueduct by the south wall, which used to supply water to Diocletian's Palace.

SOUTH TO THE MAKARSKA RIVIERA

South of Split, the Magistrala runs through some of Europe's loveliest coastal scenery. The **Biokovo Mountains** sweep precipitously up one flank in a massif of karst hulks and forested

> **⊘ Fact**
>
> Central Dalmatia enjoys the sunniest weather in Croatia, with more than 200 days of sunshine a year. However, beware the *bura*, a chilly and fierce wind that rips along the coast in the colder months, playing havoc with the ferry services.

Republic Square (Trg Republike).

ravines, while on the other, the coastline is punctuated by bays and coves, with the islands of Brač and Hvar glittering just offshore. Expect to spend the first 30 minutes of the drive out of Split trying to shake off its suburbs and the mushrooming complexes of holiday homes on the way to the heavily developed Makarska Riviera, the equivalent of the Spanish costas for Croatians, Bosnians and citizens of the former Soviet Bloc. Despite the sometimes down-market resorts and eyesores that pass for hotel developments, the glorious mountains and sea are ever present, as are long, clean shingle beaches backed by pine trees.

But before you reach the Makarska Riviera, you pass the small town of Omiš, which straddles the mouth of Cetina River and sits in the shelter of its canyon. This delightful little town is one of the most atmospheric spots to listen to klapa singing heard all along the Dalmatian coast, and here it's celebrated every summer in a particularly rousing festival in July. Listening to these melodious sounds today,

it's hard to imagine that Omiš was the home of fearsome pirates during the Middle Ages, whose exploits are still celebrated today in the Pirate Night festival held every August.

The first substantial resort of the Makarska Riviera is **Brela ❹**, probably the most tasteful and understated, though it gets very busy in high season and finding a room can be a problem. To the north and south are sweeping beaches with a line of pine trees set just back from the shingle to provide shade during the hottest hours of the day. Brela sprawls across a large area, but the old town is surprisingly compact with twisting narrow streets leading seawards.

Just 12km (7.5 miles) further south is **Makarska ❺**, a long-established resort that is big, brash and bolshy, with a dramatic backdrop provided by the Biokovo Mountains. It mainly consists of a tangle of cafés, cheap restaurants and pensions, though the waterfront Riva is a pleasant place to while away a few hours by day or to survey the smorgasbord of humanity

Ruins of the old Roman city of Salona.

cruising past by night. The standard of accommodation is rising, with smaller family-run hotels offering a more interesting alternative to the big bland monstrosities. Most remnants of the town's Ottoman and Venetian heritage are long gone, but the central Trg Kačićev does contain the Baroque **St Mark's Church** (Crkva sv. Marka), which has a fine 18th-century Venetian altar. Just outside the church look out for a work by the sculptor Ivan Rendić – a statue of the 18th-century Franciscan friar and poet Andrija Kačić Miošić. The **Town Museum** (Gradski muzej; summer Mon–Fri 9am–1pm and 7–9pm, Sat 7–10pm, winter Mon–Sat 9am–1pm) documenting Makarska's maritime past merits a visit only if you are spending a few days in town.

The area has plenty of shingle beaches on which to laze away the days. More adventurous types may want to set off to conquer some of the peaks and ridges of the Biokovo Mountains, which are easily accessible from the town and rise from the sea to afford a magnificent panorama of the Makarska Riviera and Zabiokovlje. Do not underestimate this steep range: seek local advice before setting out and take plenty of water and warm clothing. The highest peak is **Mt Sveti Jure** (1,762 metres/5,781ft), accessible from the villages of Makar and Veliko Brdo.

Other resorts on the Riviera include the very busy Blue Flag beach at **Baška Voda** and the pine-backed pebbly beach at Punta Rata, as well as **Tučepi**, **Podgora**, **Drvenik**, **Zaostrog** and **Gradac**. Accommodation tends to be geared to mass tourism and one-week minimum stays are common.

A DIP INTO BOSNIA?

South of Gradac the Magistrala bypasses the shabby port of **Ploče**, which could make a strong claim to be the least appealing settlement on the entire Croatian coastline. Rail enthusiasts and any travellers interested in visiting Bosnia can take the reopened railway line from Ploče to the Bosnian city of Mostar and on to its capital, Sarajevo.

From Ploče the Magistrala curls around the Neretva Delta, a sweeping

> ⊙ **Tip**
>
> On busy summer weekends, Brač and Hvar can be saturated with tourists. If you are looking for a relaxing day trip, consider the island of Šolta instead. It is only a short ferry trip from Split and is popular with locals for its pine-shaded walks.

Makarska's marina.

⊙ Tip

The Brač Summer Cultural Festival runs from June to September. Traditional folk music and classical concerts are held in Brač's main towns – most of them free.

plain reclaimed from the once broad river. Myriad waterways and small settlements dot the fertile valley floor, while in the background a curtain of chunky limestone hills disappears over the horizon towards Bosnia. Tourism is still very low key in this part of Croatia, but it is possible to rent a boat and explore. There are eight lakes and 12 river branches in a delta that spreads over an area of around 190 sq km (500 sq miles).

THE ISLAND OF BRAČ

For centuries, **Brač ❻**, Croatia's third-largest island, has made a living from the limestone laboriously hacked out of its rugged hills. Among the many illustrious buildings constructed from this stone are Diocletian's Palace in Split, the Hungarian Parliament in Budapest and even the White House in Washington DC. These days tourism has become equally as important as quarrying, with most visitors arriving in the island's main town of **Supetar**. The ferry from Split arrives just east of the centre, which consists of a curving bay

Omiš lies between Split and Makarska.

lined with palm trees and orange-roofed buildings dating from Venetian times. A string of pebble beaches lies within easy striking distance to the west.

The first pre-Roman settlement on Brač was unearthed on a peninsula near Supetar's beaches. The peninsula today is occupied by a cemetery with some impressively ornate tombs, many the work of Ivan Rendić, a contemporary of Meštrović. The most dramatic, the **Petrinović Mausoleum** (Mauzolej obitelji Mate Petrinović), was created in 1924 by another Croatian sculptor, Toma Rosandić, adding Byzantine influences to the range of Dalmatian styles seen elsewhere in the cemetery.

WINDSURFING OFF BOL

From Supetar, the most popular route is eastwards towards **Zlatni rat**, the Golden Horn, near the town of Bol across the mountains on Brač's southeast coast. This stark white peninsula with its backdrop of pines is a dramatic sight. One of Croatia's best beaches, it attracts huge crowds at the height of summer, but many are only

day-trippers from Split and Hvar – so it is best to stay overnight and visit outside peak season. **Bol** merits visiting in its own right. This small town of tightly packed houses has a trio of large hotels and a Dominican monastery. Skulking in the background, Vidova gora (780 metres/2,560ft) is the highest peak in the Adriatic islands. The summit is accessible from Bol, on foot or by car. Other activities include diving and windsurfing – Bol being one of the best places in Croatia for the latter.

Plans are afoot for a smooth road along Brač's southern coast, but for now the drive west is an arduous journey, not for nervous drivers, with terrifyingly tight bends and hairpins. The wild southern coastline is dotted with remote and sheltered coves.

The pretty towns of Pučišća and **Milna** are two of several places that have so far escaped development. All the classic Dalmatian components are there: a higgledy-piggledy old town, a crumbling old church, a wide waterfront and some excellent seafood restaurants, but there are few tourists,

which is probably why you will see some very smart yachts in the harbour.

The scrubby interior holds a fascinating part of Brač's history in the form of **Blaca Hermitage**, a 16th-century refuge that became home to a community of monks until as recently as 1963. The monastery grew to include the surrounding areas where the monks planted olive groves and vineyards that tumble down the stony terraces in the karst landscape between Milna and Bol.

HVAR

With its lush forests, the sweeping Sveti Nikola mountain range, the omnipresent aroma of lavender and a sprinkle of historic towns, **Hvar** ❼ is one of the most enticing of Croatia's Adriatic islands. On the downside, it is the most visited Croatian island and tends to be more expensive than other places, although prices are perfectly reasonable away from the hotspots of Hvar town. The Greeks occupied it in the 4th century, but it was the Venetians in the 15th and 16th centuries who left their stamp on the architecture, much

Lavender bags, water, oil and balm are sold all over Hvar island.

Supetar on Brač island.

Tip

The Hvar Festival runs from late June to late September in Hvar town, with theatre performances from domestic and international groups in the historic buildings, as well as open-air jazz concerts.

Lavender fields on Hvar.

appreciated by the many Italians who visit on Adriatic ferries in summer.

HVAR TOWN

Hvar town enjoys an idyllic setting in a protected island-studded bay, with the old town unfolding on a pine-covered slope that reaches to the water's edge, with clumps of wild lavender and herbs growing among the Venetian palaces. In high season, the town and its harbour are packed with shiny yachts and tour boats, and the pavement cafés and trendy bars are bursting at the seams. All available rooms usually go by mid-morning; those wanting to appreciate the island's special beauty and atmosphere would do best to visit outside the main summer season.

The best place to begin a walking tour is in front of the Palace Hotel at the **municipal flagpole** (štandarac), where government decisions used to be announced to a largely illiterate population. Directly east is **Trg Sveti Stjepana**, known locally as the pjaca (piazza), but more of a wide boulevard than a square. The main focal point of the town – and the largest square in Dalmatia – it is the setting for the nightly promenade in summer.

At the western end of the square is the 16th-century **arsenal** (oružana; high season 9am–1pm and 5–11pm, low season by appointment tel: 021 741009), once capable of housing and repairing entire Venetian warships. Unusually the upper level was transformed into one of Europe's first public theatres, a function it performs to this day, although it is temporarily closed for restoration. Far from symbolising a united and enlightened community, the theatre's genesis seems to have been a crude attempt by the town's nobles, who lived in hillside palaces, to placate the disenfranchised masses living in the maze of streets south of Trg Sveti Stjepana. The arsenal also houses a modest collection of paintings by Dalmatian artists.

ST STEPHEN'S CATHEDRAL

Strolling to the other end of Trg Sveti Stjepana, you come to **St Stephen's Cathedral** (Katedrala sv. Stjepana),

☉ LAVENDER ISLAND

The Romans are said to have believed 'As the rose is the scent of the heart, so is lavender the scent of the soul'. Whether or not the Romans first cultivated the aromatic plant on Hvar, the lavender industry – now one of the island's chief sources of income – took off in the 1930s, when the plant was brought in en masse and quickly spread across the rocky hillsides.

Conditions are perfect on an island that is the sunniest in Croatia. Today, for much of spring and summer (the harvest is in late June/early July) the scent of lavender wafts across the whole island, giving it the aroma of a luxury spa. Most of the production centres on small, family-owned plots of land, and so you are unlikely to see the great swathes of lavender fields that you find, say, in the south of France. Nonetheless, Hvar lavender, *Lavandula croatica*, is among the finest in Europe. It comes ready packaged in a bewildering array of oils, creams, bath foams and balms, which are said to aid everything from mosquito bites and sore muscles to migraine headaches and depression. For a wonderfully aromatic experience in high summer, visit the fragrant lavender stalls that line the streets of Hvar town, Stari Grad, Jelsa and Vrboska. The tiny village of Velo Grablje (full-time population: five) is the setting for an annual lavender festival at the end of June, with lavender stalls, live music and the chance to take part in the lavender-crushing process – with your feet.

visible from all over Hvar town. In 1571, the Ottomans razed the original Benedictine monastery on the site, just before their landmark defeat at the Battle of Lepanto. Today's incarnation was built in Venetian Renaissance style in the 16th and 17th centuries. The striking bell tower attached features a biforium, triforium and quatroforium. You can usually enter the cathedral shortly before Mass. If you examine the nave closely, you will notice segments of the earlier cathedral. Also worthy of attention is the understated 13th-century Madonna and Child on the altar.

Up the hillside from Trg Sveti Stjepana, on Matije Ivanića, are many of Hvar town's old family palaces, symbols of the prosperity of this Venetian trading town when it was a stopping point for northbound ships en route to the metropolis. Look out for the coats of arms lining the street above the many restaurants that have moved into the buildings. Particularly striking is a roofless palace with Gothic windows, which was never finished because of lack of funds.

The steep hike from sea level up through the hillside park to the **Spanish Fortress** (Trđava Španjola; high season 8am–10pm, low season 9am–5pm) is well worth it for the panoramic views that the ramparts offer. The town walls join each flank and Hvar town spreads around the harbour below, while Hvar's offshore islands and the island of Vis are visible further afield. The fortifications were commissioned by the Habsburg monarch Charles V in 1551; today the fort is used as a café during the day and a nightclub in the evening. It also has a collection of rare weapons.

The beaches around Hvar town are nothing special and tend to be overcrowded in summer. A better bet is a visit to the Pakleni Islands (Pakleni otoci – literally translated as Islands of Hell). Numerous boat operators run day trips and also offer taxi services out to the islands, with a one-way fare priced at about 40 kuna. The three most popular islands are **Sveti Klement**, which includes the marina and resort at Palmižana, **Marinkovac**, which has a couple of good beaches,

Hvar town with the fortress in the background.

The small village of Jelsa makes a pleasant island base.

and **Jerolim**, where clothes are very much optional.

EXPLORING THE REST OF HVAR

Stari Grad (Old Town) on Hvar's north coast earned its name on account of being the island's first major centre before the Venetians developed Hvar town. These days Stari Grad is going through something of a renaissance, fuelled to a large extent by a purpose-built ferry terminal just outside the town, which serves most of the car ferries from Split as well as services run by the Jadrolinija ferry company from as far afield as Rijeka and Dubrovnik. In contrast to its western sister, Stari Grad grew to prominence as a Greek town in the 4th century BC when it was known as Faros; although no buildings from that time remain, the structure of the town is unchanged. Since 2008, the Stari Grad Plain has been a Unesco World Heritage Site. The plain, lined with olive groves and vineyards, was laid out by Greek colonists in the 4th century BC and has hardly changed since then.

Hvar town's main square.

Stari Grad was the home of the 16th-century Croatian poet and visionary Petar Hektorović, who possessed a social conscience rare amongst his fellow nobles of the time. Hektorović's best work was the epic *Ribanje i ribarsko prigovaranje* (Fishing and Fishermen's Conversations), though islanders perhaps best remember him for his attempt to build a sanctuary in which citizens could seek refuge when the town came under attack.

Work on the **Tvrdalj** (daily May–Oct, for hours tel: 021 765068) began in 1520, though it was damaged by the Turkish attack of 1571. Unfortunately the building was never completed and in the 19th century it underwent a facelift that smoothed over the delicate Renaissance facade. The Tvrdalj now doubles as an ethnographic museum as well as a memorial to the poet – look out for his etchings in Croatian, Latin and Italian, which are carved into the walls and around the fish pond in the garden.

Next door, housed in the former palace of the Biankini family, is the

nautically themed **Stari Grad Museum** (Muzej Staroga Grada; http://msg.hr; May–June and Sept–Oct Mon–Sat 10am–1pm, July–Aug Mon–Sat 10am–1pm and 7–9pm, Sun 7–9pm, Nov–Apr by arrangement tel: 021 766324), which displays items retrieved from a 4th-century Roman shipwreck.

Just a short stroll away is Stari Grad's other main attraction, the **Dominican Monastery** (Dominikanski samostan; daily May–Oct, for hours tel: 021 765442), which houses a museum with a number of Hektorović's belongings, including a 16th-century collection of Petrarch's sonnets and portraits of the poet. The original building dates from the 15th century, though it has been modified over the years, with a church added in the 19th century. The church may be unspectacular in itself, but look out for Tintoretto's *Disposition* inside.

West of Stari Grad are the towns of Jelsa and Vrboska. **Jelsa** offers a far more relaxed resort experience than the maelstrom of Hvar town, despite the two large hotels that share the wooded slopes with the old fishing village. The main pleasure is strolling along the waterfront, but there are a couple of interesting churches. As in all the churches in Jelsa and Vrboska, opening times are erratic, but popping in just before a service gets under way is often the best bet. In the **Church of SS Fabian and Sebastian** (Crkva sv. Fabijana i Sebastijana), look out for a wooden statue of the Virgin Mary said to have been brought to Jelsa by Christians fleeing the Dalmatian hinterland in the wake of Turkish attacks. The Chapel of St John (Crkva sv. Ivana) dates from the 16th century.

Vrboska is even more relaxed, though the atmosphere was considerably less sleepy when the crews of Venetian vessels used to stop by to enjoy the seafood caught by local fishermen. Again, idling away the day on the waterfront is the chief attraction, where you can watch the boats in the two marinas, but there are a couple of churches worth seeing.

The Church of St Lawrence features a Madonna of the Rosary attributed

Franciscan monastery, Vis.

Hellenistic gravestones in Vis Town hint at the island's past.

Stari Grad on Hvar's north coast.

to Leandro Bassano, while St Mary's Church was built in the wake of devastating Turkish attacks, hence its sturdy construction. There are good views over Vrboska and the Adriatic from the roof of St Mary's.

Hugging the eastern edge of the island is the village of Sućuraj, its two bays sheltering several pebbly and sandy beaches. Fishing plays a big part in local life, with much of the day's catch ending up all over Dalmatia's islands. Away from the coast, the island's interior is a fragrant combination of lavender fields, olive groves and vineyards, and is becoming more popular with hikers and cyclists in the spring and autumn.

MAGICAL VIS

The island of **Vis** ❽ holds a special place in the hearts of many Croatians, as well as with many regular visitors who have discovered the last inhabited Croatian island before the Italian coastline. It is one of the least densely populated areas of Croatia, in part thanks to its being an off-limits military

base until 1989. On the approach to Vis its rugged, mountainous beauty is reminiscent of a Scottish Hebridean isle with lofty peaks and sheer rock walls looming large.

The first inhabitants were the Greeks in the 4th century BC – it was their biggest colony in Croatia – but its strategic position at the heart of the Adriatic, with views towards both the Croatian and Italian coastlines, has made it a prized possession historically and ownership has changed hands numerous times. Since the demise of the Venetian Republic in 1797, the Austrians, British, French and Germans have all battled over Vis, with the British leaving the most indelible imprint in the fortifications ringing Vis Town.

Aesthetically, **Vis Town** is not as immediately striking as some of the other Dalmatian settlements such as Hvar town or Rab town. Its hotchpotch of architectural styles is an indication of its turbulent history. There are two parts to the town: the area where the ferry docks, with its cafés, souvenir

⊘ DIVING

Thanks to Vis's long period as a military base, its surrounding waters have never been commercially fished and have a particularly lush sea life as well as six diveable wrecks. Not surprisingly, Vis offers some of the best scuba diving in Croatia with something to suit everyone, from inexperienced PADI (Professional Association of Diving Instructors) beginners, right through to seasoned divers in search of challenging deep dives as well as night diving. In addition, there are around a dozen submerged wrecks within easy reach of Vis, with everything from a World War II bomber to a Venetian galleon. There are several operators in Vis town. The season usually runs from 1 April to 1 December, although dives can still be set up during the winter months by special arrangement.

stalls and bus station, and the old aristocratic enclave of Kut, to the east around the bay.

From the ferry dock, turn right and a 10-minute walk will bring you to the 16th-century **Franciscan Monastery** (Franjevački samostan). Though of no special interest in itself, and usually closed, its cemetery is worth seeing, not least for the fine views of Vis town and the harbour, with verdant slopes rising to meet the sea on all sides. Some of the headstones are spectacular, such as a fine sculpture of a maiden watering flowers on the grave of one Toma Bradanović by the Croatian sculptor Ivan Rendić. Look out also for the mass tomb built to house a group of Austrian sailors killed during a fierce naval engagement with the French off Vis in 1866.

Heading east back past the ferry dock, you will come to a small palm-fringed park that gives way to a promenade lined with yachts on one side and cafés on the other. Keep walking away from the crowds and you will come to the 16th-century **Church of**

Our Lady of the Cave (Župna crkva Gospe od Spilica). The three-nave interior is quite striking, but in a sad state of repair. Even a solid-looking altar on the left has developed a serious crack through its centre. One fine surviving artwork is the *Madonna with the Saints* by Girolamo da Santacroce.

Just past the church is a small jetty with a pebble beach that is a good spot for a refreshing swim. Next to this, a path leads south past two hefty cannons to the old bastion that used to house a military museum. A celebration of Communist-era military might and Tito's victories did not sit well with the new independent Croatia and the bastion now functions as an **Archaeological Museum** (Arheološki muzej; June–Oct Mon–Fri 10am–1pm and 5–9pm, Sat 10am–1pm, Nov–May by appointment tel: 021 711729). On the lower level of the main building is an interesting collection of Greek and Roman artefacts, including many from Vis. Upstairs (where there are English-language signs) look out for the replica of a bronze bust of Aphrodite (the

Islands of the Adriatic just off the Vis shore.

Entrance to the cave on Vis where Tito and his Partisans sheltered for several months during 1944.

A glimpse of Komiža's harbour.

original is in storage on Vis) that is captioned 'the most celebrated Greek sculpture in Croatia'. Also interesting are vases and amphorae taken from wrecks around Vis.

Across the courtyard, another exhibition space displays amphorae recovered from a Greek wreck in 1971. Thought to date from the 4th century BC, these shed new light on when the Greeks first came to Vis, or Issa as they called it.

During 1944 Tito set up his headquarters in a cave on Vis following the collapse of Italy. Bolstered by the Allies, who were determined to stop the Nazis from recovering the Italian losses, Tito had fled to Vis from Bosnia, transported there by the British navy. The network of underground tunnels and caves made it an ideal location and Tito coordinated many a significant military operation from his cave in Mt Hum above Komiža. Even Winston Churchill visited the island to meet him.

A national shrine in Yugoslav days, it now functions as a not terribly exciting

Well-tended vineyards on Vis produce the excellent Plavac wine.

World War II museum, with carved lyrics celebrating Tito and his troops, exploring a period when the island helped to form the destiny of Yugoslavia and, in many ways, the post-war map of the Balkans.

WINE TASTING

Further towards Kut there are a number of family-run wine cellars (look for signs saying 'Prodajem domaće vino', where you can sit with different generations of local families and taste and buy some of their produce. Vis is renowned for the quality of its wines, with 20 percent of its surface area given over to viticulture. Both the ruby red Plavac and honey-hued Vugava are very drinkable and available for next to nothing. Most families also concoct their own Prošek dessert wines; these vary tremendously but the best of them are an excellent way to round off a meal or to have as an aperitif.

Kut, the old aristocratic quarter, was built by the wealthy Venetian nobles of Hvar as a retreat. The elegant Gothic **St Cyprian's Church** (Crkva sv. Ciprijana) and its bell tower preside over a hillside covered with beautiful Venetian-style homes and family palaces. Look out for the family coats of arms adorning many buildings and the decorative balconies where old women still stoop out to hang up their washing. Several first-rate restaurants have opened their doors in refurbished houses in Kut, offering lovely outdoor settings and lashings of atmosphere.

BIŠEVO, THE BLUE CAVE AND KOMIŽA

The island's main road straddles the mountains on a 10km (6-mile) route across to Komiža, the only other town on Vis, whose livelihood is based on sardines. It is even sleepier than Vis town, except during the daily rush to get the boats out to the nearby island of **Biševo**, the location of the celebrated Blue Cave (Modra špilja). This

is a grotto where the waters are illuminated with a brilliant blue light, a natural phenomenon, often compared with a similar grotto on the Italian island of Capri. The only way to get to the cave is on an organised boat tour or a scuba-diving trip (details available from the tourist office on the Riva in Komiža), with the latter providing the best view of the spectacle. Be aware that the phenomenon happens only in summer – best around 11am – and that all trips are cancelled during rough weather. After visiting the cave, most boat trips stop off for a few hours swimming at Porat Bay (Porat uvala) on the west side of Biševo; it is one of the few sandy beaches on the east side of the Adriatic.

Komiža itself is an unassuming little place with enough distractions for a leisurely few days. The town's single most impressive attraction is the **Church of St Nicholas** (Crkvica sv. Nikole), picturesquely set on a vine-covered bluff overlooking the town and the sea. The church served as a refuge for local people during pirate attacks. The original church on the site dated from the early 12th century, and a monastery has also existed here for centuries, with the present structure owing much to a refurbishment in the 17th century. Look on the church floor for the gravestones of local noble families.

Also worth visiting next door is a sprawling cemetery that enjoys fine views over Komiža, out across the Adriatic and back to Mt Hum (the highest peak on Vis); it also has a number of grand headstones and tombs. On the road up to the church, a track, signposted Plaža (beach), leads down to a series of rocky coves and secluded beaches.

Back in town, in the 16th-century Venetian tower on the promenade (Riva), the **Fishing Museum** (Ribarski muzej; hours vary by season) offers an insight into an industry that is still important to Vis. You can walk around the outer wall of the harbour and you will come across a plaque to British sailors killed off the island during World War II, when Vis was of major strategic importance.

Komiža.

Dubrovnik's harbour.

DUBROVNIK AND ISLANDS

The walled city of Dubrovnik is the most beautiful city on the Adriatic, and offshore lie some of Croatia's most enchanting islands, including Mljet with forest walks, twin lakes and a monastery.

The long sliver of Southern Dalmatia is the domain of one of the most beautiful cities in Europe. Dubrovnik, frequently hailed as the 'Pearl of the Adriatic', was one of the few medieval city-states to fend off all aggressors, ruling over the surrounding towns and maintaining its incredible walls intact.

The city's star status attracts many visitors including daily fleets of cruise ships, few of whose passengers have much opportunity of visiting the parts of the city beyond the walls, or the whole of the rest of Southern Dalmatia, a region rich in beauty and culture. In the north, Korčula is a smaller version of Dubrovnik, while the nearby Pelješac peninsula is one of the country's most bountiful larders. A short drive south are the gardens at Trsteno and quiet resorts such as Slano and Zaton. Some 17km (10 miles) south of Dubrovnik, Cavtat has a spectacular setting between the mountains and the sea. Offshore, the islands are far less developed than those off Central and Northern Dalmatia. Scheduled ferry services are geared more to the needs of local people, but a plethora of excursion boats provides a service for visitors. The most beautiful island is undoubtedly Mljet, about a third of which is a forested national park.

Dissecting the narrow strip of land, just south of the Neretva Delta, is a 10km (6-mile) corridor of land belonging to Bosnia Herzegovina. This once belonged to Dubrovnik but, as the Venetians bit by bit were taking over the coast, it was ceded to the Ottomans in 1699, in the hope that they would act as a buffer against La Serenissima's advance. Today it provides Bosnia with its only outlet to the sea, and the coast around the main town of **Neum** is overdeveloped. The road inland is poor, and visitors planning on trips to **Mostar**, with its famous bridge over the Neretva, need to go back up the Magistrala

Main Attractions
Dubrovnik
Elaphite Islands
Mljet National Park
Cavtat
Ston
Korčula
Trsteno botanical gardens

Maps on pages 198, 200

Cannon guarding the harbour, Dubrovnik.

Tip

There are three places to swim under the Dubrovnik city walls: on the Porporela breakwater by the old port, through a doorway in Ispod Mira Street by St Stephen's Tower and in Od Margarite Street beneath the Buza Café.

to pick up the E73 at Opuzen. Plans by Croatia to build a bridge to skirt around this corridor by hopping across the Neretva Channel (Neretvanski kanal) to the Pelješac peninsula have been debated for some time.

DUBROVNIK

The most attractive settlement on the whole of the Croatian seaboard, **Dubrovnik ①** has prospered within its walls for centuries. The city – Ragusa – was settled in the 7th century by the citizens of nearby Epidaurum (Cavtat), who fled here when it was a small island, to escape invasion. Over the centuries, Slavs settled on the hillside on the mainland opposite, and gradually links between the two settlements grew stronger. In the 11th century, the channel separating the island from the mainland – today's Stradun – was filled in and the two towns became one.

Backed by sweeping limestone cliffs and flanked on three sides by the sparkling Adriatic Sea, Dubrovnik's setting is breathtaking. The water reflects the perfectly preserved fortifications, which, unlike those of most medieval European towns and cities, were not removed to accommodate an expanding population or rendered unnecessary when military technology moved on. The result is a living history book that feels very far from 21st-century Europe. The fact that no motorised vehicles are allowed inside the walls adds to this impression. What detracts from this, however, is the constant flow of tour groups from coach parties and the many cruise liners in the port. Even outside the busy summer months, you're likely to get caught up in a sea of bewildered tourists being rushed through the sights.

PILE GATE

The best place to start a tour of Dubrovnik is **Pile Gate ⓐ** (Vrata Pile), its most dramatic entrance, on the western side of the city. It crosses the old moat, now a leafy garden, and a stone bridge. As you enter the old town, look up to see the statue of the city's patron saint, Sveti Vlaho (St Blaise), the handiwork of the ubiquitous Croatian sculptor Ivan Meštrović.

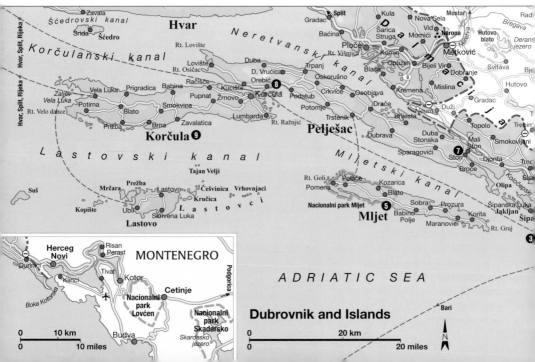

Dubrovnik and Islands

Instead of heading down the steps, take the ramp, which leads to a map detailing the attack by rebel Serbs, volunteers from Montenegro and the Yugoslav Army in 1991–2. This map details the cascade of shells that battered the old town during the fighting. The Siege of Dubrovnik made headline news around the world as the World Heritage-listed city, which had no strategic value nor any real Serb claim of ownership, was attacked from the surrounding hills. In May 1992, Serb forces withdrew, partly as a result of international pressure and partly because by then priorities had changed. Some residents of other Croatian cities, such as Vukovar and Osijek, which suffered greater damage and loss of life, feel that Dubrovnik was helped on account of its appearance and reputation. The fact that Dubrovnik is a World Heritage Site has certainly helped with reconstruction. However, there is no doubt that the residents, who lived for months without electricity and running water, suffered greatly. More than 40 of them, mainly young men, gave their lives in defence of their city and many more were traumatised.

The main artery through the old town is **Stradun** ⓑ (Placa), a wide boulevard of marble that has been polished by the feet of millions of visitors. To take the pulse of the city and soak up some of its ambience, sit for a while on the terrace of one of its cafés (the Café Festival is a good place to start); watch the crowds and admire the architectural details that help the thoroughfare retain its beauty: mellow-stoned buildings with uniform arched doorways and window shutters in the same shade of dark green, and lamp-posts all of the same design.

At the western extremity of Stradun is the **Large Fountain of Onofrio** ⓒ (Onofrijeva fontana), the culmination of a system that has brought fresh water to the city since 1444. The circular domed well, with its 16 water-spouting stone heads, is named after its designer, Onofrio della Cava, an Italian who worked in the Dubrovnik region for a number of years. During the siege it was seriously damaged,

Pile Gate provides the most dramatic entrance to the old town. During the days of the republic, the city gates were locked at 6pm and opened at 6am.

City walls, Church of Our Saviour and Large Fountain of Onofrio.

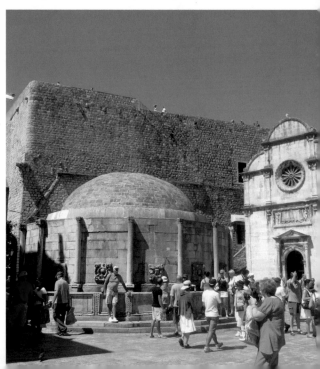

Orlando's Column.

but has now been fully restored. Some tourists consider it lucky to drink at the well, but it was originally intended merely for washing on entering the city. A second fountain, known as the **Small Fountain of Onofrio**, is at the far end of Stradun, next to the clock tower.

Just across Stradun from the well is the **Church of Our Saviour ❹** (Crkva sv. Spasa), built in Renaissance style, and one of the few buildings to survive the great earthquake of 1667. It is usually closed during the day, but is the venue for chamber recitals several evenings a week in summer.

FRANCISCAN MONASTERY

Next door is the **Franciscan Monastery and Museum ❺** (Franjevački samostan; daily Apr–Oct 9am–6pm, Nov–Mar 9am–5pm). If possible, plan an early or late visit to avoid the crowds. On the left as you enter is a delightful little pharmacy, which has been here for centuries and is still functioning today. The lovely Romanesque-Gothic cloisters, which survived the 1667 earthquake, are the work of master stonemason Mihoje Brajkov of Bar. There are double pillars with ornamental capitals, a garden, once used to grow herbs for the pharmacy, and a 15th-century well.

Among the most intriguing exhibits in the **museum** are 14th- and 15th-century objects from the pharmacy, but there are also some fine paintings, among which a 15th-century polyptych featuring St Blaise, by Lovro Dobričević, stands out. The **church** has Baroque altars, replacements for those destroyed in the earthquake, and a plaque commemorating the revered Dubrovnik poet Ivan Gundulić (1589–1638) who is buried here.

LUŽA SQUARE

Continue on down the Stradun, saving until later the little lanes that break away to the north and south, and you will come to the 16th-century **Sponza Palace ❻** (Palača Sponza; daily, opening times vary; free) on the far side of lively **Luža Square**. The palace, a mixture of Venetian Gothic and Renaissance, has had many roles. The word *Dogana* on the

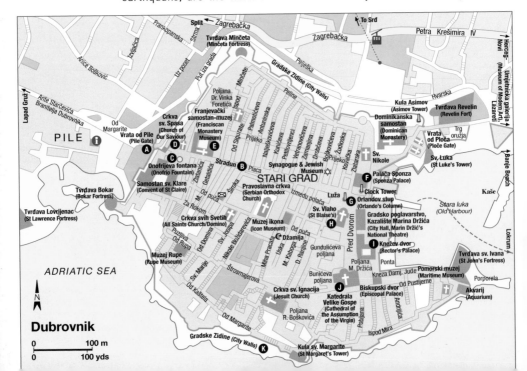

metal studded door indicates that it was once the customs house. The courtyard houses temporary art exhibitions, and is one of the most atmospheric venues for musical performances during the Dubrovnik Festival. Look out for an inscription that served as a warning to shady traders: 'We are forbidden to cheat and use false measures. When I weigh goods, God weighs me.'

To the left of the entrance is the **Memorial Room of Dubrovnik Defenders** (daily May–Oct 9am–9pm, Nov–Apr 10am–3pm; free), with photos of those who died in defence of the city during the 1991–2 siege, some of them little more than boys. Above them are pictures of burning boats and buildings, while a video plays scenes of devastation.

In the centre of Luža Square is **Orlando's Column** Ⓖ (Orlandov stup), also known as Roland's Column. The carved figure of a knight represents Roland, who is said to have helped Dubrovnik vanquish Saracen pirates in the 9th century. Although this is highly unlikely, the statue is a symbol of freedom, and very dear to the city.

It was once used for public proclamations, when citizens of Ragusa came to hear news and decrees, and criminals were exhibited at its foot. Directly in front of the column (if you are facing east, towards the harbour) is the **clock tower**, whose bell is chimed by hammers of little green men.

Behind the column is the 18th-century **Church of St Blaise** Ⓗ (Crkva sv. Vlaho; opening times vary; free), named after the patron saint of Dubrovnik. Above the high altar stands a silver figure of Sv. Vlaho that is paraded through the streets on 3 February each year. The saint is portrayed holding a scale model of the city, providing one of the few records of how Dubrovnik looked before its destruction in the 1667 earthquake. The attractive stained-glass windows, depicting saints Peter and Paul, Cyril and Methodius, are by Ivo Dulčić (1916–75), Dubrovnik's most renowned modern artist.

THE RECTOR'S PALACE

To the left of the church are the imposing buildings of the Town Hall (**Gradska**

⊘ **Tip**

High on Mount Srd above Dubrovnik, the Museum of Croatian War of Independence (daily late Mar–early Nov 8am–6pm, early Nov–late Mar 8am–4pm) has been established in the remains of a Napoleonic fort. The 1960s cable car that had been destroyed in the war has been rebuilt and speeds visitors up to the top for some stunning views.

Cloister of the Franciscan Monastery and Museum.

The colonnaded facade of the Rector's Palace. The rector was a civil leader chosen from the city's nobility.

Stradun.

vijećnica), the **Marin Držič Theatre** and the **Gradska Kavana Arsenal** (The City Café), within the arches of the old arsenal. Next door is the **Rector's Palace ❶** (Knežev dvor), which also houses the Cultural History Museum (Kulturno povijesni muzej; www.dumus. hr; daily 22 Mar–2 Nov 9am–6pm, 3 Nov–21 Mar 9am–4pm). The first palace on the site was erected in 1200, but it was destroyed and rebuilt several times over the centuries. The current palace, incorporated into the remains of an earlier one by Florentine Michelozzo Michelozzi (1396–1472) has a stunning loggia with intricately carved capitals – both Gothic and Renaissance – atop pillars of Korčula marble. Dubrovnik's well-developed democracy limited the rector's term of office to a month, forbade his family to move in with him and banned him from leaving the confines of his palace for anything other than official business. Just in case he should forget his responsibilities, an inscription in the palace also reads: 'Forget personal worries, worry about public matters.' The beautiful atrium is the venue

for summer concerts by the Dubrovnik Symphony Orchestra, and the acoustics are excellent. The staterooms display period furniture and paintings – among them a lovely *Baptism of Christ* (1509) by Mihajlo Hamzić – as well as an unusual collection of clocks.

Outside the palace you will see, to your left, the Baroque **Cathedral ❶** (Katedrala Velike Gospe; usually 8am–8pm; free). Legend has it that the original 12th-century cathedral (all but destroyed in the 1667 earthquake) was commissioned by a grateful Richard the Lionheart, said to have been saved from a shipwreck on the island of Lokrum by the citizens of Ragusa during a journey back from the Crusades.

There are three naves with solid Baroque altars, and a severe, modern, main altar (the earlier one was destroyed in another earthquake in 1979), above which is a School of Titian polyptych. The **Treasury** to the left of the altar is packed with revered objects. Chief among them are an enamelled gold reliquary of St Blaise's head, and reliquaries in delicate gold and

silver filigree of his arms and one leg, which are carried in procession around Dubrovnik on the saint's day, 3 February.

Behind the Cathedral, Gundulić Square (Gundulićeva poljana) is the site of a lively fresh **produce market** every morning except Sunday. A flight of steps leads from the south side of the square to the imposing bulk of the **Jesuit Church** (Crvka Sv. Ignacija; daily 7am–8pm; free), which was completed in 1725, its interior modelled on the Gesù Church in Rome.

DUBROVNIK'S WALLS

The best way to get an idea of the lay-out of the old town is to walk around the **City Walls** ⓚ (http://citywallsdubrovnik.hr; daily June–July 8am–7.30pm, rest of the year times vary). There are entrances by the Pile and Ploče gates and another by St Ivan's Fort in the harbour. The 2km (1-mile) walk can be arduous in the heat of a summer's day and is not recommended for anyone who suffers from vertigo. Early evening is the best time for ambling around the old fortifi-cations, as the fading light softens the

hard lines of the stone and casts peachy hues across the terracotta-tiled roofs. There is surprisingly little evidence of war damage, but look closer and you will see the different shades of the roof tiles. The older tiles were sourced from a local quarry that has long since closed down, so restorers had to import as close a match as they could get from Slovenia and France.

North from the Pile Gate is the high-est point on the walls, the **Minčeta Fortress** (Tvrđava Minčeta), designed by the Florentine artist Michelozzo Michelozzi, though local luminary Juraj Dalmatinac executed his plans. From atop the fort there are great views of the old town rooftops, gardens, domes and spires. Head along the northern wall, peering down into the narrow lanes below, and you eventually come to the **Ploče Gate** (Vrata od Ploča) from where you can see the busy harbour and most southerly bulwark, **St Ivan's Fortress**, which houses the **Maritime Museum** (Pomorski muzej; www.dumus. hr; 22 Mar–2 Nov Tue–Sun 9am–6pm, 3 Nov–21 Mar 9am–4pm). Laid out over

View from Dubrovnik's city walls.

Eat

Those wanting to splash out on a truly memorable dinner in Dubrovnik may like to head for the Nautika restaurant outside Pile Gate. It has great views of the city's fortifications and the Adriatic lapping below.

two spacious floors, the cool, air-conditioned museum gives an interesting glimpse into the history of this maritime city.

As you circle the southern walls, the Adriatic lies on one side while Dubrovnik spreads towards the limestone hills on the other. Eventually you come to the **Bokar Fortress** (Tvrđava Bokar), another creation of Michelozzi and Dalmatinac, from where you can descend to street level, back where you began near the Pile Gate. (If you keep your ticket you can leave the walls and return to them at any of the three entrance points.)

Other sights worth visiting include the **Dominican Church and Monastery** (Dominikanska crkva i samostan; daily 9am–6pm), just inside the Ploče Gate. You enter through a peaceful cloister, where late-Gothic arcades are embellished with Renaissance motifs. In the centre is a huge well that was last used to supply water for the besieged city in 1991–2. There are some excellent paintings by artists of the 16th-century Dubrovnik School in the museum, while

Peeking through the city walls.

the church has a number of modern art works, including a bronze *Virgin and Child* by Ivan Meštrović. The small **Synagogue and Museum** (Sinagoga muzej; May–Sept daily 10am–8pm, Nov–Apr Mon–Fri 10am–3pm) in Žudioska – one of the narrow streets leading north between Stradun and the restaurant-lined Prijeko – is also interesting.

Venture outside the Ploče Gate to visit the **Museum of Modern Art** (Umjetnička galerija; www.ugdubrovnik.hr; Tue–Sun 9am–8pm), a few hundred metres/yds along Frana Supila, which runs beside the sea. It is housed in a beautiful building that looks pure Renaissance but was actually built in 1935 for a wealthy ship owner. The gallery's collection, housed over four floors, with sculpture in the airy courtyard, is rotated, but includes works by Ivo Dulčić and by Vlaho Bukovac (1855–1922), who was born in Cavtat (see page 207).

When your sightseeing is done, join local people and visitors in the pavement cafés on Stradun, where people-watching is the main activity, especially in the early evening when people dress

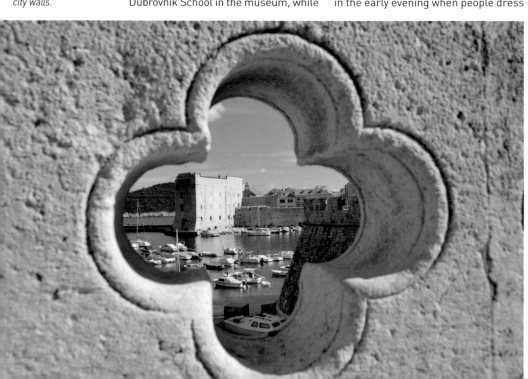

up to stroll up and down and children play on the shiny paving stones. Later, move on to enjoy a seafood dinner in the port or in one of the many restaurants in the narrow side streets of the old town.

BEYOND THE WALLS

Most people staying in Dubrovnik will be in one of the large hotels around **Lapad**, centred on a bay on the northwest of the city, an easy bus journey away. On the same side of the city is **Gruž**, the city's main harbour, where ferries go to the islands and to Italy. A few Renaissance villas remain behind high walls, and there is a daily produce market and local shops. Beyond Gruž is **Rijeka dubrovačka,** the estuary of the River Ombla, which the suspension bridge crosses. The city's main yachting marina is here.

On the opposite, south side of the city, just outside Ploče Gate and beneath the **Lazareti,** is **Banje Beach**, Dubrovnik's recreational shore. Lzareti is the former quarantine station aimed at keeping disease from the city. The half a dozen buildings are today used as workshops and cultural centres, and it is here that the local Lindo folk group regularly performs songs and dances.

Just offshore and a 10-minute boat ride from the old port is the island of **Lokrum**, which makes a pleasant excursion: take your swimming things for a dip. You pay a small charge to step ashore. The former Benedictine monastery was turned into a summer residence by Archduke Maximilian who purchased the island in 1859. There is a café, naturist beach, wooded walking trails, an old fort and peacocks roaming everywhere.

THE ELAPHITE ISLANDS

A huge range of boat trips operates out of Dubrovnik, from Gruž Harbour and Lapad, and from the Old Port. The **Elaphites** (Deer Islands) lie just north of the city. Today any deer that once lived here are long gone, and the human population is much reduced. All three of the inhabited islands, Koločep, Lopud and Šipan, are easy to visit on a day trip from Dubrovnik, but there is accommodation if you want to stay overnight.

Veliko jezero (Big Lake), Mljet.

Mali Ston village.

Fish farms at Putniković village on the Peljesac peninsula.

Nearest to Dubrovnik is **Koločep** ❷, which has two small settlements, Donje Čelo and Gornje Čelo, with just 150 inhabitants between them. The main attractions are wandering through the pine forests and olive groves and relaxing on the sands at Donje Čelo. Slightly further west is **Lopud** ❸, which has the most to offer. In the 15th century it had its own fleet of some 80 vessels and a shipyard; nobles from Ragusa often built summer houses on the island. The town, clustered around a sandy bay, has several grand old palaces, a testament to its golden age. A Franciscan monastery (currently under restoration) has a lovely cloister, and the adjoining church of St Mary of Spilica (beside the elegant Hotel Villa Vilena) can be visited. From the harbour front, lined with restaurants, a path marked Plaža Sunj leads for about half an hour through pine-scented woods, with conveniently situated benches, to the lovely sandy beach at **Sunj Bay**. **Šipan** ❹, the largest of the Elaphites and a 90-minute trip from Dubrovnik, is the most agricultural of the islands, with small vineyards and olive groves. Excursion boats stop at Sudurad and ferries also go to the little settlement of Šipanska Luka.

MLJET NATIONAL PARK

The largest of the Southern Dalmatia islands after Korčula is **Mljet** ❺, a third of which is protected as a national park. It is unspoilt, wild and beautiful and, according to myth, it was here that Ulysses was kept captive for seven years. Several other places make that same claim, but there's no denying that Mljet is as peaceful and bucolic as it comes. A fast catamaran and slower ferries go to Polače, from where a minibus will take you to the **National Park** if you buy a park entrance ticket in the kiosk near the jetty. Polače's ruined Roman walls give little clue that a palace second in size only to Diocletian's once stood here. The main attractions are the saltwater lakes of Malo jezero (Small Lake) and Veliko jezero (Big Lake), which have cycling and walking paths leading around them and off through the pine forests to the village

of Pomena, where there is the island's only hotel and a number of restaurants. Cars are not allowed in the national park, but it's very easy to rent a bicycle. There is also a small boat that goes to **St Mary's Island**, where a 12th-century Benedictine monastery houses a restaurant with tables set out on an attractive terrace.

SOUTH OF DUBROVNIK

The highway continues down the coast, heading around to **Župa dubrovačka**, a community made up of a string of small resorts around the attractive Župa Bay, where the water is beautifully clear and the white pebbly beaches a delight. A handful of small communities, hardly resorts, include Mlini, which takes its name from its water mills, and Srebreno (Silver), the administrative centre. A fragment of 10th-century Glagolithic script, inscribed in stone, has recently been found here.

The relaxed town of **Cavtat** ⑥ (pronounced 'tsavtat') is just beyond the bay. Close to the airport, this is another good springboard for Dubrovnik but it

is also a destination in its own right. There are regular boats from Dubrovnik harbour. Its picturesque houses crowd around a couple of bays that form good natural harbours, which have been attracting superyachts. The waterfront is lined with palm trees, restaurants and cafés, and a 7km (4-mile) promenade circles both bays. At one end is the Renaissance Rector's Palace, part of which contains a museum (Apr–Oct Mon–Sat 9.30am–1.30pm, Nov–Mar Mon–Fri 9am–1pm) dedicated to the scientist Baltazar Bogišić and the Baroque parish church of St Nicholas. At the other end is the **Franciscan Monastery Church** (Franjevački samostan crkva; usually open; free) with an eye-catching polyptych of St Michael (1510) to the left of the door, the work of Vicko Dobričević. The street behind the church leads up to a cemetery containing one of sculptor Ivan Meštrović's most important works, the **Račić Family Mausoleum**, built for a wealthy shipping family in 1922. Constructed of white Brač stone, it is adorned with angels, rams and eagles. From behind

A Pelješac winery.

The walls of Ston and the fortress on Podzvizd hill.

THE ADRIATIC HIGHWAY

Keep your eyes straight ahead – if you can – as you head down Croatia's beautiful but challenging coastal road that winds and curves its way along the Dalmatian coast.

The Adriatic Highway (Jadranska Magistrala) is one of the world's great corniches, heading south from its starting point in Rijeka and dramatically following the coast into Montenegro. It is a stretch on the European route E65, a chain of major roads that starts in Malmö in Sweden and ends 3,800km (2,400 miles) away in Chaniá, Greece. The Magistrala is undoubtedly the most picturesque part of it, and also the most potentially hazardous. Much of it is a single-lane road wedged between karst mountains and the sea, chasing the curves and contours of the edge of the land, with lanes tipping over the side to reach hidden villages below.

Bit by bit, new motorways are extending down the coast – and running parallel inland – though in some parts of this narrow strip of coast, there simply isn't room for another road. This is taking much of the traffic, including lorries, away from the Magistrala, but it can still be a pretty slow road, especially in

Maslenica Bridge.

high summer. Hindered by lorries and hairpin bends, drivers can become impatient and take risks. There is also a danger that a tourist, finding so much to see, forgets to concentrate on the road.

The E65 from Zagreb reaches the Adriatic at Rijeka, meeting the coast road that has swept round from Istria and the Opatija Riviera. Keeping hard by the sea, the Adriatic Highway plunges down towards Split, passing village after village and offering broad views across Kvarner. Just south of Rijeka, a turning leads off to the island of Krk, reached by a bridge that bad weather – notably the *bura* wind – can keep closed for days.

The Magistrala scurries past to Karlobag, beneath the Velebit mountains, Croatia's only biosphere reserve. (The northern part of the Velebit mountains cover 109 sq km (42 sq miles) and form the Northern Velebit National Park, the newest national park in Croatia, formed in 1999.) Ducking under the A1 main road coming down from Zagreb it then crosses into Dalmatia over the Maslenica Bridge, which had to be rebuilt after the Homeland War. This bridge may also be closed in high winds, in which case you may go back to the A1, rejoining the highway shortly afterwards to continue into Zadar.

From Zadar the road continues along the edge of the sea and through Krka National Park and crosses the River Krka shortly before arriving in Šibenik. It continues down past the fine beaches and vineyards around Primošten to Trogir and Split, which definitely need checking out. At the small port of Ploče the road skips over the islands of the Neretva Delta, returning to the coast at Kremena before sneaking through the brief seaward incursion of Bosnia Herzegovina, where you must be prepared to show your passport.

On then beneath the karst cliffs of southern Dalmatia, round the little bays of Slano and Zaton – with no sign of the famous Trsteno botanical gardens hidden down below, between the highway and the sea. Then it's over the Franjo Tuđman suspension bridge to reach the walls of Dubrovnik, scraping by the Minčeta Fortress in its northern corner. Then on to the last lap, which passes by Cavtat and Dubrovnik airport, before heading off into Montenegro where a bridge is planned to cross the Verige strait to shorten the highway around the Kotor fjord.

the cemetery there is an attractive walk all the way round the peninsula.

Halfway along Cavtat's harbour front, in a steep narrow street, is **Kuća Bukovac** (www.kuca-bukovac.hr; Apr–Oct Mon–Sat 9am–6pm, Sun 9am–2pm, Nov–Mar shorter hours), the birthplace of the artist Vlaho Bukovac. His works form the bulk of the collection, with changing exhibitions featuring contemporary artists.

The region south of here, down to Montenegro, is **Konavle**, an agricultural district where the silk moth is cultivated and the silk used in local costumes worn at the Sunday folk gatherings in **Čilipi**. Hillside hamlets make up **Pridvorje,** a town eulogised by Dubrovnik's Renaissance poets. Now a series of hamlets, the community includes a Franciscan monastery and a former palace of the rector of Konavle.

THE PELJEŠAC PENINSULA

The Magistrala is soon back in Croatia where it funnels down towards the Pelješac peninsula, whose mountains rear up on the horizon across the Neretva Channel. Pelješac is renowned for its fine food and wine: the first-rate red wines Dingač and Postup both originate from the peninsula, and the seafood is legendary, with huge mussels, lobster, oysters and many kinds of fish.

The twin villages of **Ston** ❼ and **Mali Ston** (Little Ston), either side of a narrow isthmus connecting the peninsula to the mainland, are two unspoilt little backwaters. But you can see at once from the 5km (3 miles) of fortified walls that link the two settlements across a hill that these have had glory days. The walls of the great fortress **Veliki Kaštio** are the longest in Europe, and date from 1333, when the rapidly expanding city of Ragusa (modern-day Dubrovnik) bought the town and wanted to protect it – as well as the surrounding salt pans – from attack. Sections of the walls were taken down in the 19th century, but the remaining parts withstood Serbian shelling in 1991 and an earthquake in 1997, both of which wrecked parts of the town below. While its historical merits are intriguing, most Croatians come here to eat and drink.

Korčula town.

On the beach at Slano.

View from Marco Polo Tower, Korčula.

Just offshore from the tiny fortified port of Mali Ston, fishermen can be seen working the fertile waters of the Neretva Channel in small wooden boats, and a crop of poles indicates the mass of oyster beds. Fresh from the boats, oysters, mussels and a lot of other fish and seafood are served in a handful of restaurants that hug the waterfront.

Ston, the larger of the two villages, lies a kilometre to the southwest, and it is from here that you can clamber up the wall to the Pozvizd Fortress, with views down both sides. The village is an attractive little place, with an ornate Rector's Palace and a tree-shaded central square.

The road out of Ston into the peninsula passes the great salt pans, still in use, and heads into the winelands, where produce can often be bought direct from the vineyard. There are beaches and a handful of small resorts on the peninsula. On the south side, ferries go to the island of Mljet (see page 206), while ferries cross the Neretva Channel on the north side from Trpanj to Ploče.

The largest town on the peninsula is **Orebić** ⑧, with wonderful sweeps of sandy beaches, ideal for a family holiday. Windsurfers take off from here, too. Its reputation otherwise rests on its native sea captains who were famous in the days of sail, and its seafaring past is laid out in a small Maritime Museum. The 15th-century Franciscan monastery high on the hill overlooking the town and the coast has some interesting works of art, and there are some good walks to be had in these hills.

KORČULA

From the port of Orebić, car and passenger ferries cross to the nearby island of **Korčula** ⑨ (the island also has ferry links to Dubrovnik, Hvar and Split), though many visitors leave their cars at the port and take a passenger ferry. Korčula town is the main attraction, a walled, chocolate-box ensemble of terracotta-hued roofs and spires, set on its own peninsula. The medieval town plan is straightforward and makes walking around easy: the main

thoroughfare runs right through the heart of the old centre and a waterside boulevard circles the peninsula.

The town's most impressive building is **St Mark's Cathedral** (Mon–Sat May–Sept 9am–7pm, Apr and Oct 9am–5pm, by appointment rest of the year), constructed, like most of Korčula's buildings, from the mellow limestone that made the island, and its stonemasons, famous. The tower and cupola, dating from around 1480, are the work of Marko Andijić, whose sons, Petar and Josip, worked on numerous prestigious buildings in Dubrovnik, including the Sponza Palace and the Rector's Palace. The triple-naved interior of the basilica is impressive, with a blend of architectural styles, in which Gothic and Renaissance predominate.

There is a Tintoretto altarpiece (1550) depicting saints Mark, Bartholomew and Jerome, who were credited with helping to stave off the Ottomans when they besieged the town on their way north to the Battle of Lepanto in the 16th century. The cathedral also contains a School of Tintoretto *Annunciation*.

Next door to the cathedral is the **Treasury Museum** (Opatska riznica; same hours as the cathedral), which crams a surprising number of works by an eclectic array of artists into its small confines. The building was restored in the 17th century with the addition of an attractive hanging garden. Spread across seven small halls, the museum contains works by Bassano, Carpaccio and various Croatian luminaries, as well as gold, silver and porcelain artefacts, medieval pottery and, in a stone-flagged kitchen, a huge number of Roman pots and jars, recovered from the sea in the 1960s.

The **Town Museum** (Gradski muzej; https://gm-korcula.com; July–Sept Mon–Sat 9am–9pm, Oct–June Mon–Fri 10am–3pm) is housed in an impressive 16th-century palace opposite. The story of Korčula is told here, from the arrival of the Greeks through to modern times. The stories of Korčula's famous stonemasons and shipbuilders are covered in some detail; there are costumes, furniture and photos of Tito's Partisans. Signs in English help to illuminate the collection.

Not far from the cathedral square, in Ulica Depolo, you can visit the **Marco Polo Tower** (May–June and Sept 9am–3pm, July–Aug 9am–9pm, by appointment rest of the year), adjoining the building where the explorer was said to have been born in 1254 (see page 211). There are stunning views from the top of the tower, and the attached building – a graceful, ruined palace – was renovated and turned into a Marco Polo Museum (Muzej Marka Pola; daily May–June and Sept–Oct 10am–7pm, July–Aug 9am–9pm) in 2012. The nearby church of **St Peter** (summer daily), a simple little chapel with a facade featuring reliefs by the Milanese artist Bonino, has an extremely kitsch exhibition portraying the life of Marco Polo.

⊙ MARCO POLO

A number of families today on the island of Korčula bear the name of de Polo, and it is entirely likely that Marco Polo was born here in 1254. The town has documents going back to its original communal statute of 1214, which gave the town some degree of independence from the Venetians on whom they relied for business. At the time of Marco Polo's birth, the island had come under the domain of the Venetian duke of Dubrovnik. There are documents mentioning the Polo family being from Dalmatia, and archives on the island have a document from 1430 of a Mateo Polo applying for land for shipbuilding. The Polos had shipbuilding yards on the shores on both sides of the town and there were also smiths, stonemasons, tradesmen, priests and notaries in the family. After he had returned from his legendary travels to China, Marco Polo went to live in Venice. It is thought that it was while he was on a ship in the Venetian fleet that engaged the Genoan fleet at the battle of Korčula in the Pelješac Channel in 1298 that he was captured and imprisoned in Genoa, where he dictated his book of travels to a fellow prisoner, the writer Rustichello da Pisa. He was released the following year and his book (pre-printing press) became a bestseller. The adventurer settled in Venice as a famous and increasingly wealthy merchant, where he died at the age of 70. Korčula celebrates his birthday every May.

All Saints' Church (Svih svetih), to the southeast of town, was founded at the start of the 14th century and has one of the most impressive Baroque altarpieces anywhere in the country, a *Pietà* by the Austrian sculptor Georg Rafael Donner. There is also a beautiful 15th-century polyptych by Dalmatian artist Blaž Trogiranin. The ceiling was a later addition, designed by Tripo Kokolja, an artist from present-day Montenegro, who died in Korčula town in 1713. Next door is the **Icon Museum** (Zbirka ikona; Mon–Sat June–Sept 9am–2pm, May and Oct 10am–1pm, by appointment rest of the year), housed in the Hall of the Brotherhood of All Saints.

Outside the city walls, the **Church and Monastery of St Nicholas**, on the harbour-side, were founded in the 15th century and later embellished in Baroque style. Look out for the medallions in the monastery, attributed to Tripo Kokolja.

One of Korčula's most colourful traditions can be enjoyed within the old town throughout the summer.

The Moreška sword dance has been performed in the town since the 15th century, and a dance that used to be performed only on special occasions is now seen about twice a week in the summer months. It's a dramatic spectacle as two rival kings fight over a veiled princess in a highly stylised sword fight that is compelling to watch.

After you have covered Korčula's sights, relax on the **beaches** around the town. Luka Korculanska, a safe sandy beach with shallow water, is just 15 minutes' walk away. There is also a string of good beaches near the town of **Lumbarda** to the south of the island, and at **Blato**, a pleasant village to the west. There are excellent local wines on sale all over the island, although you will really need your own vehicle if you want to explore deeper into the smaller villages and the vineyards. If you came as a foot passenger, scooters and cars can be hired in Korčula town, and there are taxis and taxi boats to take you to the beaches.

St Peter's Church, Korčula.

SLANO TO ZATON

South from Ston, the highway curls into a deep bay at **Slano** ⓾, a well-protected yachting resort. It's a small village, with just over 500 inhabitants, but it has several beaches and is in striking distance of Dubrovnik (27km/17 miles away), making it an option as a place to stay. Illyrian burial mounds and the walls of an old Roman fortress attest to Slano's historical importance, and after the village came under the control of Ragusa in 1399 villas and palaces were built here for the nobility. The Franciscan church has a triptych by the 15th-century artist Lovro Dobričević.

Another worthwhile stop on the route south to Dubrovnik is **Trsteno** ⓫, where there is an early 16th-century **Arboretum** (daily May–Oct 7am–7pm, Nov–Apr 8am–4pm). Croatia's oldest botanical gardens were created by the aristocratic Gučetić family in 1502, although local legend claims that they originated from a single oak planted by a member of a Dalmatian noble family as he set out for the Crusades. The central fountain, with statues of Neptune and nymphs, and the accompanying aqueduct, were added in 1736. Serb shelling destroyed a quarter of the gardens in 1991 and a substantial fire in 2000 further hampered their renaissance. However, painstaking reconstruction work and the rejuvenating microclimate of Trsteno have combined to bring the gardens back to life. Parking can sometimes be difficult, but you can get round the problem by parking in the private car park of the café at the garden's entrance and enjoying a drink in the shade of the lime trees.

The 18km (11-mile) drive from Trsteno to Dubrovnik runs along a beautiful stretch of coast with good views across a number of islands, including Mljet in the distance (see page 206) and the Elaphite Islands (see page 205), easily accessed from Dubrovnik. Some 8km (5 miles) from Trsteno you reach the seaside resort of **Zaton** (divided in two – Veliki and Mali), in a deep bay that causes the highway to scuttle inland around farmland. This was another choice spot for Ragusa's nobility to build summer villas.

All Saints' Church, Korčula.

MONTENEGRO EXCURSION

A small, wild, mountainous nation – neighbouring Montenegro has scenic splendour from peaks to shore and it can be visited on a day excursion from Dubrovnik.

Visitors to Dubrovnik have the opportunity of a day excursion to the Bay of Kotor (Boka Kotorska), which lies just over the border in Montenegro 40km (25 miles) to the south. Behind the bay is the old royal city of Cetinje, and further forays into the sunny mountainous country a quarter of the size of Croatia will reward the more intrepid traveller. One of the best – and certainly the cheapest – ways to stay in Montenegro is to rent a room. Montenegrins keep their doors open and are universally hospitable. Ask in any café where you can find lodgings.

The old section of Kotor.

KOTOR FJORD

A World Heritage Site, the huge **Kotor Fjord** is a sunken river canyon, 28km (16 miles) long and 30 metres (100ft) deep, with four distinct bays. It is the southernmost fjord in Europe and is a breathtaking sight, especially for anyone arriving by boat. The bay has a number of beaches, resorts and small islands, and much of the ancient architecture in the fishing and boat-building villages is from the Venetian period.

The road runs around the bay from the resort of **Herceg Novi** to reach **Risan**, the oldest settlement, adjoining a smaller, inner bay. Here are remains of a Graeco-Illyrian acropolis and some impressive Roman mosaics, particularly one representing Hypnos, the god of sleep. Beyond Risan is **Perast**, the last city in the Venetian Republic to surrender to the French. Its elegant Venetian buildings make it one of the most attractive towns in the bay, and there are even a few remaining people who speak a Venetian dialect called Perasto. Offshore are two small islands with pretty churches.

The road soon reaches **Kotor**, set spectacularly beside the bay. Kotor's delightful old town is encircled by sturdy walls and it is a pleasure to wander its music-filled streets. The most important among its impressive palaces and churches is the Romanesque cathedral of St Tryphon, which has 14th-century frescoes and a rich treasury. The excellent seafood restaurant Galion, with a view of the bay, is alone worth the trip.

The airport for the region is 4km (2.5 miles) outside **Tivat**, a largely 19th-century town in the southernmost bay. The naval base built by the Austrians is now in private hands and has been turned into Porto Montenegro, with 800 berths for superyachts and the depressing ambition of becoming the Monaco of the Adriatic.

BUDVA RIVIERA AND THE NATIONAL PARKS

Beaches and resorts continue down the coast to the Budva Riviera (Budvanska rivijera), a playground with 11km (7 miles) of fine sandy beaches. Its beauty is at great risk of being eroded, unfortunately, as development has been racing along at dizzying speed. Construction cranes are a ubiquitous sight as foreign buyers – usually Russian, judging from the advertising hoardings – fill every available space. Budva does have a very attractive walled old town, though, which was almost entirely rebuilt after an earthquake in 1978. The most picturesque place on the Budva Riviera, however, is **Sveti Stefan**, some 6km (3.7 miles) southeast of Budva. This small islet is connected to the mainland by a narrow walkway and has been turned into a five-star resort with 50 rooms, cottages and suites. Non-residents are charged an entrance fee, but the views are worth it.

Shortly after Budva, at the pretty village of Petrovac, the main road leaves the coast and heads inland to the capital, Podgorica, crossing the northern end of **Lake Skadar.** This is the largest lake in the Balkans, shared between Montenegro and Albania. Now a national park (Nacionalni park Skadarsko jezero), it has abundant birdlife and has adopted the scruffy-looking curly pelican as its emblem.

Montenegro has several other national parks. **Biogradska Gora**, based at Kolašin, has glacial lakes, streams, virgin forest and mountains topping 2,000 metres (6,500ft). At Eko Katun Vranjak, above Kolasin, you can stay in mountain huts and enjoy rural life. But the main focus of mountain tourism – climbing in summer and skiing in winter – is the **Durmitor National Park**, around the Durmitor massif, cut through with magnificent canyons such as the 80km (50-mile) Tara River Canyon, which descends 1,300 metres (4,250ft).

CAPITAL CITIES

Montenegro's capital, **Podgorica**, is a modern, workmanlike city of around 140,000. Much of it was destroyed in World War II, but there is still an old Turkish quarter and some interesting restored churches. The city has an active cultural life, and socialising takes place out of doors in the main square, Trg Republike.

Montenegro's old royal capital is **Cetinje**, on the inland road between Podgorica and Kotor, and it remains the country's cultural and educational centre. Its museums and galleries provide an idea of Montenegro and its past. These include an art museum with the most valuable murals in Montenegro. Icons can also be seen in the Museum of Cetinje Monastery. The National Museum is housed in the palace of Nikola I Petrović Njegoš, Montenegro's only king, who reigned from 1910 to 1918.

The Petrović ruling family came from Njeguši, in the nearby **Lovćen National Park**, which extends over twisting mountain roads behind Kotor. Traditional farm buildings are scattered around the park, and there are fine views over the coast that are hard to forget.

Picturesque Sveti Stefan.

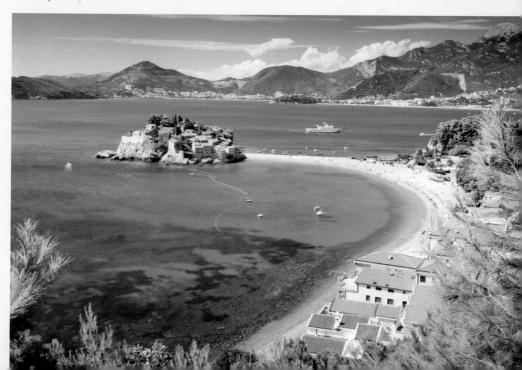

Guardian angel, Zagreb Cathedral.

ZAGREB AND AROUND

With its medieval Upper Town and elegant Lower Town, Zagreb is typical of many Central European cities. But its vibrancy is wholly its own, fuelled by one of Europe's youngest populations.

A city of over one million inhabitants, **Zagreb** ① (www.zagreb.hr) has come a long way since 1991, when Serbian rockets hit the suburbs and President Tuđman narrowly escaped assassination in a Yugoslav air raid as he sat in his presidential palace. Today, bustling Zagreb has wholeheartedly embraced capitalism and modernisation and – partly thanks to low-cost carriers – become an increasingly popular city-break destination.

The city has a scenic location, spread out on a plain with the Sava River sealing off the older parts of the city from the post-World War II suburbs and the hulk of Mt Medvednica, often visible to the north. The city's old sections in Gradec and Kaptol in the Gornji grad (Upper Town) are reminiscent of Prague or Riga, while in the Donji grad (Lower Town), a grid-like 19th-century central business district, neon lights and designer shops have moved in alongside the elegant Austro-Hungarian buildings.

Zagreb was never designed to be a capital and at times, especially in July and August when many of its residents head to the coast, it can feel more like a provincial Austrian city than a European capital. At its best, though, on a warm spring or autumn evening when the cafés are full to bursting point, it is an invigorating place to be. The young Croatians in the clubs and bars are every bit as style conscious as their counterparts in London or Milan. Expanding in parallel with Zagreb's nightlife scene and café culture are its hotel and restaurant industries, which have had huge improvements since independence. Zagreb's success as a business centre is partly due to its central location and good transport links: Austria, Hungary, Slovenia, Italy and Bosnia are all within easy driving distance.

Main Attractions

The Cathedral
Dolac Market
Lotršćak Tower
St Mark's church
Meštrović Atelier
Varaždin
Trakošćan Castle
Krapina
Samobor
Plitvice Lakes

Maps on pages
218, 220, 238

Zagreb's Dolac Market.

Zagreb and Around

0 —————— 10 km
0 —————— 10 miles

N

SLOVENIA

Maribor
Poljčane
Kozminci
Žetale
Zlogonje
Opeka
Varaždin ②
Trnovec
Nagykanizsa
Rogaška Slatina
Rogatec
Greda
Beretinec
Beletinec
Jazbina
Dvorac Trakošćan ③
Donja Voća
Bednja
Bednja
Ivanec
Lepoglava
Ljubešćica
Madžarevo
Golubovec
Novi Marof
Burmanec
Mihovljan
Krapina
Ivanščica
Mače
Donja Batina
Breznica
Sudovec
Zlatar Bistrica
Donja Bistrica
Bedenica
Marija Bistrica
Gornje Orešje
Krušljevec
Crkva Marije Bistrice ⑤
Zelina
Šelovac
Rakovec
Krkač
Donja Zelina
Sveta Helena
Belovar-Moravče
Lonja
Lonjica

Celje
Svetina
Trbovlje
Hrastnik
Zagorje
Laško
Breze
Šentjur pri Celju
Smarje pri Jelšu
Mestinje
Man Tabor
Veliki Tabor ⑥
Bežanec
④
Krapina
Rimske Toplice
Mišji dol
Lesično
Podčetrtek
Desinić
Valentinovo
Krapinske Toplice
Podkum
Radeče Hotemež
Orešje
Bistrica
Podsreda
Muzej Staro selo (Staro Selo Museum)
Kumrovec ⑦
⑧
Klanjec
Zabok
Oroslavje
Stubičke Toplice
Sljeme
Kašina
Čučerje
Sveta Helena
Breg
Bizeljsko
Veliko Trgovišće
Krapina
Donja Pušća
Medvednica
Vrhovo
Boštanj
Sevnica
Senovo
Pečice
Stara vas
Dubravica
Zaprešić
Jablanovec
Popovec
Graneština
Dugo Selo
Čatež
Trebnje
Mokronog
Zbure
Raka
Krško
Brežice
Donja Harmica
Sava
Zagreb ①
Sesvete

Dobrnič
Mirna Peč
Novo Mesto
Gmajna
Krška vas
Mokrice
Bregana
Samobor
Stupnik
Rakov Potok
Brezovica
Velika Gorica
Rugvica
Obedišće
Ivanić-Grad
Topolje
Kutina

Soteska
Podturn Dolenjske Toplice
Jugorje
Šentjernej
Dolenje Mokro polje
Šmarje
Oštrc
Vilinske jame
⑨
Galgovo
Klinča Sela
Jastrebarsko
Kupinec
Buševec
Pešćenica
Trebovec
Oborovo
Stari Log
Vrčice
Gradac
Planina
Štrekljevec
Radovica
Metlika
Kupa
Krašić
Novaki
Črna Mlaka
Bratina
Dubranec
Lukinić Brdo
Gornji Hruševec
Dužica
Trebarjevo
Sela
Palanjek
Sisak

Mozelj
Kneža lipa
Zagozdac
Dragatuš
Adlešiči
Žuniči
Donje Stative
Gornje Pokupje
Donje Pokupje
Jamnička Kiselica
Letovanić
Odra-Sava
Sisak

Laze
Stari trg
Netretić
Karlovac ⑩
Luka Pokupska
Skakavac
Sišljavić
Dugo Selo Lasinjsko
Pokupsko
Petrinja
Pračno

Vele Drage
Vinica
⑪
Turanj
Cerovac
Vukmanić
Sjeničak Lasinjski
Bović
Gornje Taborište
Gora
Taborište

Skrad
Ravna Gora
Bosanci
Vukova Gorica
Duga Resa
Belavići
Korana
Brezova Glava
Vojnić
Slavsko Polje
Gornja Čemernica
Prekopa
Marinbrod
Blinja
Jabukovac

Višnjevica
Gomirje
Trošmarija
Toplice Lešće
Generalski Stol
Budačka Rijeka
Radonja
Petrova gora
Perna
Topusko
Maja
Dodoš
Dragotina
Miočinovići

Bjelolasica
Ljubošina
Hreljin Ogulinski
Perjasica
Miholjsko
Kristinja
Veliki Obljaj
Gornji Klasnić
Donji Zirovac

Klek
Zdenac
Donji Poloj
Veljun
Dunjak
Maljevac
Velika Kladuša
Bojna
Brezovo Polje
Zrin

Ogulin ⑬
Skradnik
Hrvatski Blaga
Glina
Tatar Varoš
Cetingrad
Mala Kladuša
Zborište
Gvozdansko
Struga

Josipdol
Gornje Primišlje
Tobolić
Slunj
Donji Ladjevci
Šturlić
Bužim
Varoška Rijeka
Donji Žirovac
Ravnice
Međumajdan
Dvor

Partizanska Drežnica
Munjava
Plaški
Jezero
Gornja Močila
Tržac
Krakača
BOSNIA AND HERZEGOVINA
Bosanski Novi
Javnica

Čubrin vrch
Zrnići
Makovnik
Lipice
Lička Jesenica
Drežnik-Grad
Gornji Vaganac
Bužim
Cazin
Jezerski
Otoka
Bosanska Krupa

Krivi Put
Vratnik
Križpolje
Jezerane
Brinje
Mala Kapela
see Plitvice Lakes map
Poljanak
Plitvica
Plitvička Jezera
Plitvička jezera ⑫
Gornji Vaganac
Izačić
Donja Gata
Ostrožac
Pištaline

Prokike
Letinac
Glibodol
Dabar
Drenov Klanac
Javornik
Donji Vaganac
Donji Petrovo Selo
Grmuša
Veliki Radić
Donji Dubovik

Sveti Juraj
Žuta Lokva
Kompolje
Glavace
Zalužnica
Plitvički Ljeskovac
Homoljac
Vrelo
Bihać
Pokoj
Grabež
Zalin
Japra

Velebit
Naravni rezervat Velebitski botanički vrt
Švica
Otočac
Babin Potok
Plitvička jezera Nacionalni park
Veliki Skočaj
Gudavac
Donja Suvaja
Jasenica
Hašani

Mali Rajinac
Kuterevo
Ćovići
Rudinka
Lika
Donji Kosinj
Dreniac
Korenica
Zavalje
Veliki Skočaj
Ripač
Gorjevac
Baraka

Aniči
Naravni rezervat Zaštinjo područje
Split

ORGANISING YOUR VISIT

If time is short, one can cover Zagreb's sights in a day by spending the morning in the Donji grad and the afternoon in the Gornji grad. But this only scratches the surface of the city, as places such as the Mimara Museum and the Meštrović Atelier can take a whole day in themselves. On the outskirts are several attractive natural attractions such as Lake Jarun, Maksimir Park and Mt Medvednica, as well as Mirogoj, one of Europe's most beautiful cemeteries.

It is also worth exploring the city's cultural life. Zagreb attracts musicians and thespians from around the world and there are good venues for theatre, opera and classical music. The huge Maksimir Stadium hosts big pop and rock acts as well as football teams Dinamo Zagreb and the Croatian national team.

On a more traditional note, there is the Zagreb International Folklore Festival in July, celebrating Croatia's rich folk-culture tradition and welcoming folk groups from all over Europe.

LOWER TOWN AND KAPTOL

A good place to start a tour of the Donji grad is outside the main **railway station** Ⓐ (Glavni kolodvor), which neatly divides the most interesting parts of the city (Donji Grad and Gornji grad) to the north from the modern post-World War II suburbs to the south. From the station Zagreb's central parks are visible as well as the spires of the cathedral in the distance. Designed by the Hungarian architect Ferenc Pfaff, the station opened in 1892 when Zagreb became the main gateway to Vienna and Budapest. Its pastel-yellow neoclassical facade retains something of its original splendour and there is an old steam train on display just to the east of the passenger platforms.

Just across the tramlines in front of the station, the chunky statue of King Tomislav I welcomes new arrivals from his horse, with an outstretched sword raised in one hand. Tomislav was the first king of Croatia (925–8) and Robert Frangeš-Mihanović's depiction of the monarch

Art Pavilion in Trg Tomislava.

has become a popular central meeting place for the locals as well as one of the most recognisable symbols of the city.

Stretching north of the equestrian statue is the elegant **Trg Kralja Tomislava B**, the first of a string of parks extending north towards the city's main square and its oldest quarters. In summer Trg Kralja Tomislava is alive with students reclining on the benches, backpackers trying to catch some sleep between train rides, and inline skaters gliding around the fringes. At the northern end is the yellow Art Nouveau **Art Pavilion C** (Umjetnički paviljon; www.umjetnicki-paviljon.hr; Tue–Thu and Sat–Sun 11am–8pm, Fri until 9pm), which

holds regular temporary exhibitions and has a good restaurant. In front of the pavilion look out for the statue of the Croatian Renaissance painter Andrija Medulić by the sculptor Ivan Meštrović (see page 179).

The next park is dedicated to Bishop Josip Juraj Strossmayer (1815–1905), proponent of pan-Slavism, which contains the **Strossmayer Gallery of Old Masters D** (Strossmayerova galerija starih majstora; http://info.hazu.hr; Tue 10am–7pm, Wed–Fri 10am–4pm, Sat–Sun 10am–1pm), founded by the Slavonian prelate in 1884. Today it houses a collection of work by Italian masters such as Tintoretto and Veronese, dating from the 14th to 19th centuries,

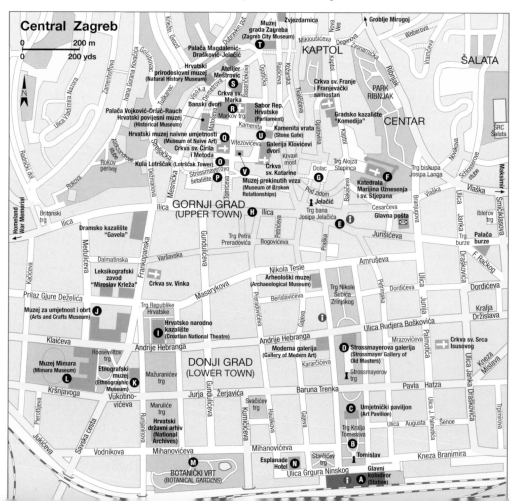

Central Zagreb

as well as paintings by Dutch masters, including Brueghel, and the less well-known Croatian painters Andrija Medulić and Federiko Benković.

Look out for the statue of Strossmayer by Ivan Meštrović, himself a campaigner for pan-Slavism, outside the gallery.

Walk north for another five minutes through the green belt of parks, past the fountains and sculptures, to Zagreb's heart, **Trg bana Josipa Jelačića ⓔ**, which rapidly dispels many preconceived notions of what a former Communist city might look like. Funky modern trams zip across a square packed with Armani-suited professionals chatting into the latest iPhones, bright-shirted students and selfie-stick-toting tourists. Presiding over the scene are the elegant facades of some of Zagreb's most impressive Austro-Hungarian-era buildings.

At the centre of the square, and a popular meeting place, is the equestrian statue of Count Josip Jelačić of Bužim, the work of Viennese sculptor Anton Dominik Ritter von Fernkorn (1813–78). When the Communists took power after World War II they removed Jelačić's statue, deeming it to symbolise the drive for an independent Croatia. But they never finished the job of disposing of the statue and it ended up in storage. During the early 1990s and the backlash against Communism, it magically reappeared to reclaim its place in the heart of Zagreb's main square.

THE CATHEDRAL

From the square take a detour from the Donji Grad, up the small Kaptol hill to the elegant **Cathedral of the Assumption of the Blessed Virgin Mary and St Stephen ⓕ** (Katedrala Marijina Uznesenja i sv. Stjepana; Mon–Sat 10am–5pm, Sun and public holidays 1–5pm), where another work by Fernkorn stands outside. This startling gold Madonna is surrounded by four equally striking angels. An earlier Romanesque church existed on the site, and the first cathedral dates back to the time of the first Croatian

Cathedral of the Assumption of the Blessed Virgin Mary, Zagreb.

⊘ MIROGOJ CEMETERY

There is no question that the smartest place to be buried in Zagreb is in the Mirogoj Cemetery (Groblje Mirogoj; www.gradskagroblja.hr) – one local joke suggests that most of its tombs are better than many homes in the city. Built in 1876, it occupies the site of the summer mansion of Ljudevit Gaj, the leader of the Illyrian Movement. After his death, the local authorities bought the land and commissioned the naturalised Croatian architect Hermann Bollé to design the cemetery, which is divided according to religion. The entrance is suitably grand, with high ivy-clad walls, neoclassical colonnades, cupolas and a large central dome. Inside lie many of Croatia's artistic, military and political luminaries, including President Franjo Tuđman, laid to rest here on 15 December 1999. His grave is not as elaborate as his character suggested it might be, but like many of the tombs it receives plenty of fresh flowers and candles.

Some of the tombs are works of art in their own right. In particular, look out for Ivan Meštrović's bust of painter Vladimir Becić (1886–1954) and work by fellow Dalmatian sculptor Ivan Rendić (1849–1932). The cemetery is also home to a collection of sculptures, giving it the feel of a huge open-air art gallery. Getting to Mirogoj is easy. Take the No. 106 bus from outside the cathedral on Kaptol (journey time 15–20 minutes). Entrance is free.

○ Eat

At 18 Ilica, Vincek sells arguably the city's finest ice cream, in myriad flavours, along with excellent cakes and pastries. The queues are slow but well worth it.

kings in the 10th century. Today's incarnation has its origins in the 13th century, but there have been countless modifications and revamps over the years, the most significant following a catastrophic earthquake in 1880. Outside the cathedral look out for the walls built to protect it from Ottoman attacks.

Inside, the high central nave appears stark and bare, but there is plenty to see. The most controversial part of the cathedral is the tomb of Archbishop Alojzije Stepinac, a man convicted under Tito of high treason and war crimes for colluding with the Nazi puppet regime established in Croatia during World War II, although later exonerated and beatified by Pope John Paul II. Whatever the politics, Ivan Meštrović's relief of Christ with the bishop is striking. Look out also for a series of 13th-century frescoes that have survived the cathedral's numerous traumas. The treasury above the sacristy is home to Baroque banners and tapestries, as well as church plate.

The neoclassical National Theatre.

Dolac Market ⒢, just a short walk down the hill from the cathedral, offers a glimpse of Zagreb life that is a world away from both the calm and order of the cathedral and the slick modernity of Trg bana Josipa Jelačića. Every morning this raffish square becomes a bustling produce market selling fruit and vegetables fresh from the countryside. There are a number of basic restaurants and cafés above the market – one open all hours – where you can have breakfast and survey the activity.

MEMORIALS AND MUSEUMS

Stretching away to the west from Trg bana Josipa Jelačića is **Ilica** ⒣, at 6km (4 miles) the longest street in Zagreb, and probably the oldest, as it dates back to Roman times. Ilica is the haunt of Zagreb's nouveau riche, who come here to buy designer-name fashion and to see and be seen. On a more sombre note, much further along Ilica (take tram Nos 6 or 11) is the **Altar of the Homeland** (Oltar domovine), with the names of

the Croatian dead inscribed across the bricks.

A 10-minute walk west of Vincek, at 18 Ilica (see margin box), and south down Frankopanska is the **Croatian National Theatre ❶** (Hrvatsko narodno kazalište; www.hnk.hr) dating from 1894. Just outside the theatre, look out for an early sculpture by Ivan Meštrović (1905). *The Well of Life*, a small fountain enclosed by a sprawl of bronze figures, lies just below street level. On the same square is fellow sculptor Fernkorn's vivid depiction of *George Slaying the Dragon*.

Just across Runjaninova is the **Arts and Crafts Museum ❶** (Muzej za umjetnost i obrt; https://en.muo.hr; Tue–Sat 10am–7pm, Sun 10am–2pm), designed by Croatia's leading architect, Herman Bollé (1845–1926), who also designed the grandiose Mirogoj Cemetery (see page 222). The exhibits include a wide range of ceramics and furniture as well as textiles. The top floor houses clocks, silverware and glass, while the second displays domestic ceramics and furniture. The

ground floor has religious art, porcelain and more furniture.

A block further south is the **Ethnographic Museum ❷** (Etnografski muzej; www.emz.hr; Tue–Fri 10am–6pm, Sat–Sun 10am–1pm), mainly devoted to costume. The ground floor displays indigenous clothing, with everything from traditional peasant attire to military uniforms, while the lower level has an eclectic range of exhibits brought to the city by adventurous Croatians from all corners of the globe. Other artefacts include weapons and musical instruments as well as fine examples of the intricate lace produced for centuries on the Kvarner island of Pag.

Behind the Ethnographic Museum is the **Mimara Museum ❸** (Muzej Mimara; July–Sept Tue–Fri 10am–7pm, Sat 10am–5pm, Sun 10am–2pm, Oct–June Tue–Wed and Fri–Sat 10am–5pm, Thu 10am–7pm, Sun 10am–2pm), founded on the 4,000-strong collection of a mysterious Dalmatian collector called Ante Topić Mimara, who died in 1987. It was never clear how Mimara

The Botanical Gardens.

The Mimara Museum, devoted to fine art and archaeology.

The short Zagreb funicular was built in 1890 and is less than 100 metres (328ft) long.

Museum of Naïve Art.

had made his fortune and the collection has been the subject of much controversy. Taken at face value, it is one of Europe's great art galleries with an exciting range of European masters, but the art world has cast doubts on the authenticity of some of the paintings. On show are works attributed to Raphael, Caravaggio, Rembrandt, Rubens, Van Dyck, Velázquez, Gainsborough, Turner, Delacroix, Renoir, Manet and Degas.

The museum, which is a work of art in itself, also has an extensive archaeological collection, again amassed by Mimara. It includes classical pieces from antiquity as well as the Vučedol Dove. The China collection contains 300 pieces of indigenous art. There is also a rich collection of sculpture, including works by Rodin, della Robbia and Verrocchio.

BOTANICAL GARDENS

Walk south towards the railway line and just before you get there head back east along Mihanovićeva to one of the city's most charming and relaxed oases, the **Botanical Gardens** Ⓜ (Botanički vrt; www.botanic.hr; Apr–Oct Mon–Tue 9am–2.30pm, Wed–Sun 9am–7pm, closes earlier in autumn; free). Though modest in comparison with the world's great botanical gardens, Zagreb's version still makes a pleasant diversion on a warm day. The gardens were opened in 1890, their design influenced by gardens in France and Britain. The network of paths, ponds and greenhouses includes some 10,000 plant species.

From the Botanical Garden it is only a five-minute stroll further east to the railway station where this tour began, but first it is worth popping into the **Hotel Esplanade** Ⓝ, occupying a prime position across from the railway station and fronted by a large fountain. Built in 1925 to cater for the discerning needs of the passengers of the Orient Express, it is regarded as Croatia's classiest hotel. The Art Deco foyer is dazzling, with funky clocks showing the time in various world cities. You can have lunch or dinner here, or just relax with a coffee

in its pavement café. At night you can return to the casino to mingle with Zagreb's influential elite.

UPPER TOWN

The Upper Town, or Gornji grad, is home to Gradec, the oldest part of the city. It still retains much of its medieval shape, though many parts of the original defensive walls have been dismantled or destroyed over the centuries. The fun way of getting to the Gradec is to take the old **funicular**, built in 1888. It rumbles up the hill from just off Ilica, revealing views of Donji grad and its blend of 19th-century and modern architecture as it goes. At 55 seconds, it is probably the world's shortest funicular ride. The funicular was initially steam powered before electrification during World War II, and it originally had first- and second-class carriages. If you are feeling energetic, you can walk up the stairs beside the tracks.

Across from the funicular terminus in Gradec is **Lotrščak Tower O** (Kula Lotrščak; June–Sept Mon–Fri 9am–9pm, Sat–Sun 10am–9pm, Oct–May Mon–Fri 9am–7pm, Sat–Sun 10am–7pm), a sturdy construction topped by an orange-tiled roof and an observation deck offering sweeping views of the city. The lower floors of the tower have a souvenir shop and a modest and regularly changing array of modern art, some of which is for sale. Be alert as it approaches midday, when a single cannon round goes off. This was originally meant to scare off the Ottoman threat; today it serves only to sort the tourists from the locals.

Walk east of the museum to enjoy the views from **Strossmayer Parade P** Strossmayerovo šetalište), built in the 19th century when the town walls were removed. You can see Donji grad falling away below, the cathedral to the left and Novi grad (New Town) spreading over the far bank of the Sava River to the south. This tree-lined boulevard has benches and old-fashioned gas lamps, as well as a silver-finished bronze figure of Modernist literary hero Antun

St Mark's Church.

The distinctive roof of St Mark's Church.

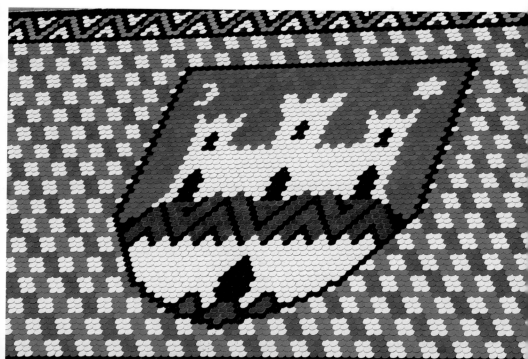

Gustav Matoš (1873–1914) reclining on a bench, the work of Ivan Kožarić.

Continue north from the terminus of the funicular and you will soon come to the **Croatian Museum of Naïve Art**  (Hrvatski muzej naivne umjetnosti; www.hmnu.org; Mon–Sat 10am–6pm, Sun 10am–1pm), housed in an old palace. The naïve tradition in Croatia originated amongst untutored painters in the rural areas and was developed by Krsto Hegedušić. He scoured the Croatian interior looking for local artists, whom he found in abundance, and the results are on show in the gallery's six rooms. Some of the key names to look out for are Ivan Generalić, Franjo Mraz and Ivan Lacković, with the most startling work a portrait of Sophia Loren – something of a departure from the traditional depictions of rural life.

ST MARK'S AND MEŠTROVIĆ ATELIER

Attending church on All Saints' Day.

Zagreb's most distinctive church, restored to glory after a 25-year project, is **St Mark's** Ⓡ (Crkva sv. Marka), which looks like something out of a Grimm fairy tale with its chequered red, white and blue roof tiles incorporating the Croatian coat of arms in its design. The roof's colourful pattern was added at the end of the 19th century, but the church dates back to the 13th century. The interior, perhaps more arresting than that of Zagreb's cathedral, includes one of Ivan Meštrović's best works, a haunting depiction of the Crucifixion with the figure of Christ stretched out in the sculptor's typical style.

After a day or two in Zagreb you may feel that you have had your fill of this Split-born artist, but the **Meštrović Atelier** Ⓢ (Atelijer Meštrović; www.mestrovic.hr; Tue–Fri 10am–6pm, Sat–Sun 10am–2pm) is worth visiting. The 17th-century house where he lived from 1924 to 1942 contains sketches and plans for some of his most significant projects, such as the Crucifixion in nearby St Mark's Church and the statue of Grgur of Nin, outside Diocletian's Palace in Split. The museum helps to fill in the blanks about Meštrović and provides a useful context for the statues, sculptures and reliefs that dot the city.

Further north on Opatička is the **Zagreb City Museum**  (Muzej grada Zagreba; www.mgz.hr; Tue–Sat 10am–7pm, Sun 10am–2pm; free guided tour Sat and Sun 11am). As the name suggests, it tells the story of the city from medieval times to the present, using well-constructed arrangements and information in English as well as Croatian. The scale models of Zagreb show how the city has metamorphosed over the centuries. The most interesting section covers Zagreb during the 1990s war.

From Gradec, a good route back down towards Trg bana Josipa Jelačića is Tkalčićeva, an old cobbled lane that hugs the old walls. Today it's lined with cafés, where the young and trendy congregate on summer evenings. Running parallel to Tkalčićeva is Radićeva, which also ends at Trg bana Josipa Jelačića, with interesting shops and a few more cafés on the way. It passes close to the 13th-century **Stone Gate**  (Kamenita vrata), the only one of four city gates still standing. It contains a small chapel, built to commemorate a fire of 1731 that razed the wooden buildings huddled about the gate but left a picture of the Virgin Mary unscathed. The chapel is a place of pilgrimage.

MUSEUM OF BROKEN RELATIONSHIPS

Before you return to Donji grad, visit one of Zagreb's most innovative and compelling attractions, the **Museum of Broken Relationships**  (Muzeij prekinutih veza; www.brokenships.com; daily June–Sept 9am–10.30pm, Oct–May 9am–9pm) near Lotrščak Tower. The humblest of objects from around the world tell poignant, funny and often bitter stories of love found and lost – from shattered mirrors broken in anger to intensely moving letters of bereavement. It's at once uplifting, thought provoking and spellbinding.

Rural landscape around Kumrovec village, in the Zagorje region.

View over Gradec, the oldest part of Zagreb, with the chequered roof of St Mark's visible.

Ⓞ DAY OF THE DEAD

Roman Catholics worldwide celebrate All Saints' Day (1 Nov) and All Souls' Day (2 Nov), also known in Croatian as Dan Mrtvih (the Day of the Dead) or Dan Spomina na Mrtve (Remembrance Day). The first is an occasion to revere all the martyrs and saints one might not have got around to remembering the rest of the year, while the second is a chance to pray for the souls of lesser mortals who might need a helping hand from the living to ease their path heavenwards. Croatians mark All Saints' Day by attending church and lighting candles over the graves of loved ones. It is a marvellous time to visit Mirogoj Cemetery – where practically the whole population of Zagreb decamps in late afternoon – to experience the eerie glow of the candles after dark.

⌕ CAFÉ CULTURE

These days, Zagreb's café culture is stronger than ever, with young citizens often preferring to spend their evenings with espressos rather than getting drunk on beer.

Coffee and café culture have been part of the fabric of social life in Zagreb ever since the days of the Austro-Hungarian occupation, when the best Viennese brews were all the rage. These days, during warmer months, all Zagreb seems to be reclining in a pavement café, as tables sprout up everywhere. Even during cooler months, at the first glimpse of sunshine locals will be out looking for a table in the sun.

A café is a *kavana* and a *kafić* is more like a café-bar, though both sell coffee and alcohol and often a variety of pastries and ice cream, and both close around midnight. *Kafići* tend to be popular with youngsters. A *slastičarnice* is a patisserie, where there is no alcohol, but a full range of coffees backed up by a wider range of snacks, ice creams and cakes than either *kavane* or *kafići* offer.

Coffee and newspapers in a café on Radićeva.

The range of coffees available in the Croatian capital is almost as confusing as the different venues for drinking it in. If you ask for a simple coffee (*kava*) you can usually expect a heart-pumping espresso, and many *kavane* open well before rush hour to allow bleary-eyed citizens their pre-work caffeine shot. *Kava s mlijekom* is an espresso slightly diluted with a dash of milk, closely related to the *macchiato* that Dalmatians enjoy. *Bijela kava* is quite simply 'white coffee', similar to a latte, while most cafés also serve up an at least acceptable cappuccino (*kapučino*). *Kava sa šlagom* is a highly calorific coffee loaded with a dollop of full-fat cream.

The city centre is the best place to experience the vibrant café culture. One of the liveliest streets, Tkalčićeva, winds down the Gornji grad's eastern edge. The street has more than a dozen cafés, many open late into the night in summer, some not getting going until after 10pm. Some of the street's best coffee is at Argentina (No. 9) and Café Bar Bonn (No. 22), while Cica (No. 8) has probably Zagreb's most comprehensive range of artisan *rakija* (fruit brandy).

If you want to fit in with the local cognoscenti on Tkalčićeva, don your trendiest clothes and begin with a quick espresso in one café, making sure everyone notices you as you go in, and then cruise up and down the cobbles a couple of times, before deigning to favour another lucky café with your presence. This time, just order an extravagant coffee creation and spin it out for an hour or so. Repeat until the cafés close, when you can move off with fellow poseurs to one of the city's chic nightclubs.

Trg bana Josipa Jelačića has a couple of notable long-established cafés that tend to be busiest during the day. Belonging to the eponymous hotel, the best is the classy Dubrovnik, a meeting place for politicians, journalists and business people. Its coffee is excellent, served in Viennese style with a glass of water, and its sumptuous cakes and ice cream are divine. There is an outdoor terrace for drinks and snacks.

Another fruitful district is Trg Petra Preradovića and Bogovićeva, where myriad cafés rub shoulders with shops and bars. Bogovićeva is the place for the peculiar Saturday ritual of *špica*, when, from 10am till 2pm, locals come out in their finest clothes just to walk around to be seen.

CITY ESCAPES

The largest park in Zagreb is **Maksimir** (www.park-maksimir.hr), a short ride east from Donji grad on tram No. 11 or 12 from Trg bana Josipa Jelačića. Covering 316 hectares (781 acres), the park owes its appearance to a makeover in 1843 that was modelled on the English garden concept. It has artificial lakes, meadows, oak forests, a zoo, a café (mobbed on summer weekends) and a large somewhat dilapidated stadium founded in 1912. It hosts the home matches of both Dinamo Zagreb and the Croatian national football team, but plans are afoot to build a more suitable replacement.

To the southwest of Donji grad, accessible by tram from Trg bana Josipa Jelačića (tram No. 17), is **Lake Jarun** (Jezero Jarun), Zagreb's 'artificial sea', another popular destination in summer. The park spreads around a rowing lake and there is a small shingle beach as well as several cafés. On summer evenings it is a favourite haunt for teenagers, who head here from the city centre at around 10pm, bringing their own drinks with them.

BEAR MOUNTAIN

To the north of the city, the bulk of **Mt Medvednica**, meaning 'Bear Mountain', beckons, its cooling breezes a godsend on a scorching summer's day. It offers a range of hiking trails and – if you are feeling particularly energetic – you can ascend to the peak of Sljeme, at a height of 1,035 metres (3,396ft), though a cable car will take you most of the way. In winter, when conditions are right, a modest ski run operates, with equipment available for hire.

It is possible to walk west from the Sljeme peak to **Medvedgrad** (Bear Town), a fortress on the forested slopes. (Allow three hours each way.) Built c.1250 to ward off Tartar attacks, it fell into a dilapidated state before a reincarnation as the Altar of the Homeland (Oltar domovine). An eternal flame burns in the interior and the site has become a controversial symbol of the rapid nation-building that has taken place in Croatia, with solemn state ceremonies and re-enactments of medieval battles held in a fortress that can claim no deep historical

⊙ Tip

For an easy escape from the heat and dust of Zagreb head down to the banks of the Sava River immediately south of the centre. Take a tram to the foot of Miramarska and descend to the riverbank from there.

View over Medvedgrad fortress and Zagreb from Medvednica mountain.

> **Tip**

You may be able to catch a football match at Varaždin's modern football stadium, where the local team Varteks inspires civic pride. The Croatian national team also occasionally plays here.

significance and was just a ruin until the 1990s. It also houses a museum and a fine restaurant with north Croatian specialities.

AROUND ZAGREB

Tourists mostly overlook it, yet this region has scenery every bit as spectacular as the coast's. Its outstanding attraction is the Plitvice Lakes region.

The Plitvice Lakes are by no means Central Croatia's only scenic attraction. Head north and west of Zagreb and you'll find rugged heavily forested hills forming a natural border with Slovenia and Hungary. These natural fortifications have put the region in the very fault line of political and religious Europe for centuries, when Christian Europe stared over the brink of the Ottoman Empire to the south. Both the Croats and the Serbs lay claim to this region, which spelt trouble in the Homeland War of the 1990s when fighting rippled through the eastern sections of Central Croatia. The conflict began around the Plitvice Lakes when the rebel Serbs overran the

Stari Grad Fortress, Varaždin.

national park, which is a Unesco World Heritage Site.

Today, the Plitvice Lakes are back on the tourism map, and the northern city of Varaždin is on the 'tentative list' for World Heritage status from Unesco. Other attractions north of Zagreb include a string of castles that used to form the old defensive line and a number of spa towns, built to cater to the 19th-century fashion for spas among Austro-Hungarians. Head farther south and the Samobor Hills are a popular weekend retreat for the citizens of Zagreb. They offer gently rolling hills, a rustic way of life, clean air and high-quality wines, produced on a pleasingly local scale.

South of Zagreb is Karlovac, once a bulwark against the Ottomans and more recently where the Croats made a desperate stand against the rebel Serbs and the Yugoslav army. Had the city fallen, the Serbs could have rolled up the motorway all the way to Zagreb. The scars of war are evident in Karlovac and the neighbouring village of Turanj, where an outdoor Homeland War museum is one of few of its kind in the country.

On the southern reaches of Central Croatia before Kvarner, travellers can choose between heading straight for the Plitvice Lakes or heading to the port city of Rijeka. Either route has plenty to recommend it.

NORTH OF ZAGREB AND THE ZAGORJE

The E71, part of the A4 motorway, runs north from Zagreb towards the Hungarian border, providing easy access to the **Zagorje**, a picturesque mountain region replete with trim villages, hilltop castles and spa retreats. Long a favourite getaway for Zagreb's inhabitants, this bucolic oasis receives few tourists and traffic is relatively light even at the peak of high season.

The city of **Varaždin** ➋ is an excellent base for exploring the Zagorje, though it is possible to access the region by taking a number of day trips from Zagreb using public transport or, more conveniently, with a hired car. Varaždin itself has enough to see to justify a few days' stay; Unesco is even considering including its historic Baroque core, popularly known as the Karlovac star (Karlovačka zvijezda), for inclusion on the list of World Heritage Sites.

The best place to start a tour of the city is at its original raison d'être, the **Stari Grad Fortress** (www.gmv.hr; Tue–Fri 9am–5pm, Sat–Sun 9am–1pm), a whitewashed 16th-century creation that looks more appropriate for a fairy tale than a battle. Scramble up the old grass mounds to get a real feel for its history, on the frontier between Christian Europe and the Ottoman Empire. When the Turkish threat finally receded, Stari Grad fell under the control of the wealthy Erdödy family, which gave it a more elaborate appearance in keeping with its new domestic purpose.

The fortress was converted into a branch of the city museum in the 1920s. This is well presented with clear displays, helpful explanations in English and friendly English-speaking staff. The exhibits, spread over several rooms, include rifles, pistols, axes and swords from the old frontier days. Look out in particular for the hallway lined with bullet-studded 19th-century wooden hunting targets that were given to the winners of local hunting competitions as trophies. In one wing is the simple St Lovro Chapel (Kapelica sv. Lovre), with its novel mobile altar and wide slits for firing cannons, which enabled a quick turnaround from chapel to artillery position. In the basement, accessed on the way to the exit, there are often temporary exhibitions showcasing the work of local artists.

From the fortress, head through the only gate that remains from the original city walls and you will come to the small Trg Miljenka Stančića, which has a hard-to-resist café and Varaždin's **Old and Contemporary Masters' Gallery** (Galerija starih i novih majstora; www.gmv.hr; Tue–Fri 9am–5pm, Sat–Sun 9am–1pm). The gallery is housed

⊘ Eat

A culinary speciality of Varaždin, usually served with coffee, is the Varaždin roll (*varaždinski klipići*), a type of breadstick made of flour, salt, milk, caraway, sugar, egg and fresh yeast. The town square is a good place to try it.

Varaždin's old town.

⊘ Tip

In September, Varaždin, itself a celebration of Baroque architecture, hosts the Varaždin Baroque Evenings (Varaždinske barokne večeri; www.vbv.hr), a 10-day celebration of chamber music in suitably period venues.

in a grand old 17th-century palace and features the modern work of local artists as well as a number of Dutch, French and German paintings.

BAROQUE ARCHITECTURE

Proceed down Kranjčevića to **Franjevački trg**, an impressive boulevard lined with restored homes of Varaždin's wealthy merchants, a sign that much has been done to restore Varaždin's Baroque splendour. The city's richest merchants and nobles used to build their ostentatious homes and palaces on Franjevački trg and their coats of arms and various symbols adorn many of the buildings.

Also on Franjevački trg is the hulk of the Franciscan church of **St John the Baptist** (Crkva sv. Ivana Krstitelja), inside which are some interesting 18th-century frescoes. Just outside the church look out for a copy of Ivan Meštrović's *Bishop Grgur of Nin*, a much smaller version of the original statue that presides over the northern entrance to Diocletian's Palace in Split. The polished and gleaming toe is

The church of St Mary of Bistrica.

evidence of local faith in the efficacy of the statue as a good luck charm.

Head east along Franjevački trg and you will come to the expanse of **Trg kralja Tomislava** and its brace of pavement cafés. Lording it over the square is the Town Hall (Gradska vijećnica), dating from 1533, though today's incarnation is largely a Gothic reconstruction. During civic events the local guard, the Purgari, don their immaculate blue uniforms and parade proudly past the Town Hall. Local pageantry also takes over on Saturdays with an elaborate changing of the guard ceremony. On the same square look out for the **Jaccomini House** (Kuća Jaccomini), an old confectionery shop whose interior is adorned with stucco decorations bearing the initials of its original owner.

A short stroll southeast is Varaždin's **cathedral** (katedrala), whose opening times are erratic, though you can always peer into the interior through the windows of the main door. This portal bears the coat of arms of the Drašković family, local nobles who were

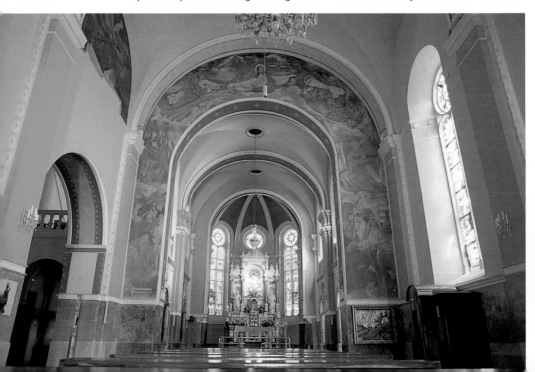

influential in the region for centuries. Inside, the highlight is the extravagant multicoloured altarpiece with its panoply of saints, angels and cherubs.

The most bizarre museum in Varaždin is without doubt the **Entomological Museum** (Entomološki odjel; www.gmv.hr; Tue–Fri 9am–5pm, Sat–Sun 9am–1pm), housed in the Herzer Palace. More than 10,000 insects, painstakingly mounted and displayed by Franjo Košćec, make up the collection. Košćec was a local high school teacher who dedicated much of his life to his unusual hobby, opening the museum in 1954 and bequeathing it to the city in 1959. His daughter, Ružica Košćec, herself a biology professor, took up the reins from 1962 until 1980 and further expanded the collection.

Varaždin is also a good place to try the cuisine of the Zagorje, especially as dining out here is shockingly cheap by Croatian standards. The city's bakers have a formidable reputation. Culinary specialities include a stodgy but very popular snack called *štrukli*, a cottage-cheese pastry. Also often on the menu are turkey with *mlinci* (a form of pasta) and buckwheat porridge. Those with a sweet tooth may want to try the traditional sugary cake *zlevka*. And as well as the local wines there is the tasty local Knaput beer.

TRAKOŠĆAN CASTLE

The Zagorje is renowned for its gloriously Baroque castles, which line this mountainous region, some just crumbling old ruins and others spruced up as tourist attractions. Arguably the most impressive castle and less than an hour's drive west of Varaždin is **Trakošćan Castle** ❸ (Dvorac Trakošćan; www.trakoscan.hr; daily Apr–Oct 9am–6pm, Nov–Mar 9am–4pm), parts of which date from the 13th century. The castle is associated with the ubiquitous Drašković dynasty, who lorded over Trakošćan from the 16th century right through to the early part of the 20th. Today's incarnation owes much to a late 19th-century reworking, which nearly bankrupted the family. Some point out that their rather outlandish tastes mean that some of the embellishments

Trakošćan Castle.

The impeccable ramparts of Trakošćan.

Statue of Tito in the Staro Selo Ethnographic Museum, Kumrovec.

have more in common with Disney than defence, but that does not deter the citizens of Zagreb and Varaždin, who make secular pilgrimages here in droves on summer weekends.

Once most visitors have delved inside the castle they head straight back to their cars and return home, but it is worth exploring the castle grounds too. The narrow tree-shrouded lake offers an opportunity to escape the crowds, good views of the castle and also, if you are lucky, encounters with the resident deer. The only noise to break the bucolic calm are the annoying pedalos that thump around the lake – great for kids, but an aural intrusion for others.

HUŠNJAKOVO

A short drive further east from Trakošćan Castle is the town of **Krapina ❹**. It is home to one of the most important Palaeolithic sites in the world, **Hušnjakovo**, on a hill on the edge of town. The bones of dozens of Neanderthals and various animals, as well as a scattering of artefacts such as

scrapers and stone axes, possibly dating from 30,000 BC, were found here in the late 19th century. The Krapina Neanderthal Museum (Muzej krapinskih neandertalaca; www.mkn.mhz.hr; Apr–June and Sept Tue–Sun 9am–7pm, July–Aug Tue–Fri 9am–6pm, Sat–Sun 9am–7pm, Mar and Oct Tue–Sun 9am–6pm, Nov–Feb Tue–Fri 9am–4pm, Sat–Sun 9am–5pm) re-creates Neanderthal and Stone Age life in innovative multimedia displays in a cave-like structure, while the grounds outside the museum invite you to follow trails through the woods thought to be used by prehistoric man.

Krapina itself is an appealing town in one of the prettiest parts of the Croatian Zagorje. The old core of the town is a little ramshackle, with nothing much to do apart from try one of the cafés or restaurants. A short walk away from the centre is the Franciscan monastery (Franjevački samostan) and the attached church of St Catherine. Look out for the coat of arms above the entrance, the symbol of the Keglević family who paid for its construction

⊘ WINE TASTING

Croatia overflows with vineyards, with the most celebrated wines coming from Dalmatia and Istria. All over the country, though, there are tiny pockets in which top-quality wine is produced in inauspicious surroundings. One of the best areas is the Samobor Hills, a short drive out of Zagreb to the southwest, where the quite sweet white wine is similar in some respects to German Riesling.

Many Zagreb citizens like to spend their weekends in the rolling hills, stocking up on wine. The hills are covered in vineyards, with a number of wine cellars open to the public (makeshift signs welcome visitors). In Croatian, wine cellar is *kleti*; so look out for signs pointing you towards the small-scale, often family-run, operations.

Public transport around the Samobor Hills is not very extensive or efficient; you need your own wheels to explore the area. If you want to stay the night, there are several good-value hotels dotted around the road from the town of Samobor towards Jastrebarsko (which eventually joins up with the motorway south to Karlovac).

The hearty local food is well worth trying and works well with the local wines. A scenic spot for lunch is the Restoran Ivančić in the village of Plešivica. Its pleasant terrace offers sweeping panoramic views out over the Samobor Hills.

in the 17th century. Also outside the town, in and around the Krapina and Sutla rivers, are opportunities for hunting and fishing, which one can organise from the town. Krapina also has a livelier cultural scene than most of the other settlements in the Zagorje, with regular classical concerts and exhibitions.

After Krapina, those on a day trip may want to head back south on the motorway to Zagreb, possibly making a relaxing stop off at the spa town of Krapinske Toplice on the way (see page 236) or to the pilgrimage church of **St Mary of Bistrica** ❺ (Crkva Marije Bistrice), southeast of Krapina, whose Black Madonna, dating from the late 15th century, draws hundreds of thousands of pilgrims each year. The statue was discovered in 1684, immured in the church wall, where it had been hidden from the Ottomans some 34 years previously. Apparently, a miraculous beam of light had indicated its presence. The current church, designed by Hermann Bollé, architect of Zagreb's cathedral and Mirogoj Cemetery, is a good place to see Croatian piety in action – in particular the many women who come to petition the Madonna. Regular buses run direct from Zagreb.

TOWARDS SLOVENIA

It is well worth exploring the area bordering Slovenia. One of the most dramatic features of this region is **Veliki Tabor** ❻ (www.veliki-tabor.hr; Apr–Sept Mon–Fri 9am–5pm, Sat–Sun 9am–7pm, Mar and Oct Mon–Fri 9am–4pm, Sat–Sun 9am–5pm, Nov–Feb daily 9am–4pm), a ruggedly impressive fortress presiding over the surrounding countryside. The original fortifications on the site date back to the 12th century, though today's version is mainly the result of a 15th-century renovation. The sturdy construction and orange slate roof may not be as magical as Trakošćan, but the castle feels more real and there are fewer visitors.

Further west and a little south, close to the border with Slovenia, is the unassuming village of **Kumrovec** ❼ (direct bus and rail connections with Zagreb). It would have remained

Veliki Tabor fortress.

Grapes on the Samobor Hills.

Samobor is renowned for its vineyards.

as sleepy and unheralded as any other village in this hilly region were it not for its most famous son, Josef Broz (Tito), who was born to a local peasant family in 1892 when the region was part of the Austro-Hungarian Empire. The house where the future Yugoslav president was born is said to have been the first brick building in the village. In 1947 it was revamped by the Zagreb Museum of Arts and Crafts and in 1948 a statue of Tito by the Croatian sculptor Antun Augustinčić (1900–79) was erected. Those travelling to Kumrovec just to visit the house may be a little disappointed, as there is little to see bar one of his old uniforms and some mementoes.

More interesting is the **Staro Selo Ethnographic Museum** (Muzej staro selo; www.mss.mhz.hr; Apr–Sept daily 9am–7pm, Mar and Oct Mon–Fri 9am–4pm, Sat–Sun 9am–6pm, Nov–Feb daily 9am–4pm), formerly the Marshal Tito Memorial Museum, which was set up in the old quarter of Kumrovec in 1953. This open-air attraction has more than 40 19th- and

early 20th-century buildings that shed light on the way of life in Tito's day. On show are dwellings, a blacksmith's, a toy shop, a pottery, a gingerbread-maker's and a vintner's, as well as a school, displays on local wedding traditions and musical instruments. There are even a few rooms for those who want to stay the night in Tito's old stamping ground, and a restaurant serving local dishes.

KRAPINSKE TOPLICE

As well as the castles and pretty scenery, Zagorje has some wonderful spas. Many came to the fore during the 18th and 19th centuries when spa bathing was all the rage for the moneyed classes of the Austro-Hungarian Empire. One of the best spa towns, conveniently located if you are on the way back to Zagreb, is **Krapinske Toplice** ❽. The temperature in its thermal pools varies from lukewarm to extremely hot, with the cooler pools large enough to swim in.

The most obvious way of getting back to Zagreb is by joining the Slovenia–Zagreb motorway, but there is an alternative. After Krapinske Toplice spa, avoid the motorway junction and instead head south on the minor road that runs alongside the motorway for a while before rambling off through the countryside. This old main road is a lot quieter and much more enjoyable for those not in so much of a hurry, as it takes a far more languorous approach to the capital.

SOUTH OF ZAGREB AND THE SAMOBOR HILLS

Heading south of Zagreb the temptation is to join Croatia's busiest road, the motorway to Karlovac, which is fine if you are in a rush to get to the coast. However, if you have your own transport and want to take a more interesting route, head southwest out of Zagreb towards the vine-clad Žumberak region and specifically the Samobor Hills. Just

20km (12 miles) from Zagreb, the town of **Samobor** ❾ is a scenic little place. It is known for a number of epicurean treats, such as *samoborska kremšnita*, a delicious warm vanilla custard cake, *bermet*, a deep red aperitif that is something of an acquired taste, and *samoborska muštarda*, a fine mustard that has been produced in the town for more than a century and which goes well with a range of local meat dishes. The town also has a lively pre-Lenten carnival, with parades, traditional masks and a firework display.

If you want to take your exploration of Samobor beyond eating *kremšnita* in one of the glut of cafés on Trg kralja Tomislava, then you will find that the town has an interesting history. In the Middle Ages it was on a par with emerging Zagreb and it came to prominence in the 19th century when composer Ferdo Livadić was part of the movement to awaken Slavic consciousness amidst the confines of Austro-Hungarian domination. His story unfolds in his old house, which Franz Liszt once visited, on Trg kralja Tomislava, now the **Town Museum** (Tue–Fri 9am–3pm, Sat 10am–2pm, Sun 2–7pm in summer/10am–5pm in winter). It also contains paintings of local luminaries, as well as displays of crude farming implements gathered from the surrounding fertile farmland.

If you are keen to work off the effects of the *kremšnita* further, then you can also head out on one of the hiking trails around Samobor. Hiking is popular with the citizens of Zagreb, who gather here on summer weekends. Tito held one of his first clandestine Communist Party meetings near Samobor under the guise of the annual hiking festival. The easiest trail is just up from the town to its old medieval castle, but there are many different options, though for some of them you may want to drive farther on to the village of Veliki Lipovec and set off from there.

Delving further south, the road cuts through picturesque scenery with rolling hills, tiny churches, villages of little more than a few houses and husband-and-wife farming teams on ancient tractors. The area is also covered in

A walkway brings visitors close to spectacular falls in the national park.

Try local foodie treats in Samobor.

⊘ Drink

Karlovac is home to what many beer-lovers rate as Croatia's number one brew. Karlovačko is a 5.2 percent full-flavoured lager with a pleasant aftertaste and few additives. According to locals, it will not give you a hangover.

Hundreds of species of flora grow in the park.

vineyards and is renowned for the excellent quality of its wine, something that few tourists really discover. The best times to visit are at weekends when the vineyards are open to visitors – the many cars from Zagreb will provide guidance on where to go (see page 239).

The road through the Samobor Hills leads south and ultimately joins the motorway to **Karlovac** ⑩, a city often overlooked by tourists as they sweep past on their way to the Adriatic Sea. Karlovac is well worth a stop off, though, both for its Austro-Hungarian heritage and for its pivotal role in the Homeland War. In Croatian terms, Karlovac is something of a new arrival, built by the Austro-Hungarians in 1579 as a bulwark in the frontier defences against the Ottoman Empire. Though the historic centre had its moat drained and walls torn down in the 19th century, the moat is now part of a leafy greenbelt and the charm of the old town is still intact. Many of its buildings, though, were damaged during Serb shelling, which was at its peak

between 1991 and 1992 but resumed in 1993 and did not stop until the Croatian Army ousted Serb forces from the city's outskirts in 1995.

The centre of Karlovac is Trg bana Josipa Jelačića, still not completely restored after bomb damage. Also patched up on the edge of the square is the Holy Trinity Church (opening times vary), whose sturdy exterior conceals an interior with good Baroque frescoes. Nearby, the **Town Museum** (Gradski muzej; www.gmk.hr; Tue, Thu–Fri 8am–4pm, Wed until 7pm, Sat 10am–4pm, Sun 10am–noon) is housed in one of the city's oldest buildings, the 17th-century Baroque Frankopan Palace. On display is a collection of traditional costumes from the region, as well as swords, guns and military paraphernalia. The most interesting exhibit is a scale model of the original fortifications that shows the virtually impregnable star-shaped design.

Just 5km (3 miles) south of the city is the battle-scarred village of **Turanj** ⑪, which was at the front line during the Homeland War and fell under Serbian

Plitvice Lakes National Park

occupation. An open-air museum (daily 24 hours) dedicated to the events of 1991–5 has a large collection of military hardware and other relics of the conflict. It is one of the few official places in the country where visitors can find out more about the war. Perhaps the most poignant exhibit is a tractor that was converted into an armoured vehicle by desperate local people as they tried to halt the advance of the Serb tanks. Across the road from the museum, a simple marble memorial commemorates the local dead.

SOUTH TO THE PLITVICE LAKES

From Turanj the drive south to the **Plitvice Lakes** ⑫ (Plitvička jezera; www.np-plitvicka-jezera.hr), one of Croatia's most popular tourist attractions, is a fairly uneventful one. You can break it, though, with a stop off at one of the restaurants that line the road side. These are good value and of an excellent standard, specialising in spit-roasted lamb and pork. Just keep a keen eye on the upcoming road and

choose a place that suits – the most attractive look out over meadows or gurgling streams.

Call them emerald, call them turquoise, call them what you will, but the tumbling waters of Plitvice are undeniably a visual circus as they bubble and churn their way through a series of 16 densely forested lakes. Already protected as a national park, Plitvice Lakes earned a place on the Unesco World Heritage List in 1979, a fact that failed to deter rebel Serbian forces from trashing the park and looting its hotels between 1991 and 1995. Today Plitvice has recovered its tranquillity and it makes an excellent place to spend a day or, better still, several days. A variety of wildlife, including the occasional bear, shares the park with humans in relative harmony.

The best places to stay are the three park hotels (some rooms have views of the park and lakes), as negotiating the car parks and fighting for a space can be a problem for those travelling in from outside. There is also a campsite. Getting around the park is

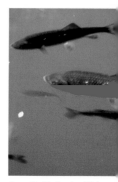

Aquatic life is plentiful in Plitvice National Park and fishing is forbidden.

Rainbow formed in the spray of the Great Falls at Plitvice Lakes.

The lakes are linked by bridges and encircled by raised wooden footpaths.

straightforward once you have paid the admission fee, which includes using the boats and tourist trains that aid getting around. There's a variety of trails, all linked by the trains and boats, and plenty of information assistants are on hand at the two entrances.

Try to visit the most popular parts of the lakes in the early morning or late evening when there are fewer people and the ever-changing light creates fabulous effects on the greeny-blue waters. To escape from fellow visitors, try heading for the more remote upper lakes to the south by taking the boat across **Lake Kozjak** Ⓐ (the park's largest lake) from Entrance 2 and following the path that skirts Lake Gradinsko. Just past the lake is a series of spectacular waterfalls. From here proceed on the trail south past the Labudovac Falls to Lake Prošćansko.

The vast, tree-shrouded **Lake Prošćansko** Ⓑ looks more like something that you would expect to find in the US or Scandinavia than in this corner of Europe. Be careful not to follow the rickety wooden walkway around the lake as this leads to a dead end requiring a dangerous jump on to the lake shore. Instead, head for the train pick-up point and then keep on south past the waiting passengers. Alas there is no lakeside trail and so you have to make do with the road, but there are few other visitors up here. A little way along there is a disused wooden pier where you can relax and take in the view in peace.

From Lake Prošćansko it is also possible to embark on a 7km (4-mile) trek up to one of the sources of the water that runs through the park. Ask at the park information kiosks as the main maps do not mark this route.

With the lower lakes so overrun by tourists in high season it is tempting just to stay in the quieter southern half, but in doing so you would miss out on some of the most impressive scenery. Again, take a boat from the hotels near Entrance 2 across Lake Kozjak, but this time take the boat heading north to the far end of the lake, where you can stop for a lunch of spit-roasted chicken before carrying on. There is a small beach here but, as in the rest of the

park, swimming is strictly prohibited. The path cuts away from the boat landing and down a series of waterfalls and small lakes that are criss-crossed by paths and wooden walkways, the scene hemmed in by limestone cliffs on both flanks. The culmination is **Veliki slap Ⓒ**, the park's largest waterfall, a spectacular drop that sprays onlookers with a gently cooling mist.

While one can negotiate the park on a rushed day trip, it is a much better idea to allow a couple of days. That way you can plan on an early morning start and beat the worst of the crowds and also enjoy a relaxed evening spent on a balcony overlooking the lake, watching the sun set and complete calm descend over the park. The rerouting of the main highway between Zagreb and Zadar (which used to cut right through the heart of Plitvice) was a welcome move. There are also long-term plans to discourage day-trippers, while providing more facilities and detailed information for people staying longer. Such measures should ease the current problems of overcrowding.

SOUTH TOWARDS RIJEKA

Instead of heading from Karlovac for the Plitvice Lakes, it is possible to take the old road across the mountains towards the Kvarner port city of Rijeka, although there is also a less scenic motorway. Be aware that the winding old road can be tortuous and the tight bends and crawling trucks make overtaking dangerous and difficult, even without the icy conditions prevailing in winter. If in a hurry you can fly; otherwise go carefully, taking time to enjoy the scenery and visit the small towns and villages along the way.

THE GORSKI KOTAR REGION

The road and rail routes from Zagreb both run straight through the heart of the wild and relatively unspoilt **Gorski kotar**, the aptly named 'wooded region', a rugged landscape of thickly wooded forests and deep river valleys that swirls around the Slovenian border from Karlovac right down to the very edge of Kvarner. The region is scattered with small roadside villages where you can savour the produce of

The lakes are known for their deep turquoise colour.

the local countryside, with spit-roasted pork a ubiquitous speciality.

One of the highlights of the Gorski kotar is the area around the town of **Ogulin** ⓭, 55km (34 miles) south of Karlovac, on the main rail line and not far from the chief road artery south. The town clusters around a 16th-century castle that in the 1930s served as a prison for Tito. On the edge of the old town is Dula's Abyss (Dulin ponor), a steep fall in the River Dobra named after a local girl who hurled herself to her death here after a tragic love affair. When the Dobra joins the Mrežnica River they combine to form two lakes offering opportunities for fishing, swimming and sailing. Parts of the River Dobra are used for white-water rafting.

Ogulin is also a good base for tackling the peak of Klek, which rises 1,184 metres (3,885ft) above sea level in the Velika Kapela mountain range. It is hard to miss the distinctive presence of Klek, as it is visible for miles around. Ascending the mountain is easy – you can either tackle it the

long way from Ogulin (a 4-hour trek) or from the tiny village of Bjelsko, where there is a well-marked trail that takes around two and a half hours each way.

From Klek you can see a familiar sight if you have been watching Croatian TV, **Mt Bjelolasica**, which always appears on TV weather reports. At 1,530 metres (5,022ft) above sea level, the mountain is much higher than Klek and it is a relatively straightforward ascent, though long and tiring in summer. The Croatian government is trying to push the Bjelolasica Olympic Centre as a ski resort, but although it may be one of the best ski resorts in Croatia, it doesn't compare with anywhere in the Alps or even in neighbouring Slovenia. The facilities are basic, but include overnight accommodation and a chairlift, which gets busy only in the brief ski season that runs any time between December and February depending on conditions. The resort caters for beginners and intermediates, and there is a good fast run for more experienced skiers.

Veliki slap, the park's highest and most dramatic waterfall.

FLORA AND FAUNA OF THE PLITVICE LAKES

The Plitvice Lakes are home to a remarkably rich diversity of flora and fauna – from brown bears and wolves to beech and sycamore trees.

The harsh karst land that ripples across Central Croatia generally supports only sparse vegetation and forms a formidable natural barrier that cuts off the Northern Dalmatian coast. But in the heart of this rugged terrain, in the midst of the mountains of Mala Kapela and Plješivica, is the lush wonderland of the Plitvice Lakes (Plitvička jezera), a Unesco World Heritage Site since 1979. The lakes were formed through the process of travertine sedimentation as limestone deposits and moss and fungi reacted to build up the travertine beds and divert the water flow of the Bijela (white) and Crna (black) rivers. Instead of smoothly flowing rivers they become an 8km (5-mile) -long network of dams, caves and waterfalls that tumble down in a series of 16 lakes and countless streams and brooks. The travertine process is ongoing as the landscape evolves, making the area the focus of scientific research.

The size of the national park is roughly 300 sq km (115 sq miles), with 230 sq km (85 sq miles) of that area covered in thick forest and 220 hectares (540 acres) sunk under fresh water. The bulk of the forests are made up of beech, fir and spruce trees, but the unique microclimate also encourages the flourishing of more exotic species, such as hop hornbeam, white Italian maple, flowering oak and sycamore.

If anything, the park's array of fauna is even more impressive. The highlights are the brown bears that thrive in and around the park. After losing their natural suspicion of humans in recent years, the bears have become bolder – not least because of irresponsible visitors ignoring regulations and leaving food for them – and even a little troublesome. The park authorities are keeping a close eye on them.

Packs of wild wolves, extinct in many of their natural habitats in Europe, also find sanctuary here. Other animals include otters, foxes, lynx, wild cats, badgers and pine martens.

On recent estimates there are at least 126 bird species in Plitvice, and of those at least 70 are thought to be nesting within the confines of the reserve. Species include owls, cuckoos, thrushes, starlings, kingfishers, wild ducks, grouse, capercaillie and the rarely spotted black storks, as well as wild ospreys. A wide variety of butterfly species also thrives and makes for a spectacular sight in summer as they flit around the edges of the lake. Plitvice is also renowned for its large and particularly picturesque orchids.

Life also flourishes beneath the water in the form of a large population of trout as well as fire salamanders and various crustaceans. But keen fishermen will be frustrated as fishing, like hunting, is banned within the park's boundaries and the trout have grown fat and lazy as a result. Zoologists are at a loss to explain why the lakes have quite so many of them.

If you want to get a feel for the park's flora and fauna throughout the year, plan at least two trips to cover different seasons. The park is open year round and there is no bad time to visit. The Plitvice Lakes on a baking hot summer's day are altogether different on a bright spring morning when life is returning after the chill of the winter. In winter, the park is caked in a sheet of snow and ice clogs up many of the waterways.

A European brown bear snoozing in the park.

Bjelovar.

CONTINENTAL CROATIA

Continental Croatia is not the rural backwater it first appears. Its towns and cities – most gloriously, Osijek – are rich in Baroque architecture, and it has significant natural resources, not least a huge untapped tourist potential.

While the 1990s war often feels like a distant bad dream in much of Croatia, many of the people of Continental Croatia are still living with the all too real consequences of a conflict that did not see all of the region handed back by the Serbs until 1998. The region remains Croatia's poorest, with the highest unemployment rate and lowest GDP per head among other unenviable economic indicators, although job prospects for land-mine disposal experts remain healthy. Many visitors choose to avoid this troubled part of the country and stick to the idyllic towns and balmy waters of the coast, but in doing so they miss an undiscovered part of Europe where tourists are very much a novelty. If you have any desire to learn more about the conflict and the way in which it has shaped the national consciousness, then a visit is highly recommended. Far from being considered ghoulish war tourists, such visitors can expect a hearty welcome from most locals. Aside from the legacies of war, which are all too evident in Osijek, Slavonski Brod and especially shattered Vukovar, Continental Croatia also has two of Central Europe's finest cathedrals, a string of historic old towns and its own Slavonian cuisine.

There are also the natural attractions of the Kopački Rit and the Lonjsko Polje nature parks and the broad sweep of the

Danube, which cuts through the region creating a natural border with Serbia. Much of Continental Croatia, especially the segment east and northeast of Zagreb (see page 248), is of little scenic interest compared with other destinations in the country, with large areas of flat land, punctuated by a few rolling hills, perfect for farming but of little real interest to tourists. Also, conditions on some of the minor roads are poor and routes are prone to flooding at all times of year. Most visitors make a beeline east along the motorway from Zagreb

⊙ Main Attractions

Lonjsko Polje Nature Park
Jasenovac Memorial
  Museum
Slavonski Brod
Đakovo
Osijek
Vukovar
Ovčara, Ilok and Hlebine
Kopački Rit

Map on page 248

Stork's nest in Lonjsko Polje Nature Park.

straight to the Slavonia region, where places of interest are located.

Today Continental Croatia undoubtedly has its problems with high unemployment, the decline of traditional industries, uncleared minefields and the ethnic tensions between Croats who suffered through the war and Croatian Serbs who sat out the war in Serbia or assisted the attacking forces. But for visitors the only remaining danger is the threat of (mostly well-marked) minefields that make the war more real than anywhere else in the country. It is wise not to express any strong opinions you have on the Balkans in this part of Croatia, though once the local people feel comfortable they are often more than happy to fill visitors in on the personal stories behind the TV news reports.

EAST OF ZAGREB

There are a handful of worthwhile diversions to break the journey to the Slavonia region, where most of the interesting parts of Continental Croatia are. **Lonjsko Polje Nature Park ❶** (www.pp-lonjsko-polje.hr), less than

100km (60 miles) along the motorway from Zagreb, is a worthwhile diversion. Hugging the banks of the River Sava with Bosnia to the south, this long, thin area of seasonal wetlands is not really set up for overnight visitors, and so it is ideal for a few hours or even as a day trip from Zagreb. Visitors are advised to bring their own food and drink, to wear anti-mosquito spray, long trousers, shirts with long sleeves and a sunhat. The birdlife includes storks, which swoop in every summer, herons and the rarely encountered white-tailed eagle. With more than 600 pairs of storks, Lonjsko Polje has the greatest concentration in Europe. On land, semi-wild Posavlje horses, the spotted Turopolje pig, wild boar, deer, beaver and wild cats can also be seen. The pigs have adapted to their watery environment by being excellent swimmers. **Sisak** is a useful base for exploring the area as it has places to stay and restaurants; the villages inside the reserve, such as Čigoč and Lonja, are not as well equipped for visitors. However, there is an information

A typical house in the Podravina region.

point and education centre in Čigoč (tel: 044 715115).

JASENOVAC

It is possible to follow the old road from Sisak (22km/13 miles west of the motorway, called *autocesta* in Croatian) through the wetlands to **Jasenovac 2** (also just 10km/6 miles south of the *autocesta* itself). Visiting the town is not a trip that many Croatians recommend – indicative perhaps of the fact that Croatia still has to come to terms with what happened at Jasenovac and to accept some measure of national responsibility. Jasenovac was a Croatian Ustaše-run concentration camp in World War II where anything from 70,000–1 million (depending on whose figures you believe) Serbs, Jews, Gypsies and political prisoners were executed by Croatians only too keen to follow and even exceed the Nazi blueprint. Even Hitler's representative in Zagreb, General Edmund Glaise von Horstenau, was shocked at the conditions in the camps, describing them as 'the epitome of horror' and

admonishing the Ustaše in letters to his superiors. Today there is little left of the original camp, but the voluminous grass void tells its own story. At its heart is a huge cement sculpture – *Stone Flower* – a monument to all who perished in the camp.

The **Memorial Museum** (Javna ustanova Spomen-područje Jasenovac; www.jusp-jasenovac.hr; Mar–Nov Mon–Fri 9am–5pm, Sat–Sun 10am–4pm, Dec–Feb Mon–Fri 9am–4pm; free) has three permanent exhibitions, including a list of individual victims. The village of Jasenovac saw war return in 1991 when the local Serbs, backed up by the Yugoslav Army, took the town, expelled Croatian residents and dynamited the Catholic churches. In a vicious circle of retaliation that was repeated throughout Croatia in 1995, the Croatian Army and Croatian irregulars sought their revenge by expelling Serbs and defacing the Orthodox churches.

INDUSTRIAL BELT

Continuing along the *autocesta*, you reach **Slavonski Brod 3**, 180km (112

A sign warning of the danger of land mines, leftovers from the Croatian War of Independence.

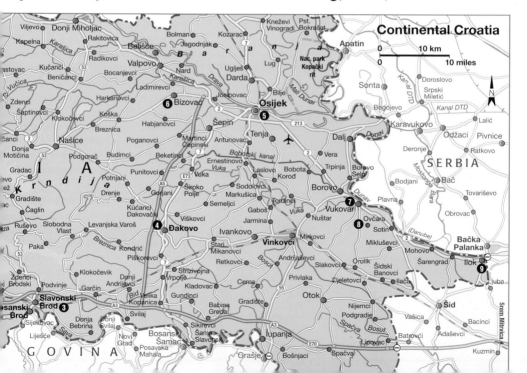

Osijek's main square.

Đakovo's cathedral.

miles) from Zagreb. Before the war, few tourists ever breezed into this industrial city and the trickle stopped completely during the fighting as the city lies right on the River Sava, which forms a natural border with Bosnia. The local authorities are trying hard to rebuild the city centre and attract tourists.

The highlight is the Baroque 18th-century **Brod Fortress**, once a pivotal bulwark against the Ottoman Empire, with much of the original perimeter in the Vauban style still standing today. As late as the Homeland War it retained its original purpose, housing soldiers of the Yugoslav Army. An ongoing reconstruction is designed to breathe life back into what was once the focus of the town, with school buildings, local government offices and a rebuilt chapel taking shape inside the old walls and the former moat refilled with water for its new role as a town park. Progress so far has been impressive if slow, because of lack of funds, and it is a sign of the town's determination to shake off the effects of a conflict whose bullet holes still scar many

public buildings, not to mention civilian apartment blocks.

Other things to see in Slavonski Brod include the Ružić Gallery (Galerija Ružić), opened in 2004 inside the largest building in the fortress with a collection of modern Croatian art and sculpture, as well as the work of the late Croatian sculptor Branko Ružić, who was born in the town and died in Zagreb. The House of the Brlić Family (Kuća Brlićevih) is a neoclassical building, whose original occupants entertained many of Croatia's leading luminaries of culture and politics. It is now a museum and art gallery. The **Brod Regional Museum** (Muzej brodskog posavlja; www.muzejbp.hr; Mon–Fri 10am–1pm and 5–8pm, Sun 10am–1pm) spreads across two buildings and houses artefacts dug up from all over Slavonia. Exhibits include fossils of an elephant, Bronze Age pieces and leg armour dating back to Roman times. The Baroque 18th-century Franciscan Monastery is another Slavonski Brod highlight.

STROSSMAYER'S CATHEDRAL

Another 35km (22 miles) along the *autocesta* (major highway) and then a 30km (18-mile) drive north along a minor road is the town of **Đakovo** ❹, which would have remained fairly anonymous were it not for one of Croatia's most colourful religious figures, Bishop Strossmayer. The bishop's epic vision of a pan-Slavic nation at a time when the region was firmly suppressed under Austro-Hungarian rule is echoed in the voluminous sweep of the twin towers of the cathedral that he commissioned. As you approach Đakovo, the towers loom like huge space rockets awaiting lift-off; the interior is equally eye-catching, with large, brightly coloured paintings of biblical scenes stretching along the walls, the work of Alexander and Ljudevit Seitz. The **cathedral** (daily 6.30am–noon, 3–7.30pm; free) was built in the 19th century in the Gothic style by Baron Friedrich von Schmidt. Look out for the tomb that holds the remains of

the controversial bishop and also, in the road opposite, for the statue of Stross-mayer pointing proudly towards his architectural legacy, described by Pope John XXIII as 'the most beautiful church between Venice and Istanbul'.

If you want to take your interest in this turbulent priest further, then head next door to the **Memorial Museum of Bishop Strossmayer** (Spomen-muzej biskupa Josipa Jurja Strossmayera; Mon–Fri 8am–6pm, Sat 8am–1.30pm) with its small collection of his scrib-blings and other artefacts that give a taste of his life. Continue down Kralja Tomislava, a pedestrianised thorough-fare that has a number of attractive outdoor cafés where you can have a coffee or savour the local Slavonian beer, Osječko. At the end of the street is a squat church that was built into an old mosque. Continue in the same direction and you will come to a mod-ern sculpture, *The Three Crosses*, erected in 1991. This gleaming tangle of steel provides an interesting visual counterpoint to the spires of the cathe-dral at the other end of town and com-memorates all those who died in the Homeland War.

OSIJEK: SLAVONIA'S LARGEST CITY

Half an hour farther north by road is **Osijek ❺**, Slavonia's largest settle-ment and an intriguing city that justi-fies a stay of a few days, especially if you are using it as a base for exploring the rest of the region. The history of the city dates back to the Romans who breezed through town in the first cen-tury, though barbarian attacks wiped out all traces of Roman Osijek. Osijek went on to serve as a fortress town for the Austro-Hungarian Empire in its efforts to keep the Ottoman Empire at bay, and there are many 18th-century reminders of that period as well as some handsome 19th-century build-ings. The Hungarian influence also lin-gers in the region's cuisine.

Although memories of war rarely fade quickly in this corner of Europe – Osijek endured a nine-month bat-tering at the hands of the Serbs, which left around 1,000 inhabitants dead and many buildings badly scarred – the city's once legendary cosmopolitan café life and joie de vivre are return-ing, especially in summer when the waterfront is once again crowded with people relaxing in its cafés and bars.

UPPER, LOWER AND OLD TOWN

The city is split into three distinct areas that huddle on the banks of the fast-moving Drava River: Gornji grad (Upper Town), the Tvrđa old town and Donji grad (Lower Town), the first two of which are of most interest to visitors. The cen-tre of Osijek is still dominated by the **Cathedral of St Peter and St Paul** (Kat-edrala sv. Petra i Pavla), commissioned by Bishop Strossmayer, who was born here. This voluminous red-brick edifice, with its 90-metre (300ft) tall tower, was designed by German architect Franz Langenberg, but his original plans had to be modified after his sudden death in

Fountains and the Cathedral in Osijek's main square.

1895 and the Viennese architect Richard Jordan took over the reins. The interior is graced with impressive stained-glass windows and brightly coloured paintings by Mirko Rački.

Walk further away from the Drava on the same street and you will soon come to the **Croatian National Theatre** (Hrvatsko narodno kazalište), whose ground floor has been occupied, much to the chagrin of many locals, by a well-known international fast-food chain, but its facade has been impressively restored. A marvellous example of the Venetian-Moorish style, the theatre was built in 1866, and is one of only four national theatres in Croatia.

Head back past the cathedral to Trg Ante Starčevića and then walk east and you will come to Europska avenija, once one of Croatia's grandest boulevards and still a superb ensemble of Art Nouveau architecture. On both sides, wealthy Austro-Hungarian and German families erected grand testaments to their fortunes, each with their own unique and often delightfully overblown decorative touches. Nos 12

and 22 are particularly fine. The thoroughfare was badly damaged during the Homeland War, but painstaking restoration work has brought it back to its former glory. Financing this work remains a problem: larger investment interests such as banks are able to renovate but, as in much of central and eastern Europe, there is not enough state or private money to cover the rest. The **Museum of Fine Arts** (Muzej likovnih umjetnosti; www.mlu.hr; Tue–Fri 10am–8pm, Sat–Sun 10am–1pm) at No. 9 is one of the country's finest showcases of Croatian painting from the 18th century onwards.

BAROQUE FORTRESS

A brace of Osijek's 17 parks envelops Europska as it heads east towards Tvrđa – look out for the plaque to the left marking the spot where Croatian forces dynamited a statue of a woman cradling a child that commemorated all victims of World War II, including local Croats and Serbs. As you walk through the park, the Baroque fortress of **Tvrđa** rises up on the riverside. Built in stages in the first half of the 18th century, the fortress was intended to prevent the Ottomans from ever occupying the town again – the Turks having been forced out of Osijek as late as 1687.

After World War II the Yugoslav Army used Tvrđa as a base and it fell into disrepair before suffering further in 1991–2 when the same forces bombarded it with shells from outside the city. Money from the Croatian government has helped in the rebuilding process and the Catholic Church has helped to address the severe beating meted out to Tvrđa's churches. Life has returned to Tvrđa with Osijek University moving into several of the former barracks and old administration blocks. Further restoration work could result if Osijek is successful in its attempt to get Tvrđa placed on the Unesco World Heritage List.

The centrepiece of Tvrđa is **Trg svetog Trojstva**, a grand square

Tvrđa old town, Osijek.

surrounded by impressive Austro-Hungarian military buildings. At its heart is a plague column commissioned in 1729 by the wife of a local commander in thanks for the city being relieved of an outbreak of the disease. On the western flank of the square is the main guard building with a clock tower, a colonnaded exterior and a couple of small cannons. A sprinkling of cafés and bars now also occupy one end of the square, and at night the laughter and rowdy escapades of local students breathe life into the area.

Also in Tvrđa is **St Michael's Church** (Crkva sv. Mihaila), with its signature twin towers; its gleaming appearance inside and out is the result of an almost total reconstruction.

Back past the main square, the church of Tvrđa's **Franciscan Monastery** (Franjevački samostan) has been impressively renovated. Although the monastery is rarely open to the public, you can see the dimly lit Baroque interior, with its impressive 15th-century statue of Mary and Judas, through the glass.

From the monastery head downhill towards the only one of the four original gates still left standing, with the single surviving Tvrđa defensive tower nearby. Leaving the gate brings you out on to the banks of the Drava River, in its final flourish before the mighty Danube swallows it up just downstream. Look across the water and there is the surreal apparition of the ambitiously named Copacabana – a modest stretch of riverside sand, backed up with swimming pools, a water slide and a restaurant. However, hardcore beach lovers may be better off looking a little bit farther along the coast.

SPA TREAT IN BIZOVAC

The legacy of war, sparse tourist facilities and long distances on the motorway can make visiting Slavonia a gruelling experience, but there are two great places to recuperate near Osijek. You can either spend a day or two in the Kopački

Rit Nature Park, just 7.5 (8 miles) from Osijek (see page 254); or in the spa of **Bizovačke Toplice** in **Bizovac** ❻, 20km (12 miles) west of the city. From a depth of 2km (1 mile) below the earth's surface, bubbling water gushes forth into four indoor and two outdoor pools. The waters are said to be of particular benefit for skin conditions and stress disorders. In addition there are swimming pools, whirlpools, a small water park with slides and tennis courts. It is easy to visit the spa on a day trip, but it is more relaxing to stay at one of the onsite hotels.

Hunting is bringing more tourists to Slavonia, with organised trips to hunt boar and deer in hunting grounds such as Spačva and Tikveš. Wine tourism is building too, particularly in the so-called Golden Valley north of Slavonski Brod. Wine routes link vineyards such as Požega-Pleternica and Kutjevo, with more wine makers opening their doors both for accommodation and dining.

BATTLE-SCARRED VUKOVAR

Today it takes around 30 minutes to drive south from Osijek to **Vukovar** ❼; during

⊙ Tip

Good-value accommodation is slowly coming to Continental Croatia, particularly in Osijek. But as many hotels cater mainly for business people, with prices to match, a good bet is to ask at the local tourist office for details of residents who let out rooms in their homes.

St Michael's Church, Tvrđa area of Osijek.

☉ Fact

Eastern Croatia is rich in natural gas and petroleum. Including hydro power, it can supply 60 percent of the country's primary energy needs.

the war in the early 1990s the journey through the flat cornfields was suicidal. Vukovar is a name synonymous with Croatian suffering, a name that evokes a reaction in every Croat when it is mentioned. For three months in 1991, the lightly armed inhabitants of the Baroque town of Vukovar, which hugs a picturesque bend in the River Danube, were subject to the sort of savage and devastating siege not experienced in Europe since World War II (see page 257).

Visiting is not an enjoyable experience as such, but by and large the locals are very keen on outsiders coming to learn more about their experiences and to bring in some much-needed cash to help in the rebuilding work. Visiting the town is completely safe: all ordinance has been removed and all central areas de-mined, though walking around the surrounding cornfields is dangerous. Venturing into the embittered Serbian suburb of Borovo Selo is also inadvisable without local contacts.

Today Vukovar is trying to rebuild, but its population lives in segregated conditions, with separate schools and other institutions. While Croats make up more than half of the population, the Serbian minority is more than a third, and neither group is mingling much with the other. Many of the 20,000 Croat refugees who left in 1991 have shown little interest in returning to the economically depressed town, where jobs and accommodation are in short supply.

An essential first stop is the tourist office on the main street, which can give information on current rebuilding projects and, with a few days' notice, provide English-speaking guides (tel: 032 442889; www.turizamvukovar.hr).

A FALLEN CITY

Vukovar town centre is a sad shadow of its former self. Most of the buildings have new roofs and the roads have been resurfaced, but many beautiful Baroque buildings are skeletons, including Radnički dom (House of the Workers), where one of the first meetings of the Yugoslav Communist Party took place in 1920. The jumble of ruined buildings leads down to the river and a memorial,

Kopački Rit Nature Park.

☉ KOPAČKI RIT

Kopački Rit Nature Park is a must for ornithologists but also a wonderful day trip for less committed bird lovers. One of the largest inland wetlands in Europe, sprawling across 180 sq km (70 sq miles) at the confluence of the Danube and Drava rivers, it has more than 260 bird species, including white-tailed eagles, woodpeckers, kingfishers and black storks. The waters teem with at least 40 fish species from pike and perch to carp and catfish. The park is also home to deer, pine martens, wild cats and wild boar.

During the 1990s war, the park was heavily mined. Most areas have been cleared but it is essential to stick to trails designated as safe. The best way to discover the park is to hire a guide or join an organised tour. For further information, visit www.pp-kopacki-rit.hr.

where many Croats who watched the plight of Vukovar unfold on their television screens, come to lay flowers. Do not enter abandoned buildings, which may still have land mines or be in danger of collapse, and take care to stick to footpaths on the edge of town.

Before the war, Vukovar's most graceful 18th-century building was the Eltz Palace, built by a local noble family and reconstructed after the war. It now contains a modern and interactive **Town Museum** (Gradski muzej; Tue–Sun 10am–6pm) containing prehistoric and Roman pieces, portraits of local nobles and luminaries from the 18th-century golden age of Vukovar and ethnographic and cartographic collections, as well as those devoted to the history of Vukovar. Much of the museum's collection was looted in the war and returned from Serbia in 2001 after painstaking diplomacy, and many of the paintings were donated by artists around Europe.

Uphill from the town centre is the **Franciscan Monastery** (Franjevački samostan). The Franciscans were hugely important in the history and culture of Vukovar and had seven monasteries here in the Middle Ages. The exterior has been impressively renovated, disguising the sad dereliction of the interior, although regular services once again take place here. As with many projects in Vukovar, the original rush of funds to shore up buildings has dried up. One structure that may never be renovated is the voluminous water tower, visible from many parts of the town.

Another symbol of the war is the **Place of Memory** (Mjesto sjećanja; Županijska ulica 35; Mon–Fri 8am–3pm) in the basement of the city hospital that kept going through heavy shelling, with exhibits poignantly recapturing life under the siege.

On a plain on the outskirts of Vukovar is the **war cemetery** (Memorijalno groblje žrtava iz Domovinskog rata), separated between the defenders of Vukovar and civilians, though the division between the two during the siege was blurred, as many had little choice but to become involved. In the centre are hundreds of white crosses marking those whose bodies were never found.

OVČARA

Close to the border with Serbia, 7km (4 miles) from Vukovar, is **Ovčara ❽**, where one of the worst atrocities of the war took place. On capturing Vukovar, Serbian forces removed around 300 hospital patients from under the noses of the International Red Cross. After being badly beaten, the prisoners were held for three days and then taken off and shot. A simple memorial now marks the spot where they were murdered. Some of the higher-ranking officers involved have been indicted by the Hague War Crimes Tribunal, but some Croat residents of Vukovar complain that the ordinary soldiers and irregulars involved were never brought to justice. There is no public transport to the memorial and the minor road there is difficult to follow, so it is advisable to

Wooden statues in Hlebine, a centre of naïve art in Croatia.

The memorial to prisoners murdered by Serbian forces in Ovčara.

Post-war Vukovar.

get detailed instructions from the tourist office before setting out.

ILOK

Heading 29km (18 miles) further east from Vukovar you reach **Ilok** ❾, a small town – Croatia's easternmost – with a real frontier feel, overlooking the Danube and right on the Serbian border. Before the war, this ethnically mixed town with large Slovak, Serb and Hungarian minorities was a prosperous agricultural centre renowned for the quality of its wine – Traminer, Burgundy and Graševina. Wine production has picked up again, and some of the wine makers from the surrounding vineyards offer tastings from their wine cellars in town.

Architecturally, the town is also interesting, with Islamic styles blending into the traditional Pannonian buildings, a legacy of the days when Ilok was a tolerant multi-ethnic hub. It is encouraging to witness the residents of a town, who have every reason to feel bitter and depressed, getting back on their feet.

NORTHERN AREA

From the Osijek region, the only possibility is to turn around and travel back. For a change of scene you can return via the northern route rather than along the *autocesta*, initially flanking the Drava River and the Hungarian border and cutting south at **Đurđevac**, which has a medieval castle, to **Bjelovar** with its superb farmers' market (Mon–Sat) or the pleasant town of **Varaždin**, a good base for exploring the Zagorje (see page 230). The agricultural flatlands of corn and sunflowers interrupted by tidy villages and towns have few sights and even fewer hotels, but the route gives an insight into rural life.

One such insight is to be found at **Hlebine**, near the administrative centre of Koprivnica on the way to Varaždin. This typical Podravina village evolved into a centre for naïve art following the discovery of the work of the self-taught painter Ivan Generalić by the Paris-trained artist Krsto Hegedušić in the 1930s. Its **Hlebine Gallery of Naïve Art** (Galerija naivne umjetnosti Hlebine; Tue–Fri 10am–4pm, Sat–Sun 10am–2pm) contains the work of many naïve artists, including Generalić and his son Josip. Among the most notable paintings on display is Ivan Generalić's *The Tower*.

The Hlebine School, which evolved from a local art club, explores rural themes, using intense colours and metaphor. It was championed by the Croatian Peasant Party and viewed as an authentic expression of Croatian culture free of Western influences.

Koprivnica also has a showcase of naïve art, the **Koprivnica Gallery** (Galerija Koprivnica; Tue–Fri 8am–4pm, Sat–Sun 10am–2pm), as well as a 17th-century Franciscan monastery and an 18th-century Orthodox church catering to the town's large Serbian minority.

🔍 THE SIEGE OF VUKOVAR

Since World War II, few places in Europe have been better witness to the worst aspects of nationalism and the futility of war than Vukovar.

It is hard to comprehend the full horror of the Siege of Vukovar. For three months, the might of the Yugoslav Army, with more than 40,000 troops and 600 tanks, was brought to bear on a Baroque town whose residents scraped by with no electricity or running water and precious little food. Almost every building was shattered, 2,000 citizens were killed and more than 4,000 wounded as the town was razed to a shadow of its former self.

The determination of Vukovar's residents to resist the attacks was replayed nightly on Croatian TV, but international media attention was concentrated on the less bloody siege further south in Dubrovnik. Inevitably the town fell. The stiff resistance of Vukovar, though, slowed up the Serbian advance, weakened Yugoslav Army morale and dispelled any notions that dragging Eastern Croatia into 'Greater Serbia' was going to be easy.

Before the conflict, Vukovar had more than 44,000 citizens, roughly 44 percent Croat and 37 percent Serb, with significant Bosnian, Hungarian, German and Slovak minorities. As tensions rose around the rest of the country, attempts were made to mediate between local Croats and Serbs, but the Serb population clandestinely received arms from elements of the Yugoslav Army and the Serb-dominated suburb of Borovo Selo became a no-go area for Croats.

On 2 May 1991, a busload of Croat policemen was ambushed and massacred in Borovo Selo. The Yugoslav Army became involved on the pretext that it was there to separate the skirmishing Croats and Serbs. However, the army joined forces with Serb irregulars and mounted a ferocious siege using mortars, howitzers, bomber jets and navy gunships, surrounding the Croats on all sides.

The defenders of Vukovar were armed with little more than hunting rifles or old World War II relics. The battle lines were drawn across the mined cornfields on the town's perimeter, and while the defenders were able to confront the infantry and tank attacks they could do little about the shells raining in from afar. At the height of the siege, up to 10,000 explosives a night pummelled Vukovar, driving the residents to their cellars. Both the Yugoslav Army and Serb irregulars thwarted repeated attempts by international organisations to relieve Vukovar and evacuate the wounded. For those not fit or rash enough to make the dangerous dash for freedom across the cornfields, there was no escape.

By the start of November, the dwindling number of defenders could offer less and less resistance. On 18 November, the Serbs rolled into Vukovar. Men of fighting age were rounded up and there were summary executions. More than 2,000 people are still listed as missing.

The irony is that the Serbian victory was a hollow one. The town they inherited was virtually worthless and Serbia handed it back to Croatia in 1998 through the UN. As the international community began to comprehend the extent of the atrocities that had been committed, there was a stiffening resolve to avoid 'another Vukovar'.

On the eastern approach road to Vukovar, one the biggest mass graves in Europe assembled since World War II – with 938 white crosses – is an eerie aspect of a visit to the town.

The memorial by the river in Vukovar.

📷 NAÏVE ART

A speciality of Croatia, 'peasant' painting on glass has never gone out of fashion – so much so that the genre is becoming more popular with collectors.

If anything is guaranteed to cheer you up, it is a visit to the Croatian Museum of Naïve Art in Zagreb on the second floor of the 18th-century Raffay Palace. It opened with state finance in 1952, and was hailed as the first museum of naïve art in the world. Its collection of life-affirming works of art date from the 1930s and the Hlebine School (see page 259) to the present day.

The style is deeply rooted in Central European peasant painting mixed with a touch of Brueghel. These delightful scenes of rural life are rich in imagination and exquisitely executed. The earlier, prewar paintings had a serious side, depicting social injustice. Later works became dreamier and more abstract, but retained their essential peasant soul, with fetes and weddings, harvests and winter landscapes, and animated scenes of village life.

Many are *sous verre*, painted in oils in reverse on glass, a tricky technique that emerged in Central Europe and around the Ottoman Empire in the late 19th century. It involves putting the final touches on the glass first and working up into the background. This technique gives the colours, viewed through the glass, a luminous quality.

The town of Hlebine, near the Hungarian border, birthplace of the great Ivan Generalić (1914–92) and fellow artists Franjo Mraz (1910–81) and Mirko Virius (1889–1943), also has a collection of its eponymous school associated with the town.

These paintings today can command high prices. In 2008, 100 works of Croatian reverse-glass naïve art were a highlight of the prestigious Art Basel in Miami, and prices exceeded $5,000. A few months earlier, a Generalić sold at auction for just over $10,000.

'White Birds', painted by Ivan Generalić in 1969.

The artistic tradition is encouraged around the country – Grožnjan holds an annual art competition.

'Farm in the Snow', by Ivan Lacković (1932–2004) from Padrovina, one of many self-taught artists who found international acclaim.

The Croatian Gallery of Naïve Art in Hlebine, centre of the 20th-century movement.

The Hlebine School

Krsto Hegedušić, the founder of Croatia's 20th-century naïve art movement, was born in 1901 into a family who came from the village of Hlebine on the misty Pannonian plain near the Drava river. On entering the Arts and Crafts College in Zagreb at the age of 19, he began painting his home village from memory. A few years afterwards, on a scholarship to Paris, he became entranced by the work of Pieter Bruegel. On his return to Croatia he organised an exhibition at the Zagreb Art Pavilion for a prolific 17-year-old artist from Hlebine – this was Ivan Generalić, the son of local peasants whose thatched, single-storey, mud-rendered building looked out over a pond where geese and pigs roamed. A member of Zemlja (soil), a group of Marxist artists, Hegedušić founded the Hlebine School in 1930. After the war he became a professor at the Zagreb Academy, illustrating books and designing theatre sets, while his protégé, Generalić, went on to become the finest exponent of Croatian naïve art.

This painting in the Croatian Naïve Art Museum is by Emerik Feješ who used matchsticks instead of paintbrushes.

Patchwork landscape by Ivan Rabuzin (1921–2008).

Wood carving in the naïve art park at Ernestinovo, near Osijek, where a colony was founded in 1974 by Peter Smajić.

Looking towards Nin's old town.

CROATIA

TRAVEL TIPS

TRANSPORT

By air

Flights from Europe

Zagreb's small but functional airport, situated 17km (10.5 miles) south of the city, is Croatia's main international airport. The country has another six international airports at Split, Dubrovnik, Pula, Rijeka, Osijek and Zadar. Croatia's national airline Croatia Airlines (www.croatiaairlines.hr) and its partners connect the country to more than 30 European destinations including London, Paris, Brussels, Rome, Vienna, Zurich, Frankfurt and Munich. British Airways (www.ba.com) flies from London Heathrow to Zagreb, Split and Pula, and from London Gatwick to Dubrovnik. No-frills airlines with direct flights from the UK and Ireland include easyJet (www.easyjet.com), which flies from London Luton to Zadar; from London Gatwick, Stansted, Luton, Manchester, Glasgow, Newcastle and Bristol to Split; and from London Gatwick, Stansted, Luton, Bristol, Belfast and Edinburgh to Dubrovnik; and from London Gatwick and Bristol to Pula; Wizz Air (www.wizzair.com), which flies from London Luton to Split; Jet2.com (www.jet2.com), from London Stansted, Belfast, Newcastle, Leeds Bradford, Manchester, Edinburgh, East Midlands and Glasgow to Dubrovnik; from London Stansted, Birmingham, Leeds Bradford, Manchester, Edinburgh and East Midlands to Split; and from London Stansted, Manchester, Leeds Bradford and Edinburgh to Pula; Flybe (www.flybe.com) connecting Dubrovnik and Zadar with London Southend and Zagreb with Birmingham, Edinburgh and Manchester; and Ryanair (www.ryanair.com), linking Bristol, Glasgow,

Manchester and London Stansted with Zadar, and Stansted with Pula and Rijeka.

Other cheap options include indirect flights to Zagreb, Dubrovnik, Split, Rijeka, Pula and Zadar via various airports in Germany with TUIfly (www.tuifly.com) or Eurowings (www.eurowings.com), or flying to Pescara, Bari or Ancona in Italy and taking a catamaran to Dalmatia.

Some useful price-comparison websites for airfares are www.skyscanner.net, www.kayak.com and www.momondo.com.

Airport information

Dubrovnik
Tel: 020 773100
www.airport-dubrovnik.hr
Osijek
Tel: 031 514400
www.osijek-airport.hr
Pula
Tel: 060 308308
www.airport-pula.hr
Rijeka
Tel: 051 841222
www.rijeka-airport.hr
Split
Tel: 021 203555
www.split-airport.hr
Zadar
Tel: 023 205800
www.zadar-airport.hr
Zagreb
Tel: 060 320320
www.zagreb-airport.hr
Travel to and from the airport
Bus services from Zagreb airport to the city's bus station, run by Pleso prijevoz (tel: 01 633 1982; www.plesoprijevoz.hr), operate almost every half hour daily from 7am to 8pm, with additional services after later flights have landed. In the return direction services run from 4.30am to 8.30pm (Monday until 9pm and Sunday until 9.30pm) but also leave 90 minutes before aircraft departure on domestic flights and 120 minutes

on international flights. At the bus station, look for the Croatia Airlines terminal sign. It takes around 30 to 45 minutes and costs 30 kuna.

Taxis collect passengers from outside the international arrival hall. Fares to the city are usually between 150 and 250 kuna, depending on distance and hour. It is best to order a cab on tel: 970.

Croatia's other international airports also have bus connections to the city centre. Distances and journey times are as follows:

Split 24km (14 miles), 35 minutes; Dubrovnik 18km (11 miles), 20 minutes; Osijek 3km (2 miles), 10 minutes; Zadar 15km (9 miles), 15 minutes; Rijeka 27km (17 miles), 35 minutes; Pula 7km (4 miles), 10 minutes. Check airport websites for the most up-to-date information.

Airlines

Dubrovnik
Croatia Airlines
Terminal A
Dubrovnik Airport
Tel: 020 773232

Pula
Croatia Airlines
Pula Airport
Tel: 052 218909

Rijeka
Croatia Airlines
Jelačićev trg 5
Tel: 051 330207

Split
Croatia Airlines
Hrvatskog Narodnog preporoda 9
Tel: 021 362997
www.croatiaairlines.hr

Zadar
Croatia Airlines
Zadar Airport
Tel: 023 250101

Zagreb
Croatia Airlines
Bani 75b, Buzin
Tel: 01 667 6555
www.croatiaairlines.hr
Air France
1st Floor
Hotel Westin, Kršnjavoga 1
Tel: 01 489 0800
www.airfrance.com
Aeroflot
Andrija Hebranga 4
Tel: 01 487 2055
www.aeroflot.ru
Austrian Airlines
Maksimirska 112a
Tel: 01 626 5900
www.austrian.com
Lufthansa
Bantel Travel Lufthansa City Centre,
Ilica 191
Tel: 01 390 7284
www.lufthansa.com
Turkish Airlines
Zagreb Airport
Tel: 01 626 5158
www.turkishairlines.com

Flights from Australia, New Zealand, Canada and the US

There are no direct flights from the US, Canada, Australia or New Zealand to Croatia. However, Croatia Airlines has representatives in Australia and New Zealand and connections are possible through various European cities. Three useful websites for planning flights and comparing prices are www.skyscanner.net, www.kayak.com and www.momondo.com.

Taxi boat in Trogir.

⏱ Timetables

A useful resource for domestic and international bus timetables as well as domestic ferry routes is www.autobusni-kolodvor.com.

Sky Air Services (GSA)
7/24 Albert Road
South Melbourne
Victoria 3205
Australia
Tel: +61 (3) 9699 9355
Email: lidia@skyair.biz
CTTravel Limited NZ Ad
182 Lincoln Road
Henderson
Auckland
New Zealand
Tel: +64 (9) 837 9897
Email: croatiaairlines@cttravel.co.nz

By sea/ferry

International car ferries connect Italy to Croatia. Jadrolinija operates the majority of these services. The main routes are from Ancona to Zadar, Ancona to Split and Stari Grad (Hvar) and Bari to Rijeka via Dubrovnik, Korčula and Split. Jadrolinija offices are usually close to the ferry dock.

Jadrolinija offices at main ports:
Dubrovnik, tel: 020 418000
Pula (Activa Travel), tel: 052 215497
Rijeka, tel: 051 211444
Split, tel: 021 338333
Zadar, tel: 023 254800
Other offices are listed on Jadrolinija's website: www.jadrolinija.hr.

From mid-June to early September, SNAV operates international car and passenger ferry services between Ancona and Split. **SNAV** also operates a service from late July to the end of August from Pescara to Split via Stari Grad. From early April to the end of October BlueLine Ferries sails from Ancona to Split, with some services also stopping in Stari Grad or Vis. From June to September Jadrolinija operates a ferry from Bari to Dubrovnik. From mid-April to mid-October Venezia Lines runs ferries from Venice to Rovinj via Poreč, and from mid-July to the end of August from Venice to Pula and Mali Lošinj and from early June to late September from Venice to Rabac. From the end of May to mid-September it also runs ferries from Venice to Rovinj via Piran (Slovenia). A useful ferry-booking website is www.traghettiweb.it.

SNAV (Società Navigazione Alta Velocità)
Ancona
Ancona Maritime Station
Tel: +39 (0) 71 207 6116
www.snav.it
Tickets are also available from Jadroagent in Split.
Tel: 021 460999
www.jadroagent.hr
BlueLine Ferries (sales agents)
In Capita, Gat sv. Duje, Split
Tel: +385 021 352533
Blue Line Marittima, Ancona Maritime Station
Tel: +39 (0) 71 204041
www.blueline-ferries.com
Elite Travel, Dubrovnik Maritime Station
Tel: 020 358200
www.elite.hr
Venezia Lines
V. Dorsoduro 1473A, Venice
Tel: +39 (0) 41 847 0903
Call centre for Croatia: 052 422896
www.venezialines.com

By train

There are direct international rail connections to Zagreb and Rijeka from Italy, Austria, the Czech Republic, Slovakia, Germany and all neighbouring countries except Montenegro. EuroCity services to Zagreb run from Munich via Salzburg and Ljubljana, from Villach and from Belgrade. InterCity services link Vienna to Zagreb via Maribor, Budapest to Rijeka and Zagreb and Budapest to Osijek, while EuroNight sleeper services connect Venice and Ljubljana with Zagreb and Budapest with Split.

⊘ Taxis

Taxis can be caught at ranks, hailed on the street or booked by telephone. Reputable taxis have meters. As a general guide, the starting fare is 10–25 kuna and each additional kilometre costs 5–10 kuna, depending on the city. Fares for long journeys should be agreed in advance. Hotels, restaurants, tourist offices and travel agencies all carry flyers for local taxi firms. Compared with other living costs in Croatia taxis are expensive.

From mid-July to early September there is also a daily train from Prague to Split via Brno, Bratislava, Szombathely and Split, with sleepers and couchettes available. A less obvious international rail option is the 13.75-hour train from Zagreb to Ploče, the nearest station to Dubrovnik, travelling via Mostar, Sarajevo and Banja Luka in Bosnia Herzegovina.

From London to Zagreb the most convenient route involves changing in Paris and Munich and takes about 24 hours. Comfortable sleeper accommodation with showers is available on the overnight *Cassiopeia* train between Paris and Zagreb.

Croatian Railways provides timetable and station information in Croatian and English on its website, www.hzpp.hr and by telephone, tel: 01 378 2583. Two useful websites for planning European railway travel are www.seat61.com and www.sbb.ch.

Zagreb's tram system.

Various InterRail and Eurail passes that cover Croatia (for European and non-European residents respectively) are available. However, train fares in Croatia are low and it is generally better value to buy point-to-point tickets. See www.eurail.com and https://uk.voyages-sncf.com for details.

Bus/coach

International coach services connect Croatia to its neighbouring countries as well as Macedonia, Austria, Hungary, the Czech Republic, Slovakia, Italy, Germany, France and Switzerland.

Eurolines, with its extensive network, is the biggest international service provider. Its local partner in Croatia is Eurotrans (www.autotrans.hr), although there are also other companies running international services. Links to individual country websites are available through the main site www.eurolines.com.

International bus terminals

Dubrovnik
Obala pape Ivana Pavla II 44A
Tel: 060 305070
www.libertasdubrovnik.hr
Osijek
Trg Lavoslava Ružičke 2
Tel: 060 334466
Pula
Istarske divizije 43
Tel: 052 500012
Rijeka
Žabica 1
Tel: 060 888666

Šibenik
Draga 14
Tel: 060 368368
Split
Obala Kneza Domagoja 12
Tel: 060 327777; (+385 (0) 21 329199 from outside Croatia)
www.ak-split.hr
Zadar
Ante Starčevića 1
Tel: 023 211555
Zagreb
Avenija Marina Držića 4
Tel: 01 600 8600
www.akz.hr

GETTING AROUND

Choosing transport

Travelling around Croatia is gradually becoming less of a frustrating experience it used to be. For decades it had suffered from a dearth of motorways, but there are more dual carriageways forming arteries in central parts of the country. However, the main coastal road between Rijeka and Dubrovnik, the Jadranska Magistrala (Adriatic Highway), still has stretches of single lanes, which can make driving a white-knuckle experience.

A viable alternative is to catch a bus. Villages, towns and cities are well connected by extensive national and local bus services, but these stop frequently for rest breaks, a joy for smokers, drivers and the incontinent but a pain for many others. The standard of vehicle also varies from luxury air-conditioned coaches to run-down buses with poor ventilation.

Domestic train travel is not really an option if you want to get around Croatia quickly, as the Austro-Hungarian rulers were more interested in connecting Croatian cities to Austria and Hungary than to each other. Little changed under Yugoslav rule and many lines became damaged or fell out of use during the war. Split, Pula and Rijeka all have a direct rail link by diesel train to Zagreb, but services are slow and those requiring connections are subject to backtracking and long waits. Many lines remain non-electrified and single track, there is no direct rail link between Istria and the rest of

Croatia, and Dubrovnik has no railway station. Unsurprisingly most locals scarcely use the railway, though for rail buffs the run-down system can be fun to ride. There is a night train between Split and Zagreb, taking eight hours and with comfortable if not very spacious sleeper accommodation in one-, two- or three-berth compartments.

Travelling by ferry can also be exasperating. Jadrolinija has a near monopoly over ferry travel in Croatia, with infrequent and oversubscribed services to destinations along the coast and on the islands, especially in summer. Foot passengers can buy tickets for immediate or future travel on any service; however, those driving cars often experience lengthy waits. So book in advance, if possible. The timetables and regulations are confusing. It's best to get local advice.

By air

Domestic flights with Croatia Airlines connect Zagreb to Bol (Brač), Dubrovnik, Osijek, Pula, Rijeka, Split and Zadar. Taxi flights from destinations in Croatia, Germany, Austria, Slovenia, Italy, Bosnia Herzegovina and other countries in the region also land in the small airport at Mali Lošinj. Airport information for international airports is included in the Getting there section (see page 262).

Brač Airport
Tel: 021 559711
www.airport-brac.hr
Lošinj Airport
Privlaka 19
Mali Lošinj
Tel: 051 231666
www.airportmalilosinj.hr

By Bus/coach

It is possible to travel almost anywhere in Croatia by bus or coach. Autotrans (tel: 051 660660; www.autotrans.hr) is the main company operating domestic services. Buy tickets at the local bus station or – if you are not boarding at a station – from the conductor. Fares are not especially cheap, with three to four journeys costing at least 100 kuna, with an extra charge on most journeys of 10 kuna for baggage stowed under the bus. Hand luggage is free of charge.

By train

Most Croatians rarely travel by train. The network is small with few connections between major towns and cities. Where connections do exist, services are often much slower than the bus. Tickets are cheap and available from railway stations. There is rarely any need to book ahead.

The main routes are between Zagreb and Split and Split and Rijeka. Croatia's dreamiest railway journey is from Zagreb to Split, cutting through the heart of the country and culminating in the harsh karst mountains of the Dinaric range. Journey times are about six and a half hours. There is also a slower night train, all second-class, bearing reasonably priced sleeper carriages with one, two or three berths as well as seats. For arrival and departure information, visit the Croatian Railways (Hrvatske željeznice) website at www.hzpp.hr or tel: 060 333444.

Pula Railway Station
Kolodvorska 5
Rijeka Railway Station
Trg kralja Tomislava 1
Šibenik Railway Station
Fra Jerolima Milete 24
Split Railway Station
Obala Kneza Domagoja 10
Zadar Railway Station
Ante Starčevića 3
Zagreb Railway Station
Tomislavov trg 12

Island-hopping

There are two ways to island hop in Croatia. The first is to use the regular passenger- and car-ferry services that connect towns and cities along the coast and many of Croatia's islands. The second is to charter a yacht.

The main car and passenger service provider is Jadrolinija (www.jadrolinija.hr), whose main offices are listed in the Getting there section (see page 263). Local offices are near the ferry dock. Jadrolinija provides more than 30 direct connections, with the main tourist routes being: Krk-Cres, Krk-Rab, Mali Lošinj-Ilovik, Prizna-Pag, Zadar-Mali Lošinj, Zadar-Dugi otok, Split-Trogir, Split-Brač, Split-Hvar, Split-Vela Luka, Split-Vis, Pelješac-Mljet and Split-Dubrovnik via Hvar, Bol and Korčula.

The following is a list of selected routes, some of which are seasonal:

Jadrolinija services
Biograd na moru-Tkon
Brestova-Porozina
Dominče-Orebić
Drvenik-Sućuraj
Drvenik Veli-Trogir
Dubrovnik-Split
Dubrovnik-Suđurađ
Makarska-Sumartin
Prapratno-Sobra
Šepurine-Šibenik
Šibenik-Vodice
Šibenik-Zlarin
Šibenik-Žirje
Split-Drvenik Veli
Split-Hvar
Split-Jelsa
Split-Rogač
Split-Stari Grad
Split-Supetar
Split-Ubli
Split-Vela Luka
Split-Vis
Zadar-Brbinj
Zadar-Bršanj
Zadar-Ist
Zadar-Mala Rava
Zadar-Mali Lošinj
Zadar-Molat
Zadar-Preko (Ugljan)
Zadar-Premuda
Zadar-Rava
Zadar-Sali
Žigljen-Prizna

Tickets for cars and their passengers can – and in summer should – be purchased in advance, because traffic queues to board the ferry are lengthy, with waits of up to four hours frequently reported.

Foot passengers do not face the same problems and can purchase tickets immediately before departure. Tickets cannot be purchased on board and those requiring seats or cabins on the journey between Rijeka and Dubrovnik are also advised to book well ahead.

Bura Line & Off Shore
Put Porta 19, Slatine
Tel: 095 837 4320
http://buraline.com
Operates between Trogir and Split via Slatine.
G&V Line
Vukovarska 34, Dubrovnik
Tel: 020 313119
www.gv-line.hr
This Dubrovnik-based company operates the following route: Dubrovnik-Luka Šipanska-Sobra (Mljet)-Polače (Mljet)-Korčula-Ubli (Lastovo).

Miatrade
Vrata sv. Krševana, Zadar
Tel: 023 254300
www.miatours.hr
Runs services from Zadar to Olib via Premuda and Silba.

Rapska Plovidba
Hrvatskih branitelja domovinskog rata ½, Rab
Tel: 051 724122
www.rapska-plovidba.hr
Runs services from Stinica to Mišnjak (Rab).

Split Tours
114 brigade 10, Split
Tel: 021 352533
www.splittours.hr
Runs services from Split to Rogač and Žirje-Kaprije-Šibenik.

UTO Kapetan Luka
Poljička cesta-Krilo 4, Jesenice
Tel: 021 645 476
www.krilo.hr
Runs services from Korčula to Split via Hvar.

Chartering a yacht

Numerous companies offer yacht charters in Croatia. Contacts for some of the bigger companies are listed below. To charter a yacht you need a qualified skipper who must hold a navigation permit. (People who have held a captain's certificate for at least three years can take an examination to gain their permit.) For those without formal qualifications it is usually possible to hire a skipper through the various yacht charter companies.

ACI (Adriatic Croatia International Club)
M. Tita 15, 51410 Opatija
Tel: 051 271288
www.aci-marinas.com
Charters boats throughout Croatia.

Adriatic Yacht Charter
Braće Leonardelli 33, Pula
Tel: 098 366721
www.ayc.hr

ACI Marina Dubrovnik
Dubrovnik
Tel: 098 335554
www.ayc.hr

⏻ Distances from Zagreb

Karlovac = 56km/35 miles
Varaždin = 87km/54 miles
Rijeka = 166km/103 miles
Slavonski Brod = 190km/118 miles
Pula = 267km/166 miles
Osijek = 280km/173 miles
Dubrovnik = 606km/377 miles

Asta Yachting Ltd
Put Murata 1a, Zadar
Tel: 023 316902
www.asta-yachting.hr

Club Adriatic
Tel: 01 467 7395
www.clubadriatic.com

Driving

Main routes

Croatia's expanding motorway network connects Zagreb northwards to Varaždin and beyond to the Hungarian border, eastwards to Slavonski Brod and Osijek, southwards to Rijeka, and further southeast via Knin to Split and then inland roughly parallel to Hvar. All motorways are toll roads. Croatia's other main route is the Jadranska Magistrala connecting Rijeka and Dubrovnik (subject to roadworks and further expansion). For the latest traffic news, check out www.hak.hr.

Car hire

It is fairly expensive to hire a car in Croatia – around €280 (£245 or $330) per week for a small car in high season. This will include unlimited mileage, third-party insurance, collision damage waiver and theft waiver, and local taxes. For the international car-hire firms, it generally works out cheaper to hire in advance of arriving in Croatia, but you may manage to get a good deal on the spot from a local company.

Drivers must be at least 21 years old and have held a full driving licence for two years; they also need a valid passport or national identity card. When hiring your car, check the insurance carefully to be clear about any excess charges that may be applied in case of accident.

Major hire companies such as Budget, National and Avis have offices throughout Croatia, with many at major transport terminals. It is best to book through a central reservations number or online.

Avis
Tel: 01 467 3638
www.avis.hr

Budget
Tel: 01 467 3638
www.budget.hr

Europcar
Tel: 052 390090
www.europcar.com/hr

Insurance

When hiring a car it is advisable to purchase collision damage waiver (CDW) and theft protection (TP) for the duration of the hire. Personal accident insurance (PAI) is optional. Damage to a vehicle must be reported to the police immediately (tel: 92), otherwise the insurance becomes invalid, leaving the hirer liable for the repair bill.

Rules of the road

To enter Croatia by car, drivers need a valid licence, an automobile registration card and evidence of insurance cover. Official speed limits are 50kmh (30mph in built up areas, 80kmh (50mph) outside residential areas, 100kmh (62mph) on major roads and 130kmh (80mph) on motorways. However, many Croatians drive faster. Buses and vehicles with a trailer have a maximum speed of 80kmh (50mph).

The wearing of seat belts is compulsory and dipped headlights must be on at all times. Using mobile telephones that are not hands-free is banned. It is a legal requirement to inform the police about traffic accidents (tel: 92) and to use a hazard warning triangle. A variety of violations, including speeding, not wearing a seat belt and not observing the right of way, incur an on-the-spot fine. Fines range from 100 kuna to 500 kuna depending on the severity of the incident. Drivers under the influence of alcohol will have their licence revoked.

Many of Croatia's old towns are officially closed to traffic except for those accessing residential property. Although there is lax enforcement of this rule, old town streets are very narrow, hard to navigate and can become unexpectedly blocked.

In case of a breakdown, tel: 987. The Croatian Auto Club (Hrvatski Autoklub – HAK; tel: 072 777777, www.hak.hr) can provide more information about toll roads, driving in Croatia and traffic updates

Parking

Car parks in Croatia are well signposted with a white 'P' inside a blue square. The main car parks in many of Croatia's historic towns are just outside the pedestrian zones and cost 4 to 7 kuna an hour. Parking is usually available for 24 hours.

A

Accommodation

Choosing a hotel

Croatia has hotels to suit all tastes and budgets, from vast concrete resorts that were built in the Communist era to small luxury hotels and even renovated lighthouses. The country is also in the process of developing high-quality small-scale accommodation, with more focus on design. Prices and facilities vary greatly, but most hotels offer spacious, clean rooms. The star system can be confusing, as the criteria for each category have yet to be standardised. You might find yourself in a hotel that awarded itself three stars but has very few or even no private bathrooms. It is highly advisable to book in advance in high season. For those travelling on a tighter budget, Croatia has a wealth of private accommodation and camping grounds with excellent facilities. Except in Zagreb and some five-star hotels, hotel prices are seasonal, being highest in July and August and up to 40 percent less off-season. In Zagreb prices rise during trade fairs. You can find a list of trade fairs in Zagreb at www.zv.hr. Hotel prices are often better if booked online.

Private accommodation

Private accommodation is popular in Croatia, and many resorts, villages and towns throughout the country have more beds in private accommodation than in hotels. The standard of private accommodation varies considerably, ranging from simple rooms in private houses (called *sobe*) to self-contained studios or apartments, ideal for longer visits. Although it is common for people to approach travellers at transport terminals offering rooms, it is best to go through an agency.

The concept of agrotourism is developing in Croatia, particularly in Istria, where farmers are opening their doors to guests and offering home-cooked food featuring their own produce. While it's not as widespread as in Italy, agroturizam, or eko farm, as it's known, it is becoming more popular for people who want a real taste of rural life.

The cheap rates for a room can be hiked by supplements for short stays (30–100 percent depending on the location) taxes, registration fees and single occupancy. *Generalturist*, *Atlas* and *Kompas* are among the biggest agents and have offices throughout Croatia. A useful resource is www.hostelworld.com.

Holiday rental companies are expanding rapidly and constantly adding new Croatian properties to their lists. Some firms offer luxurious villas, such as Croatian Villa Holidays (www.croatianvillaholidays.com) and James Villas (www.jamesvillas.co.uk). Other rental companies have an enormous range of properties, from studio apartments in the heart of a city to large villas with private pools. Companies worth checking out include Online Croatia (www.online-croatia.com), Holiday Lettings (www.holidaylettings.co.uk), HomeAway Holiday Rentals (www.homeaway.co.uk) and Only Apartments (www.only-apartments.com). Vintage Travel (www.vintagetravel.co.uk) has properties in Istria.

Lighthouses

For a unique holiday experience you can stay in one of 11 renovated lighthouses in Croatia. Located on beautiful islands and promontories they offer a real getaway. Most lighthouses have their own keeper and a stay of seven days, from Saturday to Saturday, is required (three days out of season). More information is available on tel: 021 390609, www.plovput.hr.

Camping

Croatia has more than 500 campsites with accommodation in tents or mobile homes, categorised on a star system from one to four. They can range from small family-run sites to large holiday parks. Some cater to naturists. Facilities are generally good and include hot water, showers and toilets as a minimum. Larger campsites will have swimming pools, playgrounds and organised activities for children and adults. Camping is seasonal and the campsites listed are open from April through to October. The **Croatian Camping Union** can provide information. Pionirska 1, Poreč, tel: 052 451324, www.camping.hr.

Youth hostels

Hostels affiliated with Hostelling International are prefixed YH and can be booked at www.hfhs.hr. If you don't have a membership card, expect to pay a nominal guest fee per night.

Admission charges

Most Croatian museums charge an entry fee between 10 and 40 kuna, with half-price entry for children, students and senior citizens, although a few have occasional free-entry days. For one day around the end of January, many institutions in Croatia participate in Museum Night, which offers free entry to museums and galleries from 6pm to 1am. Many museums have restrictions on still or video photography. In Zagreb, the Zagreb Card (www.zagrebcard.fivestars.hr) offers free or discounted access to nearly all the city's museums and many other venues, as well as free public transport. It is available for either 24 or 72 hours.

Budgeting for your trip

Here are some average costs. Note that costs in Zagreb and Dubrovnik are generally higher than elsewhere and many prices increase in high season (July and August).
Croatian beer (half a litre) or a glass of house wine (125ml) in a bar or café: around 15 kuna
Main course at a cheap restaurant: 50 kuna
Main course at a moderate restaurant: 85 kuna
Main course at an expensive restaurant: 175 kuna
Double room with breakfast at a cheap hotel in high season: 500 kuna
Double room with breakfast at a moderate hotel in high season: 800 kuna
Double room with breakfast at a deluxe hotel in high season: 3,500 kuna
A taxi journey from Zagreb airport to the city centre: 180 kuna
A single bus ticket: 10–30 kuna

City transport

Tickets for local bus services are available from tobacco kiosks or from the driver at a slightly higher price. In larger towns and cities, bus services start as early as 4am and run until around 11pm, with fares ranging from 10 to 30 kuna depending on the distance travelled. Local and national bus services can be caught at bus stations or hailed at designated stops. The main bus stations are listed in the Getting there section (see page 264).

Zagreb and Osijek both have a city tram service. Trams operate a similar timetable to the buses and tickets should be purchased from a newspaper kiosk. Passengers must first validate tickets using the on-board machines.

Children

Most hotels, restaurants and cafés are very accommodating to families. In many establishments under-3s can stay free, and discounts are frequently available for accommodation, travel and food for under-12s and even under-18s. The beaches and resorts, especially Istria and its islands, offer plenty of water-based activities for children as well as dry sporting facilities for older children. One thing that Croatia is very short on, however, is sand, and most of the beaches are shingle, rock, or man-made from concrete or gravel. If you don't bring swimming shoes, they are readily available in beach resort shops.

Climate

Croatia has four seasons and two distinct climatic zones. Inland Croatia enjoys temperate weather whereas the Adriatic coastline has a more Mediterranean climate with hot, sunny summer days and mild, wet winters. The Dinaric Alps, backing onto the Dalmatian coast, have hot summers and cold winters with lots of snow. Inland temperatures drop as low as –1°C (30°F) in January and reach highs of 26°C (79°F) in August. Coastal temperatures are around 5 to 10°C (40–50°F) in January and regularly reach 30°C (86°F) in August. The sea is warm all year round with a low of 12°C (53°F) in winter and a high of 26°C (79°F) in summer.

The tourist season is April to October. Spring and summer are the best times for hiking and biking. August is the time for nightlife, but at this hot, busy time of year car drivers have to queue for hours to board ferries for the islands, and many hotels and private rooms are booked up.

What to wear/bring

Croatia is a well-developed, modern country and visitors will be able to buy most of the things they need. The type of clothing required depends on the season and intended activities. At the height of the tourist season in July and August temperatures in the sun can reach 30°C (86°F), although they usually hover around 24°C (76°F), so it is essential to wear light, loose non-synthetic clothing, sunglasses and a sunhat. Night-time temperatures are mild, making it possible to wear shorts, T-shirts and sundresses through to bedtime. Mild, humid evenings attract mosquitoes and so a supply of insect repellent with 30 to 50 percent DEET is a good investment.

In spring, early summer and early autumn, when average temperatures are lower, a sweater or light jacket is also advisable. November through to March are cold months and a good winter coat is necessary.

Although parts of Dalmatia are renowned for long dry periods, be prepared for the possibility of rain whatever the season. It is also advisable to bring sturdy walking shoes or trainers for easy walks. More serious hiking will require hiking boots.

Useful numbers

Weather forecast and road conditions: tel: 060 520520.

Crime and safety

Crime rates in Croatia are lower than in most European countries and crime against tourists is rare, violent crime extremely rare. Simple precautions such as not leaving valuables in vehicles, carrying personal belongings securely and avoiding walking alone in dark areas at night minimise the risk. Do not leave items unattended at beaches. It is advisable to photocopy the identification pages of your passport so that if it is lost or stolen the consulate will be able to issue a replacement quickly. The emergency number in Croatia is 112. Visitors to Croatia need to carry a passport or, where applicable, national ID card, at all times.

Land mines

The Croatian government was quick to remove land mines at the end of the war and most areas are completely safe. However some more remote areas around Lika and Continental Croatia are still being de-mined, including areas close to main roads. Look out for warning signs with the skull and crossbones on a red triangle with black lettering saying Ne prilazite (Do not enter), and do not stray from roads and paved areas without a local guide. Particularly avoid overgrown

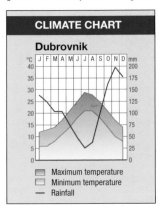

CLIMATE CHART

Dubrovnik

Maximum temperature
Minimum temperature
Rainfall

areas and abandoned war-damaged buildings. A useful resource is the Croatian Mine Action Centre (Hrvatski centar za razminiranje; tel. 044 554151; www.hcr.hr).

Customs regulations

Visitors coming from other parts of the European Union have no limits on what they can import, as long as they can prove it is for personal use. Visitors from outside the European Union can bring 1 litre of wine and 1 litre of spirits, 1 bottle of scent, 250ml of toilet water, 200 cigarettes or 100 cigarillos or 50 cigars or 250g of tobacco into Croatia duty free. If you are carrying more than a total of €10,000 in cash or cheques you must declare it at customs. The transportation of domestic currency is restricted to 15,000 kuna. It is possible to bring cats and dogs into Croatia if they have a certificate confirming vaccination against rabies, issued within the previous six months and at least 15 days before the date of entry.

D

Disabled travellers

Many of Croatia's most interesting sights lie within the country's historic old towns, where streets are generally cobbled and buildings are old with narrow staircases, hallways and no lifts, making disabled access problematic. Access to beaches can also be difficult, requiring descents over steep steps or crossing rocky outcrops, although the town of Omiš, near Split, has a wheelchair-accessible beach with special ramps to lower disabled people into the sea, and the nearby town of Ivašnjak is also wheelchair-accessible. Travellers with disabilities should plan their visits in advance and check with local tourist boards that their needs can be catered for. In general, newly built hotels are more likely to have facilities for disabled travellers.

E

Eating out

Although not always especially cheap, eating out is one of the high points of visiting Croatia and you won't have to look far to find somewhere specialising in fresh local delicacies. There are also many places serving international cuisine, especially Italian.

Taverns

In Croatian, a konoba is a tavern where fishermen would eat some of their catch. While this practice is not quite as common as it used to be, the term konoba usually indicates a historic venue serving traditional local delicacies at reasonable prices, usually doubling as a bar in the evening, although a few places have gone upmarket. If you're looking for generous helpings of authentic Croatian food lashed down with carafes of home-made wine in a cosy environment, head for your nearest konoba. If you're looking for a cheap meal, try a gablec, a workers' restaurant usually offering inexpensive set menus at lunchtime.

Cafés

Croatians have an average annual consumption of 4.9kg (10lb) of coffee per capita, and Croatia has one of the most vibrant café societies of any country in the world. Croatian even has a word – špica – to describe the traditional caffeine-laced post-shopping Saturday-morning get-together between friends. While at home Croatians drink Turkish coffee (turska kafa), in a café (kavana or, if it is small, kafić), they ape the Italians and are likely to order a cappuccino (kapućino), espresso, macchiato or simply a black coffee (crna kava) or milky white coffee (kava s mlijekom). It is rare to find bad coffee in Croatia. Fruit, herbal and black teas are also popular. But you can order just about any drink you can think of – soft or alcoholic – and almost every café also serves pastries and ice cream. A slastičarnica is a pastry shop or ice cream parlour that also sells soft drinks. There is a smoking ban in all enclosed public spaces including bars, restaurants and cafés, but since there is such a culture of outdoor dining and drinking on terraces the ban has had little effect on business, simply making finding a table inside easier.

Wine cellars

There are two main wine regions in Croatia: the continental region – covering Plešivica, Zagorje, Prigorje, Moslavina, Pokuplje, Slavonia and Podunavlje – and the coastal region of Istria and Dalmatia. Istria currently has the best infrastructure for wine tourism and there are numerous wine cellars open to the public in the region. The Istria County Tourist Association (tel: 052 452797; www.istra.hr) can provide a road map showing locations and giving contact details for each cellar.

The island of Vis is another great place for wine lovers. Alongside bigger producers such as Roki's and Rukatac, the island has lots of small wine cellars, where people go to enjoy a glass of their favourite tipple with the producer. Many vinoteke bear the sign Prodajem domaće vino (domestic wine for sale). Opening times are usually 9am–noon and 6.30–11pm.

What to eat

Croatian cuisine varies regionally. In coastal areas, fresh fish features heavily on the menu, whilst staples inland include mlinci (a type of pasta), roast lamb, roast suckling pig and boiled or baked štrukli (pastry with ham and cheese). Each region also has its own local dishes. Pršut (prosciutto), brodet (fish stew with polenta) and pašticada (beef goulash and gnocchi) are Dalmatian specialities. Istrian specialities include pršut, manestre (dried meat and vegetable broth), ombolo (pork fillets) and truffles. In Kvarner, look out for Pag cheese (hard and salty sheep's cheese). Inland specialities include kulen (paprika-flavoured salami) and češnjovka (garlic sausages from Zagorje). A useful source of information about eating and dining in rural Croatia is www.ruraltour.org.

Vegetarian food

Many restaurants offer a very small number of vegetarian dishes. Zagreb has an excellent vegan eatery. Most restaurants specialise in fish and meat dishes, and even many of the pasta staples served as starters have meat sauces. Vegetarian options are commonly available in pizzerias and in fast-food outlets that sell sandwiches.

Ordering fish

It is normal for restaurants to charge for fish and seafood by weight, although there are usually a few set-price dishes too. A typical helping is about 250g (9oz), but to avoid confusion and unpleasant surprises on the bill, it is best to specify the amount wanted when ordering.

Embassies and consulates

Zagreb

Australian Embassy
3rd Floor, Centar Kaptol, Nova ves 11
Tel: 01 489 1200
www.croatia.embassy.gov.au
British Embassy
Ivana Lučića 4
Tel: 01 600 9100
www.ukincroatia.fco.gov.uk
Canadian Embassy
Prilaz Đure Deželića 4
Tel: 01 488 1200
www.canadainternational.gc.ca
Irish Embassy
Miramarska 23
Tel: 01 627 8920
www.dfa.ie/irish-embassy/croatia
New Zealand Consulate
Vlaška ulica 50a
Tel: 01 461 2060
www.mfat.govt.nz
South African Honorary Consulate
Vinkovićeva 7
Tel: 01 468 0981
United States Embassy
Thomasa Jeffersona 2
Tel: 01 661 2200
http://zagreb.usembassy.gov

Croatian embassies and consulates

Australia
Croatian Embassy
14 Jindalee Crescent
ACT 2606, Canberra
Tel: 61(2) 628 66988
Canada
Croatian Embassy
229 Chapel Street,
Ottawa, Canada K1N 7Y6
Tel: 1(613) 562 7824
Ireland
Croatian Embassy
Adelaide Chambers
Peter Street, Dublin 8
Tel: 353 (1) 4767 181
New Zealand
Croatian Consulate
2 Akersten Street
Port Nelson 7010
Tel: 03 5282800
South Africa
Croatian Embassy
1160 Stanza Bopape (Church) Street
0083 Colbyn, Pretoria
Tel: 27 (12) 342 1206
UK
Croatian Embassy
21 Conway Street
London W1T 6BN
Tel: 44 (20) 7387 2022

US
Croatian Embassy
2343 Massachusetts Avenue
Washington, D.C. 20008
Tel: 1-202 588 5899

Etiquette

Croatians tend to be quite reserved with strangers, especially away from the main tourist areas. A few words of Croatian go a long way. When addressing strangers it is polite to use the honorific *gospodine* (for a man), *gospođo* (for a married woman) or *gospodice* (for a young unmarried woman), followed by the family name. Beachwear is not acceptable in churches and visitors should cover their shoulders and knees. As a visit to any café will quickly confirm, Croatians take their fashion seriously and do not appreciate scruffy dress. If invited to a Croatian house for a meal, it is appropriate to give the hostess an odd number of flowers, from three upwards (but not chrysanthemums, which symbolise death) and the host a bottle of good wine or a box of chocolates. Do not start eating before the host. It is polite to wait for the host to insist before accepting a second helping.

Events and festivals

Winter Carnival (Zimski karneval), Pag, January–February (from first Saturday after Epiphany to Ash Wednesday)
Every Saturday people attend masked parties in various locations. It is claimed to be the oldest carnival in the Adriatic. www.tzgpag.hr.
Rijeka Carnival (Riječki karneval), January–February
Month-long series of events including a carnival queen pageant, a children's carnival parade and various concerts. For further information, tel: 051 315710, http://www.rijecki-karneval.hr.
Cultural summer, Istria
During the summer season, outdoor venues throughout Poreč, Umag, Rovinj, Pula and Grožnjan come alive with concerts. For further information, tel: 052 452797, www.istra.hr.
Summer Carnival (Ljetni karneval), Pag, usually 27 June
This festival is another excuse to dress up in colourful costumes and party. For further information, www.tzgpag.hr.
International Children's Festival (Međunarodni dječji festival), Šibenik, late June/early July

Emergency numbers

All emergencies: 112
Police: 92
Fire Brigade: 93
Ambulance: 94
Emergency road service: 987
Coast guard: 985

A festival featuring puppet shows, ballet, art and performances by children's theatre groups. For further information, contact: tel: 022 213636, www.mdf-sibenik.com.
Poreč Open Air – Festival of Life, mid-June–mid-September
Numerous street performances as well as music, cinema and theatre events. For further information, http://porecopenair.com.
Zagreb Summer Evenings (Zagrebačke ljetne večeri), July
This festival brings traditional folklore, music, theatre and concerts to stages across the capital. For further information, tel: 01 450 1200, www.kdz.hr.
Musical Evenings in St Donat's (Glazbene večeri u sv. Donatu), Zadar, early July–mid-August
A chance to hear musicians playing classical music in this historical church. For information, contact Concert Office Zadar, Poljana Šime Budinića 3, tel: 023 627 762, www.donat-festival.com.
Summer events, Krk, early July–late August
Stages throughout Krk are illuminated with opera, plays and concerts. For further information, tel: 051 221359, www.krk.hr.
Dubrovnik Summer Festival (Dubrovački ljetni festival), mid-July–late August
One of Europe's great festivals, this annual feast of folklore, music, opera and drama takes place in numerous outdoor venues. Contact Dubrovnik Summer Festival, tel: 020 326100, www.dubrovnik-festival.hr.
Days of Opatija, mid-July–late July
Programme of musical, sporting and art events celebrating the Feast Day of St Jacob, the city's patron saint, on 25 July. For further information, visit www.opatija.hr.
Feast Day of St Theodore, Korčula, 27 July
A tradition probably brought to Korčula by traders from Spain, the *moreška* is a sword dance commemorating the triumph of Christians over the Ottomans. This

one celebrates the Feast Day of St Theodore (sveti Todor), the island's protector.

Pula Film Festival, mid-July–late July

An annual event held inside the city's Roman amphitheatre. For further information, tel: 052 393321, www.pulafilmfestival.hr.

The Summer of Split (Splitsko ljeto), mid-July–mid-August

An outdoor festival of drama, opera, ballet and concerts. For further information, contact the Croatian National Theatre Split, www.splitsko-ljeto.hr.

International Folklore Festival, Zagreb (Međunarodna smotra folklora), Wednesday–Sunday in the third week of July

Most events are free. Various venues. For further information contact Zagreb tourist office or tel: 01 450 1194, www.msf.hr.

Vinkovci Autumn Festival (Vinkovačke jeseni), two days, late September

A national review of authentic Croatian folklore. For further information, tel: 032 331072, http://vinkovackejeseni.hr.

Varaždin Baroque Evenings (Varaždinske barokne večeri), late September–early October

Opera and Baroque ensembles feature amongst the daily performances. www.vbv.hr.

H

Health and medical care

Health

A visit to Croatia does not carry any specific health risks and no vaccinations are needed. However, it is advisable to take precautions against sunstroke, sunburn and dehydration in the summer by bringing sunscreen, a sunhat, and drinking plenty of water. It is safe to drink the tap water throughout Croatia although mineral water is also widely available.

Visitors needing specific medication should take adequate supplies with them, including the packaging listing ingredients, which will help pharmacists supply replacements if necessary.

Those planning to travel for long periods in Croatia's mountains should think about vaccinating against tick-borne encephalitis, a serious disease causing the brain to swell and sometimes leading to death. Another potential hazard is sea urchins, black spiky balls about the size of a child's fist that lurk around rocky beaches. If you tread on one, the spines can become implanted in the skin, causing great pain and potentially leading to infection if not removed.

Medical treatment

Medical care in Croatia is of a high standard, with facilities on a par with those in Western Europe. Larger towns and cities have their own hospitals and most small towns have a medical centre with a doctor on call 24 hours every day. Most bigger towns and cities also have a 24-hour pharmacy. Local tourist offices and hotels can provide details of these. Also see Insurance (see page 271) for information on payment for health services.

Insurance

Citizens of Britain, Ireland and most European countries are entitled to free medical care thanks to a mutual health-care agreement. If no such agreement exists, patients pay according to a standard price list.

Credit cards often offer limited insurance when used to book a flight or holiday, and some household insurance covers personal possessions away from home including cover abroad. You should always check terms and conditions thoroughly prior to departure.

It would be unwise to rely on any of these forms of insurance alone. Without taking out adequate travel insurance you could face large medical bills, repatriation costs or expensive lawsuits.

The cover provided by travel-insurance policies varies greatly and so it is essential to read the small print and ensure that you have comprehensive cover that includes claims by a third party. Extra premiums may apply for covering adventure sports and expensive articles such as mobiles and laptops.

I

Internet

High-speed broadband and wireless internet have been spreading rapidly around Croatia. Wi-fi hotspots have become more common, particularly in marina areas along the popular coastal resorts. Bars and cafés will often offer free Wi-fi if you don't mind asking the staff for the code. Croatia's membership in the European Union led to a welcome reduction in charges for voice and data communications from mobile phones.

L

LGBTQ travellers

Croatia is a religious country with a Roman Catholic majority. As a result, homosexuality is tolerated, but not embraced. As such there are not many official gay venues and public displays of affection are not welcome, though there are LGBTQ scenes in larger cities. Every year since 2002 a Zagreb Pride march has taken place in June with the support of the city authorities, but despite a strong police presence often with a backdrop of violence from protestors. There is also a Queer Zagreb festival every spring. There are several gay rights groups in Croatia including Iskorak (www.iskorak.org) and Kontra (www.kontra.hr), a group for lesbians and bisexual women. A useful online guide to gay Croatia, listing many clubs, bars and other meeting places, is www.croatia-gay.com.

M

Media

Television

Hrvatska radiotelevizija (HRT; www.hrt.hr) operates Croatia's four public television stations: HRT1, HRT2, HRT3 and HRT4 as well as an international station aimed mainly at the Croatian diaspora. Six other private stations operate in addition to at least 20 regional stations around the country. The majority of foreign-language programmes, of which there are many, have Croatian subtitles rather than dubbed soundtracks.

Maps

Useful national maps are available from Croatian National Tourist Offices abroad, good local bookshops and also local tourist offices.

Radio

Croatia's three main radio stations are Hrvatska radio 1, 2 and 3 (HR1, HR2 and HR3). HR1 and HR2 broadcast news, weather reports, travel news music, documentaries and sporting programmes, and HR3 broadcasts classical music and radio drama. All of them are streamed live on the internet as well. During the main tourist season Hrvatska radio regularly broadcasts news, reports on road and sailing conditions in English, German and Italian. www.hrt.hr.

Print

Croatia's five main daily newspapers are *Večernji List* (www.vecernji.hr), *Jutarnji List* (www.jutarnji.hr), *24sata* (www.24sata.hr), *Novi List* (www.novilist.hr) and *Slobodna Dalmacija* (www.slobodnadalmacija.hr). The *Hina News Line* website is in Croatian and English. You can also access the *Novi list* (www.novilist.hr) and the business newspaper *Dnevnik* (www.dnevnik.hr) online, in Croatian only. The international edition of the *Guardian* and the *International New York Times* are readily available in Croatia in summer, as is a selection of other foreign-language newspapers, though they are often not available on the day of publication.

Money

Cash

Croatia's official currency is the kuna: 100 lipa make 1 kuna, although prices are frequently quoted in both kuna and euros. It is not advisable to carry large sums of money, but it is useful to keep a small emergency fund if you are planning to visit remote areas of the country (you can change euros, US dollars, pounds sterling and other major currencies at banks and exchange offices throughout Croatia). Beware of changing money unofficially as you risk picking up counterfeit notes, especially for 200 and 500 kuna.

Approximate exchange rates:
1 euro = 7.4 kuna
1 pound = 8.4 kuna
1 US dollar = 6.2 kuna

ATMs and credit cards

The easiest way to get cash in Croatia is to debit money from your bank account via one of the many ATMs, although try to avoid waiting until you reach one of the smaller islands. Debit cards carrying the Maestro, MasterCard, Visa and Cirrus symbols are widely accepted. When debiting money directly from a bank account the exchange rate is more predictable than when using a credit card, but commission charges vary greatly, with some banks charging as much as 4 percent. Credit card cash advances can also be made from ATMs.

Credit cards are a good way to settle bills, but do not assume that they will be accepted everywhere, even in the most expensive restaurants. It is advisable not to depend on one card only and to inform your bank of your travel plans to prevent cards being blocked.

Most credit card companies will replace a lost or stolen credit card within 24 hours and arrange an emergency cash advance on the same day. Western Union money transfer services are also available at more than 1,000 post offices throughout Croatia.

Tax

Value Added Tax (PDV) is applied to nearly all purchases in Croatia and charged at 25 percent. Bread, milk, medicine and technical and educational books are exempt and there is a 13 percent rate for accommodation services, magazines and newspapers. Non-EU visitors can claim this tax back on purchases over 5,000 kuna from shops that display a Tax Free Shopping logo. Some local authorities also charge a 3 percent tax on certain transactions.

Tipping

Hotel and restaurant bills usually include tax and service. However it is common practice to round the bill up to the nearest 10 kuna or leave an additional tip of 10 to 15 percent if service has been good, especially in more expensive restaurants. In cheaper places it is normal to leave any coins from the change. Unless the service has been exceptional, do not feel obliged to tip taxi drivers as they often overcharge tourists or round up the fare.

Opening hours

Office hours are generally 8am–4pm or 8.30am–4.30pm Monday through Friday. In the tourist resorts opening hours are often 8am–1pm and 5–11pm. Many large towns have a 24-hour pharmacy and some have 24-hour grocery stores. Banks are generally open 7am–3pm Monday through Friday and 8am–2pm Saturday. Opening hours for museums vary but they generally close on Monday and public holidays. Try to avoid travelling without your own wheels on national holidays, when public transport grinds to a trickle. Most public transport also has a restricted Sunday timetable. Most shops and department stores open from 8am–8pm on weekdays, sometimes with a siesta from noon to 4pm, and until 2 or 3pm on Saturday. Some open till 10pm, especially in tourist areas in high season, and from 8am–2pm on Sunday. There are a few 24-hour shops in major cities, often in or near major transport terminals.

Postal services

Croatia has an efficient postal service operated by Hrvatska pošta (www.posta.hr). It sells stamps and telephone cards, sends packages, and gives credit card cash advances and changes foreign currency. Some towns have separate post offices for sending larger packages. Post offices are generally open from 7am–7pm Monday through Friday and until 1pm on Saturday. In smaller towns the post office may close at 4pm whilst those in tourist resorts operate a split shift, opening from 7am–1pm and 7–9pm.

Religious services

Around 86 percent of Croatians are Roman Catholic and Mass is held in Catholic churches and cathedrals throughout the county. According to the 2011 census, minority groups include Orthodox 4.4 percent, other Christian 0.6 percent and Muslim 1.4 percent. The local tourist office will be able to advise visitors of service times or direct them to the office of the parish priest. Zagreb's Anglican chaplaincy hosts English-language services for Christians of any denomination at 10am each Sunday from September through June at St Joseph's Chapel on the third floor of the Jesuit Centre, Jordanovac 110. According to the constitution, Croatia is a secular republic in which all religious groups are separate from the state. However, Roman Catholicism has long played a strong part in the national identity – before it collapsed, about half the population of Yugoslavia was Orthodox, 30 percent Catholic and 10 percent Muslim – and these faiths have made a resurgence since independence.

S

Shopping

What to buy

Traditional Croatian souvenirs include handmade silk neck ties (kravate, singular kravata), Pag cheese, handmade lace, fragrant herbal remedies, stoneware and glassware. Traditional morčić jewellery from Rijeka, natural cosmetics and high-quality silver jewellery made with red Adriatic coral are also popular. Local foods, wines and spirits such as fiery Croatian fruit brandy (rakija), or šljivovica (plum brandy), truffles, honey and olive oil also make good gifts. In a nation obsessed with fashion, clothes and shoes are also a good buy. In Zagreb, Nataša Mihaljčišin and Martina Vrdoljak-Ranilović are two voguish designers running the I-GLE Fashion Studio, which distributes its lines through the world's top stores.

Shopping areas

The main shopping areas in Croatia's smaller towns and resorts are easy to locate because of the throngs of people. In most destinations it is possible to purchase high-quality jewellery, souvenirs, original artwork, candles, perfume, lace and clothing from small boutiques. Some unmissable shopping areas include Poreč's Ulica Decumanus, where the remains of Venetian villas brim with souvenir shops, and Rovinj's Ulica Grisia in the old town, where high-quality artwork and gifts abound. In Hvar, Trgovački Orbit is worth a

⊙ Time Zone

GMT plus 1 hour, with daylight saving time in summer.

visit with its boutiques and antique shops. In Split, the best place for shopping is around Diocletian's Palace and Marmontova, where designer stores abound. Zagreb is also a good place for fashion, centred in Ilica. The tourist office has a good selection of reproduction antiques and other gifts.

Markets

Most resorts, towns and cities in Croatia have both a green market – selling fresh fruit, veg, fish and meat – and a general market. Most markets in Croatia are open daily, except Sunday, between 8am and 2pm. Markets in major tourist destinations tend to have extended opening hours.

T

Telephones

You can make domestic and international direct-dial calls from any telephone in Croatia. Mobile phone numbers begin with 09 and all the digits must be dialled.

To call Croatia from outside the country, first dial your international access code followed by the code for Croatia, 385. When calling from abroad omit the initial 0 in the regional access code. For example dial 1 instead of 01 for Zagreb. You can save on telephone calls by buying a local SIM card for your mobile phone. A cheap way to make international calls is to pick up a discount telephone card from a post office.

Useful numbers

Directory enquiries: 988
International operator: 901
International directory assistance: 902
Fire, police, ambulance and other emergencies: 112

Tourist information

Tourist offices abroad

The Croatia National Tourist Office (Hrvatska turistička zajednica) provides brochures, maps and leaflets about the country's many attractions, accommodation and facilities. Detailed information is also available on its website, www.croatia.hr.
UK and Ireland
1 Farrier's Yard, 77–85 Fulham Palace Road, W6 8JA London

⊙ Public holidays

New Year's Day 1 January
Three Kings Day/Epiphany 6 January
Easter Sunday and Easter Monday March/April
International Workers' Day 1 May
Corpus Christi May/June (60 days after Easter)
Anti-Fascist Struggle Day 22 June
Croatian National Day 25 June
Victory Day/National Thanksgiving 5 August
Feast of the Assumption 15 August
Independence Day 8 October
All Saints' Day 1 November
Christmas 25 December
St Stephen's Day 26 December
Names may vary slightly according to the translation from Croatian to English.

Tel: + 44 (0) 20 8563 7979
Email: info@croatia-london.co.uk
US and Canada
P.O. Box 2651
New York, NY 10108
Email: mailto:info@htz.hr

Tourist offices in Croatia

Istria
Motovun
Trg Andrea Antico 1
Tel: 052 681726
http://tz-motovun.hr
Poreč
Zagrebačka 9
Tel: 052 451293
http://www.istra.hr/porec
Pula
Forum 3
Tel: 052 219197
www.pulainfo.hr
Rovinj
Pina Budičina 12
Tel: 052 811566
www.tzgrovinj.hr
Kvarner
Krk Town
Vela placa 1/1
Tel: 051 221414
www.tz-krk.hr
Opatija
Maršala Tita 128
Tel: 051 271310
http://visitopatija.com
Rab
Trg Municipium Arba 8
Tel: 051 724064
http://www.rab-visit.com

Rijeka
Užarska 14
Tel: 051 315710
http://www.visitrijeka.hr
Zadar and Šibenik
Šibenik
Fausta Vrančića 18
Tel: 022 212075
www.sibenik-tourism.hr
Zadar
Svetog Leopolda Bogdana Mandića 1
Tel: 023 315316
www.zadar.hr
Split and islands
Hvar Town
Trg sv. Stjepana 42
Tel: 021 741059
www.tzhvar.hr
Split
Obala Hrvatskog Narodnog Preporoda 9
Tel: 021 348600
www.visitsplit.com
Trogir
Trg Ivana Pavla II 1
Tel: 021 885628
www.tztrogir.hr
Dubrovnik and islands
Dubrovnik
Brsalje 5
Tel: 020 312011
www.tzdubrovnik.hr
Zagreb and around
Karlovac
Ulica Petra Zrinskog 3
Tel: 047 615115
www.karlovac-touristinfo.hr
Varaždin
Ivana Padovca 3
Tel: 042 210987
http://www.tourism-varazdin.hr
Zagreb
Trg bana Josipa Jelačića 11
Tel: 01 481 4051
www.infozagreb.hr
Continental Croatia
Osijek
Županijska 2
Tel: 031 203755
www.tzosijek.hr
Vukovar
J.J. Strossmayera 15
Tel: 032 442889
www.turizamvukovar.hr

Tour operators

Insight Guides
Insight Guides (www.insightguides.com/holidays) offers holidays to numerous destinations around the globe, including Croatia. You can book trips, transfers and a range of exciting experiences through our local experts, taking in the highlights of the Dalmatian Coast and all the major cities.

UK tour companies

UK companies offering charter flights and package holidays to Croatia include:
Adriatic Holidays
Prama House, 267 Banbury Road
Oxford OX2 7HT
Tel: +44 (0)1865 339481
www.adriaticholidays.co.uk
Specialises in sailing holidays along the Dalmatian coast. Offers organised trips and charters.
Balkan Escape
8 Victoria Street
Spalding, Lincolnshire PE11 1EA
Tel: +44 (0)1775 719891
www.balkanescape.co.uk
Balkan Holidays
Sofia House, 19 Conduit Street, London W1S 2BH
Tel: +44 (0)20 7543 5555
www.balkanholidays.co.uk
Chalfont Holidays
104-5 High Street, Eton, Berkshire SL4 6AF
Tel: +44 (0)1753 740176
www.chalfontholidays.co.uk
Specialist providers of naturist holidays in Croatia.
Completely Croatia
The Old Forge, Gardner Street
Herstmonceux, East Sussex BN27 4LG
Tel: 0800 970 9149
www.completelycroatia.co.uk
Exodus
Tel: (0)20 3811 6120
www.exodus.co.uk
Activity holidays including cycling in Istria, Dalmatia and Plitvice Lakes.
Original Travel
1st Floor, 111 Upper Richmond Road, London SW15 2TL21
Tel: (0)20 7978 7333
Luxury holidays in boutique hotels in Dalmatia and Istria.
www.originaltravel.co.uk
Regent Holidays
6th Floor, Colston Tower
Colston Street, Bristol BS1 4XE
Tel: +44 (0)20 7666 1244
www.regent-holidays.co.uk
Thomson Holidays
Tel: +44 (0) 203 451 2688
www.thomson.co.uk
Specialist holidays.

Croatian tour companies

Travel Agents in Croatia offer a variety of specialist tours, activities or holidays including cruising, climbing, sailing, water sports, hunting, fishing, diving, adventure holidays, horse riding, mountain biking, coach tours and wine tours. The two biggest travel agents are Atlas and Kompas; they both have branches across the country:
Atlas
Izidora Kršnjavog 1
Zagreb
Tel: 01 241 5611
www.atlas-croatia.com
Kompas
Ede Murtića 4
Zagreb
Tel: 01 488 2500
www.kompas.hr

V

Visas and passports

All foreign nationals entering Croatia must hold a valid passport, although those from EEA countries and European microstates can enter with a national ID card. For stays of less than 90 days many Europeans (including all EU and EEA citizens) and those from the US, Canada, Australia and New Zealand and many South American countries do not need a visa to enter Croatia. For longer stays the easiest way around the visa requirements is to leave the country temporarily by crossing the Croatian border with Slovenia, although a limit of 90 in 180 days applies. South Africans require a 90-day visa to enter Croatia and should seek advice from any Croatian Embassy.

Visitors to Croatia must register with the police even when visiting friends. Hotels, campsites and agencies offering private accommodation automatically take care of the paperwork. Those who do not register may experience difficulties if they need to report anything to the police. It is essential to travel with a passport at all times. Visas are not required for most nationals (EU, US and Australian) entering Montenegro.

Advice and a full list of countries whose citizens require a visa to enter Croatia can be obtained from:
Consular Department of the Croatian Foreign Ministry
Tel: 01 456 9964
www.mvpei.hr.

⊙ Weights and Measures

Metric.

LANGUAGE

PRONUNCIATION TIPS

Croatians use a customised version of the Roman alphabet, with the pronunciation of many letters being the same in Croatian and English. Every single letter is pronounced and their sounds do not change from word to word.

c like the 'ts' in 'hats'
ć like the 'tu' in 'nature'
č like the 'ch' in 'chip'
d like the 'du' in 'endure' (sometimes written dj if the correct character is unavailable)
dž like the 'j' in 'juice'
j like the 'y' in 'yacht'
lj like the 'lli' in 'billion'
nj like the 'ny' in 'banyan'
š like the 'sh' in 'lush'
ž like the 's' in 'treasure'

USEFUL PHRASES

Hello *Bok*
Good morning *Dobro jutro*
Good day/afternoon *Dobar dan*
Good evening *Dobra večer*
Good night *Laku noć*
Goodbye *Do viđenja*
Welcome *Dobro došli*
My name is... *Moje ime je...*
How are you? *Kako ste?*
yes *da*
no *ne*
Where? When? How? *Gdje? Kada? Kako?*
How much? *Koliko?*
Thank you very much *Hvala lijepo*
please *molim*
Excuse me, please *Oprostite, molim*
Do you speak (English, German, Italian, Croatian)? *Govorite li (engleski, njemački, talijanski, hrvatski)?*
I (don't) speak *(ne) govorim*
I (don't) understand *(ne) razumijem*
cheers *živjeli*

AT THE HOTEL

Do you have...? *Imate li...?*
a room *sobu*
a single room *jednokrevetnu sobu*
a double room *dvokrevetnu sobu*
with a shower/bath *sa tušem/banjom*
one night/week *jednu noć/tjedan*
bed and breakfast *noćenje i doručak*
full board/half board *pansion/polupansion*
How much is it...? *Koliko košta za...?*
per night *jednu noć*
per person *po osobi*
balcony *balkon*
terrace *terasa*

SHOPPING

Do you have...? *Imate li...?*
How much is it...? *Kolika košta...?*
bakery *pekara*
bookshop *knjižara*
butchers *mesnica*
delicatessen *trgovina delikatesen*
department store *robna kuća*
fishmonger *ribarnica*
grocer *dućan*
laundry *praonica rublja*
market *tržnica*
pastry shop *slastičarnica*
souvenir shop *suveniri*
supermarket *samoposluživanje*
price *cijena*
cheap *jeftino*
expensive *skupo*

TRAVELLING

Where is the...? *Gdje je...?*
railway station? *željeznička postaja?*
bus stop? *autobusna postaja?*
tram stop? *tramvajska postaja?*
What time does the... leave? *U koliko sati polazi...?*
train/bus/ferry? *vlak/autobus/trajekt?*
one way/return ticket *jednosmjerna/povratna karta*

Signs outside Visovac's monastery.

1st/2nd class *prva/druga klasa*
booking *rezervacija*
airport *zračna luka*
timetable *raspored*
How much is the ticket to...? *Koliko košta karta za...?*

SIGHTSEEING

Where is the ...? *Gdje se nalazi*
museum *muzej*
church *crkva*
monument *spomenik*
monastery *samostan*
cathedral *katedrala*
old town *stari grad*
exhibition *izložba*
main square *glavni trg*
palace *palača*
castle *dvorac*
How much is the ticket? *Koliko košta ulaznica?*
sightseeing *razgledanje grada*

EATING OUT

restaurant *restoran*
breakfast *doručak*
lunch *ručak*

coffee house *kavana*
drink *piće*
one portion *jednu porciju*
Have you got a table for...? *Imate li stol za... osobe?*
May I have the menu (wine list)? *Molim vas jelovnik (vinsku kartu)?*
Have you got any food for vegetarians? *Imate li nešto za vegetarijance?*
Please could you bring...? *Molim vas donesite...?*
Thank you, it was delicious *bilo je jako dobro*
The bill please *račun molim*

MENU DECODER

beer *pivo*
black coffee *crna kava*
brandy *rakija*
fruit juice *voćni sok*
mineral water *mineralna voda*
plum brandy *šljivovica*
table wine *stolno vino*
tea (with milk/lemon, rum) *čaj (s mlijekom/s limunom/s rumom)*
wine (white, red, rosé) *vino (bijelo, crno, roze)*
bread *kruh*
egg *jaje*
ham omelette *omlet sa šunkom*
honey *med*
jam *marmelada*
cheese *sir*
cold meat *hladno pečenje*
ham (raw, cooked, smoked) *šunka (sirova, kuhana, dimljena)*
olives *masline*
sausage *kobasica*
soup *juha*
cod *bakalar*
lobster *jastog*
mussels *dagnje*
shellfish *školjke*
octopus *hobotnica*
oyster *kamenica*
scampi *škamp*
squid *lignje*
beefsteak *biftek*
beef goulash *goveđi gulaš*
chicken *pile*
roast suckling pig (cooked on the spit) *pečeni odojak (na ražnju)*
pork chops *svinjski kotleti*
lamb on the spit *janje na ražnju*
turkey *tuka*
veal cutlet *teleći odrezak*
apple *jabuka*
banana *banana*
orange *naranča*
strawberry *jagoda*
beans *grah*
cucumber *krastavac*

green pepper *paprika*
mushrooms *gljive*
onion *luk*
potato *krumpir*
salad *salata*
cake *kolač*
fruit salad *voćna salata*
ice cream *sladoled*
pancakes *palačinke*
whipped cream *šlag*
rice *riža*

HEALTH

I am ill *Ja sam bolestan/bolesna sam (m/f)*
Where is the nearest...? *Gdje je najbliža...?*
chemist *ljekarna*
doctor *liječnik*
dentist *zubar*
hospital *bolnica*
I have a sore throat *boli me grlo*
I have a headache *boli me glava*
I have a stomach ache *bolove u želucu*
I have... *Imam...*
nausea *mučninu*
diarrhoea *proljev*
toothache *zubobolju*
medicine *lijek*
I'm... *Ja sam...*
asthmatic *asmatičar*
diabetic *diabetičar*
epileptic *epileptičar*

ON THE ROAD

Is this the road to...? *Je li ovo cesta za...?*
Go straight ahead *Vozite ravno*
Turn right (left) *Skrenite desno (lijevo)*
I want... litres of... petrol *Molim vas... litara... benzina*
spare tyre *rezervna guma*
My car has broken down *Moje auto je pokvareno*
I have had a car crash *Imao sam sudar*
Could you please call...? *Molim vas pozovite...?*
the police *policiju*
the ambulance *hitnu pomoć*
the tow truck *vučnu službu*
driving licence *vozačka dozvola*

EMERGENCIES

My...has been stolen *Ukraden mi je...*
money *novac*

⏱ Numbers

0 *nula*
1 *jedan*
2 *dva*
3 *tri*
4 *četiri*
5 *pet*
6 *šest*
7 *sedam*
8 *osam*
9 *devet*
10 *deset*
11 *jedanaest*
12 *dvanaest*
20 *dvadeset*
30 *trideset*
40 *četrdeset*
50 *pedeset*
60 *šezdeset*
70 *sedamdeset*
80 *osamdeset*
90 *devedeset*
100 *sto*
1,000 *tisuću*

suitcase *kofer*
car *auto*
watch *sat*
camera *foto-aparat*
passport *putovnica*
Could you please call...? *Molim vas pozovite...?*
the police *policiju*
the ambulance *hitnu pomoć*

DAYS OF THE WEEK

Monday *ponedjeljak*
Tuesday *utorak*
Wednesday *srijeda*
Thursday *četvrtak*
Friday *petak*
Saturday *subota*
Sunday *nedjelja*

MONTHS OF THE YEAR

January *siječanj*
February *veljača*
March *ožujak*
April *travanj*
May *svibanj*
June *lipanj*
July *srpanj*
August *kolovoz*
September *rujan*
October *listopad*
November *studeni*
December *prosinac*

HISTORY

The National Question in Yugoslavia by Ivo Banac (1998). An examination of the tension between Serbian nationalism, Croatian nationalism and Yugoslavianism in the Balkans from the mid-19th century to the 1921 Vidovan Constitution.

Yugoslavia's Bloody Collapse by Christopher Bennett (1995). A critical study of Milošević's role in the rise of Serbian nationalism and the collapse of Yugoslavia.

The Fall of Yugoslavia by Misha Glenny (1996). An eyewitness account of Croatia and Slovenia's struggles for independence, and the ensuing five-year war. Glenny also considers the future in an unstable region and places the Yugoslavian war within a useful historical framework.

Croatia: A History by Ivo Goldstein (1999). Goldstein takes readers on a fascinating journey through Croatia's history right up to the present day.

The Impossible Country: A Journey Through the Last Days of Yugoslavia by Brian Hall (1996). An engrossing account of the author's journey during the last days of Yugoslavia in 1991. Reveals how everyday citizens can be persuaded to think the worst of their neighbours just because they happen to come from a different ethnic background.

The Death of Yugoslavia by Laura Silber and Alan Little (1996). A riveting account of the events that contributed to the 1991 war and running on to the Dayton Accord, presented from a historical perspective.

Croatia: A Nation Forged in War by Marcus Tanner (2001). Written by the author of the history chapters in this guidebook, this is a compelling account of Croatian history that ranges from the Greeks and Romans to the present day.

Forging War: the Media in Serbia, Croatia and Bosnia Hercegovina by Mark Thompson (1999). Examines the role of the Yugoslav press in fanning the fires of ethnic hatred.

The Demise of Yugoslavia: A Political Memoir by Stipe Mesić (2004). Unique and insightful account of the collapse of the former Yugoslavia, by the federation's last president, and the first democratically elected president of the independent Croatian state.

The Yugoslav Auschwitz and the Vatican: The Croatian Massacre of the Serbs During World War II by Vladimir Dedijer (1992). Written by a former Yugoslav ambassador to the UN, this detailed and impeccably researched book covers a secret episode of the 20th century and one that many Croatians – and Roman Catholics – would prefer had remained secret. It is probably a bit too harrowing for holiday reading.

How We Survived Communism and Even Laughed by Slavenka Drakulić (2001). A collection of essays that examine different aspects of life under Communism, including censorship and consumerism.

Café Europa by Slavenka Drakulić (1996). A collection of essays written between 1992 and 1996 that takes a look at post-Communist life in Zagreb, Warsaw, Tirana and Budapest.

Balkan Express by Slavenka Drakulić (1993). A compelling insight, given through a series of essays, into the effects of the Homeland War on the lives of ordinary people.

Croatia Through History by Branka Magaš (2008). Despite being Croatian, historian and journalist Branka Magas bravely attempts to cover objectively the history of Croatia from the Middle Ages to the present and does it remarkably well.

Goli Otok – Hell in the Adriatic by Josip Zoretić (2007). The former Yugoslavia's answer to Solzhenitsyn's *One Day in the Life of Ivan Denisovich*, this vividly written memoir is a harrowing account of life in the gulag on the Croatian island of Goli otok, where the author was a prisoner from 1962 to 1969. It is essential reading for anyone believing in the widespread popular image of Tito's regime as Communism with a human face.

The Culture of Lies by Dubravka Ugrešić (1998). A collection of essays attacking the politics and culture of the Croatia that rose from the ashes of the Yugoslavian war, and of the war in Croatia and Bosnia. Also an insightful attempt to understand the nationalist aggression that triumphed at this time.

Blood and Belonging: Journeys into the New Nationalism by Michael Ignatieff (1994). The Canadian academic and former politician examines the waves of nationalism sweeping through Europe and, in particular, the former Yugoslavia in the 1990s.

⊙ Send Us Your Thoughts

We do our best to ensure the information in our books is as accurate and up-to-date as possible. The books are updated on a regular basis using local contacts, who painstakingly add, amend and correct as required. However, some details (such as telephone numbers and opening times) are liable to change, and we are ultimately reliant on our readers to put us in the picture.

We welcome your feedback, especially your experience of using the book "on the road". Maybe you came across a great bar or new attraction we missed.

We will acknowledge all contributions, and we'll offer an Insight Guide to the best letters received.

Please write to us at:
Insight Guides
PO Box 7910
London SE1 1WE

Or email us at:
hello@insightguides.com

CULTURE

A Taste of Croatia: Savoring the Food, People and Traditions of Croatia's Adriatic Coast by Karen Evenden

Selection of Croatian newspapers.

(2007). Not so much a cookbook as a well-written and lengthy love letter celebrating its subject.

My Favourite Croatian Recipes by Sandra Lougher (2005). One of very few books about Croatian food in English, this includes more than 60 recipes from all over the country.

The Best of Croatian Cooking – Expanded Edition by Liliana Pavičić and Gordana Pirker-Mosher (2003). As well as 200 recipes, the book has an introduction covering Croatia's culinary tradition and local specialities and a useful wine guide.

TRAVEL

Croatia: Travels in Undiscovered Country by Tony Fabijančić (2003). Written by a Canadian-born son of Croatian immigrants who decided to explore the back roads of his ancestral homeland, this engaging travelogue deals insightfully and affectionately with the challenges facing rural Croatians rapidly adapting to life in a modern European state.

Black Lamb and Grey Falcon by Rebecca West (1941). West's colossal and seminal account of several journeys through Yugoslavia during the 1930s remains essential reading to anyone who wants a deeper understanding of Balkan history.

FICTION

As If I Am Not There: A Novel of the Balkans by Slavenka Drakulić (1999). Set in Bosnia, not Croatia, this book takes the reader on a journey into the heart of the Balkan conflict through one woman's experiences. A harrowing and enlightening read.

Chasing A Croatian Girl by Cody McClain Brown (2015). This warm and delightful book tells of Cody McClain Brown's experiences as he adapt to life in a new country. An irresistible and humorous insight into life in Croatia, from its coffee consumption to the importance of familial bonds.

Have a Nice Day: From the Balkan War to the American Dream by Dubravka Ugrešić (1994). A fictional diary of a life in exile in the US through the eyes of a Croatian woman whose country is being destroyed by war.

The Museum of Unconditional Surrender by Dubravka Ugrešić (1991). A well-written novel that weaves an intriguing mix of humour and bitterness. This prize-winning novelist hones in on the life of a 45-year-old Croatian woman living in exile.

Croatian Nights ed. Borivoj Radaković, Matt Thorne and Tony White (2005). An eclectic and brilliant collection of short stories by Croatian and British writers, which grew out of a movement called FAK – Festival of Alternative Literature. It gives an insight into how young writers look at the country.

Zagreb Noir ed. Ivan Srsen (2015). A beautifully curated collection of harrowing tales that reveal the dark underbelly of Zagreb.

OTHER INSIGHT GUIDES

The classic **Insight Guides** series combines in-depth features and an exploration of essential sights accompanied by vibrant photography. Other European titles include Italy and Western Europe.

Insight Explore Guides provide precise routes and recommendations from local expert writers. Titles include Croatia, Dubrovnik, Prague and Venice.

Insight Pocket Guides are the perfect companion to your trip, featuring all you need to know on where to go and what to do. Pocket guides to the region include Croatia, Slovenia and Vienna.

Insight Fleximaps combine clear, detailed cartography with essential travel information. The laminated finish makes the maps durable, waterproof and easy to fold. Fleximaps Croatia and Dubrovnik make useful companions to our guidebooks.

CREDITS

INSIGHT GUIDE CREDITS

Distribution
UK, Ireland and Europe
Apa Publications (UK) Ltd;
sales@insightguides.com
United States and Canada
Ingram Publisher Services;
ips@ingramcontent.com
Australia and New Zealand
Woodslane; info@woodslane.com.au
Southeast Asia
Apa Publications (SN) Pte;
singaporeoffice@insightguides.com
Worldwide
Apa Publications (UK) Ltd;
sales@insightguides.com
Special Sales, Content Licensing and CoPublishing
Insight Guides can be purchased in bulk quantities at discounted prices. We can create special editions, personalised jackets and corporate imprints tailored to your needs.
sales@insightguides.com
www.insightguides.biz

Printed in China by CTPS

All Rights Reserved
© 2018 Apa Digital (CH) AG and
Apa Publications (UK) Ltd

First Edition 2007
Fourth Edition 2018

Every effort has been made to provide accurate information in this publication, but changes are inevitable. The publisher cannot be responsible for any resulting loss, inconvenience or injury. We would appreciate it if readers would call our attention to any errors or outdated information. We also welcome your suggestions; please contact us at:
hello@insightguides.com

www.insightguides.com

Editor: Helen Fanthorpe
Authors: Magdalena Helsztyńska-Stadnik and Mary Novakovich
Head of Production: Rebeka Davies
Update Production: Apa Digital
Picture Editor: Tom Smyth
Cartography: original cartography Berndtson & Berndtson, updated by Carte

CONTRIBUTORS

This new edition of *Insight Guides Croatia* was commissioned and edited by **Helen Fanthorpe**. It has been updated by **Magdalena Helsztyńska-Stadnik**, building on the work of travel writer and journalist **Mary Novakovich**. Novakovich has a particular interest in the countries of the former Yugoslavia (Croatia, Serbia and Montenegro), where her family is from.

Contributors to previous editions also include **Roger Williams**, **David St Vincent**, **Dorothy Stannard**, **Marcus Tanner**, **Robin McKelvie**, **Jennifer McKelvie** and **Jane Foster**.

The book was indexed by **Penny Phenix**.

ABOUT INSIGHT GUIDES

Insight Guides have more than 45 years' experience of publishing high-quality, visual travel guides. We produce 400 full-colour titles, in both print and digital form, covering more than 200 destinations across the globe, in a variety of formats to meet your different needs.

Insight Guides are written by local authors, whose expertise is evident in the extensive historical and cultural background features. Each destination is carefully researched by regional experts to ensure our guides provide the very latest information. All the reviews in **Insight Guides** are independent; we strive to maintain an impartial view. Our reviews are carefully selected to guide you to the best places to eat, go out and shop, so you can be confident that when we say a place is special, we really mean it.

Legend

City maps

	Freeway/Highway/Motorway
	Divided Highway
	Main Roads
	Minor Roads
	Pedestrian Roads
	Steps
	Footpath
	Railway
	Funicular Railway
	Cable Car
	Tunnel
	City Wall
	Important Building
	Built Up Area
	Other Land
	Transport Hub
	Park
	Pedestrian Area
	Bus Station
	Tourist Information
	Main Post Office
	Cathedral/Church
	Mosque
	Synagogue
	Statue/Monument
	Beach
	Airport

Regional maps

	Freeway/Highway/Motorway (with junction)
	Freeway/Highway/Motorway (under construction)
	Divided Highway
	Main Road
	Secondary Road
	Minor Road
	Track
	Footpath
	International Boundary
	State/Province Boundary
	National Park/Reserve
	Marine Park
	Ferry Route
	Marshland/Swamp
	Glacier Salt Lake
	Airport/Airfield
	Ancient Site
	Border Control
	Cable Car
	Castle/Castle Ruins
	Cave
	Chateau/Stately Home
	Church/Church Ruins
	Crater
	Lighthouse
	Mountain Peak
	Place of Interest
	Viewpoint

INDEX

Zagreb

0 ——————— 500 m
0 ——————— 500 yds

N

JELENOVAC

ZELENGAJ

Stube V.
Mandekića

Voukova

Pantovčak

Goljak

Novi Goljak

Zelengaj

Zelengaj

Zelengaj

Paunovac

Dubravkin put

Tuškanac

Jabukovac

Goljački ogr.

Šilobodov put

Kriažin Gvozd

Goljak

Ilica Vladimira Nazora

Ivana Gorana Kovačića

Dubravkin put

Ilin

Muzej
grada Zag...
(Zargreb
Museum)

Palača Magdalenić-
Drašković-Jelačić

Atelijer
Meštrović

Crkva sv.
Marka

Hrvatski
prirodoslovni
muzej

Zamenhoffova

Ivana Gorana Kovačića

Tuškanac

Demetrova

Visoka

Banski dvori

Sabor
Hrvats
(Parlia

Palača Vojković-Oršić-Rauch
Hrvatski povijesni muzej

Markov trg

Kamenita

Streljačka

Hrvatski muzej
naivne umjetnosti

Crkva sv.
Ćirila i
Metoda

Ga

Aleksandrove stube

Kula Lotrščak (Lotrščak Tower)

Rokov perivoj

Rokova

Dežmanova

Mesnička

Tomićeva

Strossmayerovo
šetalište

Muzej prek...
(Museum of
Relationshi

Britanski
trg

Crkva sv.
Ćirila i
Metoda

Ilica

GORNJI GRAD
(UPPER TOWN)

Homeland War Memorial

Vinogradska cesta

Kosirnikova

Ilica

Istarska

Hercegovačka

Jelenovac

Buča rova

Jarunska

Buča rova

Podolje

Nad lipom

Hercegovačka

Badalićeva

Pantovčak

Pavlinovićeva

Bukovačka

Buconjićeva

Ilica

Ilica

Ilica

Radnički dol

Ivana Kukuljevića

Radnički dol

Dramsko kazalište
"Gavela"

Medulićeva

Frankopanska

Trg Petra
Preradovića

Bog

Varšavska

Dalmatinska

Leksikografski
zavod
"Miroslav Krleža"

Crkva sv. Vinka

Masarykova

Preradovićeva

Ilica

Slovenska

Čanićeva

Reljkovićeva

Austrije

Krajiška

Kordunska

Prilaz Gjure

Kačićeva

Deželića

Trg Republike
Hrvatske

Institut
za turizam

Trg Vladka
Mačeka

Grada Mainza

Filipovića

Talovčeva

Republike

Klaićeva

Muzej za
umjetnost i obrt
(Arts and Crafts
Museum)

Hrvatsko narodno
kazalište
(Croatian National Theatre)

Gundulićeva

Trg Francuske
republike

Fonova

Hanuševa

Jagićeva

Klaićeva
Rooseveltov
trg

Andrije Hebranga

DONJI GRAD

And

Mažuranićev
trg

Zapadni kolodvor
(Train Station)

Hochmanova

Muzej Mimara
(Mimara Museum)

Etnografski
muzej
(Ethnographic
Museum)

Magazinska

Nova cesta

Jonkel

Pavletićeva

Petračićeva

Andrije Žaje

Brozova

Jukićeva

Pierottijeva

Kršnjavoga

Savska cesta

Vukotino-
vićeva

Marulićev
trg

Jurja

Gundulićeva

Žerjavića

Svačićev
trg

Kumičićeva

Dom
Sportina

Metalčeva

Andrije Žaje

Valjavčeva

Novotnijeva

Kučerina

Božidara Adžije

Hrvatski državni arhiv
(National Archives)

Mihanovićeva

Runjaninova

Mihai

Espla

Metalčeva

Pašarčeva

Kalnička

Bisačka

Kranjčevićeva

NK
Zagreb

Vodnikova

Crnatkova

BOTANIČKI VRT
(BOTANICAL GARDENS)

Miran...
podv...

Samobor

Čakovečka

Krapinska ulica

Kenovečka

Grebengradska

Gotalovečka

Beletska

Loborska

Trakoščanska

Nova cesta

Ogrovečka

Badalićeva

Tratinska

Tehnički
muzej
(Technical
Museum)

Sportska dvorana
"Dražen Petrović"

Koturaška

Ursa

Bednjanska

Koturaška

Sutlanska

Plitvička

Zelinska

Miranska

Miranmarska

Taborska

Ozaljska cesta

Trešnjevački
trg

Richtmanova

Garićgradska

Kamengradska

Florijana Andrašeca

Ilodska

Tratinska

Ozaljska cesta

Magiška
Dobojska

Zvonička

Drenovačka

Srebre-
nička

Ostrovička

Ključka

Višegradska

Cernička

Gagarinov put

Ulica grada Vukovara

Savska cesta

Miškine P. TV.

Ulica grada Vukovara

Alagina

Bošnjakovićeva

Stožena

Vraničeva

Polička poljana

Ivana Lučića

Alexandera von Humboldta

Narodno
sveučilište

Čazmanska

Kolča

TRNJE

Jarun